Social Welfare and Responsibility

The issue of social welfare and individual responsibility has become a topic of international public debate in recent years as politicians around the world now question the legitimacy of state-funded welfare programs. David Schmidtz and Robert Goodin debate the ethical merits of individual versus collective responsibility for welfare. David Schmidtz argues that social welfare policy should prepare people for responsible adulthood rather than try to make that unnecessary. Robert Goodin argues against the individualization of welfare policy and expounds the virtues of collective responsibility.

David Schmidtz began his teaching career at Yale University in 1988 and is now Professor of Philosophy and joint Professor of Economics at the University of Arizona. His research interests include environmental ethics, moral theory, and rational choice theory.

Robert Goodin took his D.Phil. in Politics at Oxford and spent a decade teaching government at the University of Essex before taking up in 1989 his present post as Professor of Philosophy at the Research School of Social Sciences, Australian National University. Goodin is author of various books on political theory, public policy, and applied ethics.

For and Against

General Editor: R. G. Frey

For and Against offers a new and exciting approach to the investigation of complex philosophical ideas and their impact on the way we think about a host of contemporary social and political issues. Two philosophers explore a topic of intense public interest from opposing points of view. This approach provides the reader with a balanced perspective on the topic, but also serves to introduce the reader to the deep philosophical conflicts that underpin these differing views. The result is both a series of important statements on some of the most challenging questions facing our society as well as an introduction to philosophy. Each essay is compact and nontechnical, yet avoids a simplistic, journalistic presentation of the topic.

Social Welfare and Individual Responsibility

David Schmidtz

Robert E. Goodin

CAMBRIDGE
UNIVERSITY PRESS

PUBLISHED BY THE PRESS SYNDICATE OF THE UNIVERSITY OF CAMBRIDGE
The Pitt Building, Trumpington Street, Cambridge, United Kingdom

CAMBRIDGE UNIVERSITY PRESS
The Edinburgh Building, Cambridge CB2 1RP, UK   http://www.cup.cam.ac.uk
40 West 20th Street, New York, NY 10011-4211, USA   http://www.cup.org
10 Stamford Road, Oakleigh, Melbourne 3166, Australia

First published 1998

Printed in the United States of America

Typeset in Meridien 10.5/14 pt. in LaTeX 2_ε [TB]

A catalogue record for this book is available from the British Library

Library of Congress Cataloging in Publication Data

Schmidtz, David.
    Social welfare and individual responsibility / David Schmidtz,
Robert E. Goodin.
        p.   cm. – (For and against)
    Includes bibliographical references (p.   ) and index.
        ISBN 0-521-56416-6 (hardback). – ISBN 0-521-56461-1 (paperback)
        1. Social justice.   2. Responsibility.   3. Social policy – Moral
and ethical aspects.   4. Public welfare – Moral and ethical aspects.
5. Welfare state – Moral and ethical aspects.   I. Goodin, Robert E.
II. Title.   III. Series: For and against (Cambridge, England)
HM216.S296   1998
361.6'1 – dc21   97-52782
                                                                    CIP

ISBN 0-521-56416-6 hardback
ISBN 0-521-56461-1 paperback

Contents

Series Editor's Introduction   *page* xi

Preface   xv

1   Taking Responsibility   1
     David Schmidtz

1.1 The Tide of Wealth   3
     1.1.1 How Things Are and How Things Change   4
     1.1.2 Individual versus Collective Responsibility: Not the
            Real Issue   7
     1.1.3 Assigning Blame: Not the Real Issue   10
            1.1.3.1 Federal Deposit Insurance   12
     1.1.4 How to Make Sure the Poor Are Left Behind   14
     1.1.5 How to Minimize Suffering   20
     1.1.6 Responsibility and Welfare   21

1.2 Why Isn't Everyone Destitute?   24
     1.2.1 Original Appropriation: The Problem   25
     1.2.2 Original Appropriation: A Solution   28
            1.2.2.1 Appropriation Is Not a Zero-Sum Game   29
            1.2.2.2 The Commons before Appropriation Is Not
                     Zero-Sum Either   31
            1.2.2.3 Justifying the Game   33
     1.2.3 What Is It Like to Be Poor?   36

1.3 Responsibility and Community   44
     1.3.1 The Unregulated Commons   46
            1.3.1.1 The Communal Alternative   48
     1.3.2 Local versus Remote Externalities   49
            1.3.2.1 Small Events   50

	1.3.2.2 Medium Events	50
	1.3.2.3 Large Events	51
	1.3.3 Jamestown and Other Communes	53
	1.3.4 Governance by Custom	56
	1.3.5 The Hutterite Secret	58
1.4	Mutual Aid	60
	1.4.1 Friendly Societies in a Sometimes Hostile World	63
	1.4.2 Could Friendly Societies Work Today?	69
	1.4.3 The Possibility of Political Disarmament	73
	1.4.4 Babies Born Destitute	77
1.5	But Is It Just?	80
	1.5.1 The Concept of Justice	80
	1.5.2 When, If Ever, Does Equal Respect Mandate Equalization?	82
	1.5.2.1 Equal Opportunity	84
	1.5.3 Consequences Matter	86
	1.5.4 Escaping the Status Quo	88
	1.5.4.1 An Alternative View	91
	1.5.5 Real Self-Esteem	93
	1.5.6 The Bottom Line	94
2	Social Welfare as a Collective Social Responsibility	97
	Robert E. Goodin	
2.1	The Policy Context	99
	2.1.1 What's the Problem?	100
	2.1.2 Some Blunt Facts about Social Policy	106
2.2	Some Key Words in Context	116
	2.2.1 Dependency, Reliance, and Social Welfare	116
	2.2.2 Dependency from the Dependent's Perspective	123
	2.2.3 Reliance, Planning, and Prudence	127
	2.2.4 Self-Reliance: But Who Is the "Self"?	133
	2.2.5 The Costs of Moralized Definitions	139
	2.2.6 Family Values: An Aside	141
2.3	Collective Responsibility	145
	2.3.1 Alternative Kinds of Collectivism	145
	2.3.2 Two Senses of Responsibility	149

2.4   The Classic Case for Collectivization Restated   155
   2.4.1 Fault and the Folly of Disentangling Causes   156
   2.4.2 The Collectivization of Risks   158
   2.4.3 The Efficiencies of Collective Provision   168

2.5   The Morality of Incentives and Deterrence   172
   2.5.1 Deterrence: Punishing the Blameless   173
   2.5.2 Opportunities versus Incentives   177
   2.5.3 Offers You Can't Refuse   180
   2.5.4 Welfare as Compensation for Structural
       Unemployment   184

2.6   The Point of Politics   190
   2.6.1 Rising Tides, Wasted Lives: Money Is Not Like Water   192
   2.6.2 Who We Are and What We Stand For   193

References   196
Index   211

Series Editor's Introduction

SINCE the mid-1960s, the application of ethical theory to moral, social, political, and legal issues has formed a growing part of public life and of the philosophical curriculum. Except perhaps during the 1950s and the flowering of ordinary language philosophy, moral philosophers have always to some extent been concerned with the practical application of their theories. On the whole, however, they did little more than sketch implications or draw provisional conclusions with regard to practical issues based upon some distant familiarity with a few empirical facts. Today, the opposite is the case: they have come to immerse themselves in the subject matter of the issues with which they are normatively concerned, whether these come from law, medicine, business, or the affairs of social and political life. As a result, they have come to apply their theories in a much broader and deeper understanding of the factual setting within which the issues in question arise and have become of public concern.

Courses in applied ethics now figure throughout the philosophical curriculum, including, increasingly, within philosophy components of professional education. More and more periodicals – philosophical, professional, popular – devote space to medical and business ethics, to environmental and animal rights issues, to discussions of suicide, euthanasia, and physician-assisted suicide, to surrogate motherhood and the rights of children, to the ethics of war and the moral case for and against assisting famine victims, and so on. Indeed, new periodicals have arisen devoted entirely to applied issues, from numerous environmental quarterlies to the vast number of journals in medical ethics that today feature a compendium of philosophical, medical, and sometimes popular authors, writing on a diverse array of issues ultimately concerned with life, quality of life, and death.

What is striking about the *best* philosophical writing in all these areas (I concede that there is much chaff amongst the wheat) is that it is factually informed and methodologically situated in the subject areas under discussion, to a degree that enables specialists in those areas, be they doctors, lawyers, environmentalists, or the like, to see the material as both engaging and relevant. Yet, the writing is pitched at the level of the educated person, comparatively free of technicalities and jargon, and devoted to matters of public concern. Much of it, whether by philosophers or others, such as economists and political and social scientists, is known outside the academy and has had the effect, as it were, of taking philosophy into the public arena.

Interest in applied ethics will continue to grow, increasingly as a result of technological/scientific developments, enacted social policies, and political/economic decisions. For example, genetic engineering raises a number of important moral issues, from those that concern human cloning, illnesses, and treatments to those that center around alteration in animal species and the "creation" of new animals. Fetal tissue research holds out the promise of help for diabetics and those with Parkinson's disease, but even using the tissue, quite apart from how we acquire it, is a controversial affair. Equally contentious is the bringing to term of severely deformed fetuses who will die almost at once, in order to use their organs for transplant. But, so, too, is xenograph, or cross-species transplantation, in which animals are treated as repositories of organs for humans.

Social, political, and legal decisions always spur ethical interest. Topics such as obscenity, pornography, and censorship are of perennial interest, as are straightforwardly economic/political issues to do with capital punishment, equality, majoritarian democracy, the moral assessment of capitalism, and the provision of societal welfare. Today, some comparatively new issues have come to figure in this ethical landscape, from the place of children in society and all manner of interest in educational policy and practice to population policy and the relation of this to the distribution of various societal resources. And it is obvious that, throughout the world, issues to do with nationalism, political and judicial sovereignty, and immigration are of massive interest to educated persons and raise all kinds of moral questions.

This new series, For and Against, aims to cover a good many of these applied issues. Collectively, the volumes will form a kind of library of applied ethics.

Philosophy is an argumentative discipline: among its best practitioners, whom this series will feature, it proceeds by the clear and careful articulation, analysis, and assessment of arguments. Clashes of arguments, ideas, principles, positions, and theories are its very lifeblood. The idea behind the series is very simple: it is to capture this clash. Two or more philosophers, in opposition on some moral, social, or political issue, will state and defend their positions on the issue in as direct and powerful a manner as they can. Theory will be involved, but the general aim is not to have two authors differ over the development or worth of a philosophical theory. Rather, it is to show the application of philosophy to practice, with each author using as much theory as necessary to state and defend a position on the topic. Educated people generally should be able to read and assess the success of the authors.

The volumes will be polemical but in the best sense: each author will dispute and defend a position on some controversial matter by means of clear and careful argument. The end, obviously, is that each volume will exhibit to the full the best case each author can muster for his or her respective side to the controversy.

The first volume in the series is the present one, *Social Welfare and Individual Responsibility*, by David Schmidtz and Robert Goodin. It makes for a splendid beginning. In a direct and careful manner, in a prose that is enormously readable and at times impassioned, Dave and Bob sift the issues that swirl around state provision of welfare. No social issue has emerged from the 1980s as more important to the definition of the kind of society we should all like to live in than that of social welfare, yet no issue has proved more politically difficult to achieve even a moderate consensus over. What separates intelligent and thoughtful people on this issue of state provision of aid to the poor? I know of no more lucid, accessible, and compelling answers to this question than are to be found here, in Dave's discussion of internalizing responsibility for one's life and of viewpoints and institutions that foster that internalization, and in Bob's discussion of why social welfare is and must remain a collective social responsibility.

R. G. Frey

Preface

W HEN I was a child, I saw a movie in which the Soviet Union blew up the Alaska pipeline. The bombing was in response to a U.S. grain embargo that had led to widespread starvation in the Soviet Union. The president telephoned the premier to denounce him for the bombing. The premier responded that the president had fired the first shot.

Amazed, the president said, "You mean to say that when we decide not to give you our grain, you think that gives you the right to bomb our pipeline?"

The premier responded, "It's not your grain. It's the world's grain."

That scene showed me something that, as a young boy, I had not imagined possible: unresolvable disagreement about (what I took to be) a basic fact, namely who had fired the first shot. That revelation remains fresh in my mind.

Bob Goodin and I are like the characters in that movie. In some way, we are alien to each other. Nonetheless, I have come to have the highest respect for him and, indeed, to think of him as a friend. Each of us has more to say about responsibility and welfare than can be said in these few pages, of course. Interested readers would be well advised to consult Goodin's other works. They set the standard for philosophical reflection on the topic of social welfare.

I thank the Earhart Foundation for a grant in the fall of 1996 that helped me to finish on schedule, and Cambridge University Press for permission to use material from "Guarantees," *Social*

Philosophy and Policy 14 (1997), and "The Institution of Property," *Social Philosophy and Policy* 11 (1994). For generous advice and comments, I thank Bob Goodin and Ray Frey, and also Scott Arnold, Paul Bloomfield, Allen Buchanan, Tom Christiano, Andrew Cohen, Dale Cooke, Tyler Cowen, Patrick Fitzgerald, Michael Hechter, Uri Henig, David Kelley, Barry Macleod-Cullinane, Tom Palmer, Terry Price, Linda Radzik, Daniel Shapiro, David Sobel, Christopher Wellman, Elizabeth Willott, and especially Steve Scalet. I thank Karl-Heinz Ladeur and Peter Köller for opportunities to discuss work in progress at, respectively, the European University of Florence and the 1996 Wittgenstein Symposium in Kirchberg. I also thank participants in my seminar in the spring of 1996 when I was just getting started, especially those who most fearlessly took issue with the positions I was trying to develop: Kristen Hessler, Scott LaBarge, Avery Kolers, Dan Russell, David Truncellito, and Mark Wunderlich.

I dedicate my portion of this book to my parents. We left our farm in Saskatchewan when I was eleven, partly so my younger brother and I could get an education. Dad worked as a janitor, then as a bartender. Mom was a cashier in a fabric shop. They taught me, by example, that the most important thing is not what you do but how well you do it. In the end, that was what I needed to know.

David Schmidtz
Tucson, January 1997

T HIS BOOK is not the veritable "dialogue of the deaf" that it may seem. Certainly Dave Schmidtz and I do not "join issue" in all the ways that readers of a "For and Against" debate might ordinarily expect – and it is greatly to the credit of the series' editor, Ray Frey, that he did not insist that we exaggerate our differences, just for the sake of that form. But we are not literally "alien" to one another, either. What each of us is ardently "for" in this debate the other does not so much dispute as merely takes for granted. I am not against people's assuming responsibility for their own lives, any more than Dave is against taking care of people who are unable to care for themselves. Our differences are ones of emphasis, of what we think needs be said emphatically and what ought simply be taken to be business as usual. Differences of emphasis sometimes make a big difference to policy, of course, and that is precisely what we are debating here. Beyond any more particular points each of us hopes to carry in that debate, we hope to show that you can have that debate in a sensible and spirited way without denying the obvious and important truths that the other side claims as its own.

In the process of writing this book, Dave and I have exchanged drafts and comments, and (thanks to the hospitality of the Austrian Ludwig Wittgenstein Society) a fair few liters of dubious Sylvaner and one particularly memorable trout. Whether it was the force of our disputations that caused David Gauthier to shed his last baby tooth will never be known, but we are grateful to him and various other companions in those revelries for their contributions to our conversations. I have also received useful comments on my portion of the book from Brian Barry, Abram de Swaan, Claus Offe, Ray Frey, Amy Gutmann, Jennifer Hochschild, Desmond King, Eva Feder Kittay, Julian Le Grand, Andrew Levine, Jane Lewis, Mark Philp, Stein Ringen, Bo Rothstein, Alan Ryan, Cass Sunstein, and most especially Diane Gibson, whose touch on these issues is in so many ways surer than my own. Since the Research School provides me with no undergraduates of my own, I am also grateful to Daniel Shapiro and Marian Simms for letting me try out these materials on them and their students.

My immediate family history is no match for Dave's. Like him, however, I dedicated my earlier attempts to grapple with these issues to my parents. It was they who taught me the importance of "protecting the vulnerable": my father from the noblesse oblige perspective of his upper Hudson Dutch forbears, filtered through midwestern small-town aristocracy; my mother from the perspective of her own mother, who left school aged eight to tend the family when her mother died, and for whom "the poorhouse" always constituted a vivid prospect rather than merely a florid figure of speech. What turned those family teachings into a powerful social message for me was my time doing outreach work from the office of Indianapolis Mayor Richard G. Lugar. Accordingly, it is to him that I dedicate my portion of this book. In a better world, he would have been president. In a better world still, he would not have needed to be.

Robert E. Goodin
Canberra, November 1996

1 Taking Responsibility

David Schmidtz

1.1 The Tide of Wealth

MARKET SOCIETY is sometimes described as a tide that lifts all boats. In many ways, the metaphor is apt. It reminds us that the key to prosperity in a market society is to produce what other people value. Profits normally are not made at other people's expense. People get rich when they market the light bulb, telephone, or computer not because such inventions make people worse off but rather because they make people better off.

People tend to see human commerce as a zero-sum game – a game in which wealth is redistributed but not created. If society were a zero-sum game, though, we would be born in caves. Our teeth would fall out before we turned thirty, and we would die soon thereafter, as our ancestors did when human society was in its infancy. We fare better today because human commerce is not zero-sum. There is a tide. It is lifting boats. In principle, it could lift them all.

What I do not like about the metaphor is its suggestion that the tide lifts us all unconditionally or indiscriminately. There are tides in market society that lift virtually all boats, of course. Market society has given us telephones and light bulbs, and few of us would be better off without them. Nevertheless, as a general rule, material progress does more for some people than for others. The tide lifts the boats it touches; the rest are left behind. They are not left living in caves, but still they are left behind, at least in relative terms.

To see why the tide does not touch everyone, we first need to see why it touches anyone. If we try to force the tide to lift everyone, without understanding how the tide works, we are likely to end up with more poverty rather than less, a few decades down the road. The first question, then, is not why some people still live in caves but, rather, Why doesn't everyone? Why is there such a thing as material progress in the first place?[1]

The basic answer is that progress occurs because people produce. People perceive a need. They take responsibility for meeting it. And in meeting that perceived need, they produce things of value. Their productivity creates and constitutes the tide of material progress. That explains in the most general terms why there is a tide, and why some people are lifted by it. The tide tends to lift people when they contribute to it. The tide is not an external force. People are not merely *lifted* by the tide; they *are* the tide. Or, at least, some of them are.

1.1.1   How Things Are and How Things Change

Unfortunately, those who do not produce do not contribute to the tide. They are not part of the tide. And the tide tends to leave them behind. The tide tends to offer less to those who, sometimes through no fault of their own, fail to produce what other people value.[2]

This essay's purpose is to explain how individual responsibility contributes to the welfare of people in general.[3] Thus, while

---

[1] Why focus on material progress? Some say, "Money isn't everything. Failing to take responsibility for one's own welfare is psychologically as well as financially crippling, and the bigger problem is not its incompatibility with wealth but rather its incompatibility with self-respect." I completely agree, but I focus on material progress in this essay because it is the production and distribution of wealth that people are arguing about when they argue about social welfare.

I might add that material progress is never merely material. Where commerce flourishes, so do the arts. For an engaging look at the history of the arts in market society, see Cowen (1998).

[2] People can value X in the sense of being willing to offer something of value in return for X. That is how I use the term here.

[3] Philosophers will be all too aware of how thankless a task it is to try to define terms like 'social welfare' precisely. I use the term in a nontechnical sense, not presupposing any particular way of aggregating individual utilities. Chapter 7 of Schmidtz 1995 explains how I characterize the common good, but this essay does not presuppose that account.

this essay is to some extent about people whom the tide leaves behind, it is more fundamentally about what produces the tide in the first place. My role in this book is to argue that people are better off thinking of their welfare as their own responsibility rather than as the government's responsibility. They are better off living (and their children are better off growing up) in communities where people take responsibility for their own welfare. The following chapters look at why some societies, cultures, and institutions have led to prosperity while others have not. I talk about incentives and how people respond to them, but nothing in this essay presumes that individuals are egoistic, or that they are maximizers, or that real-world markets are perfectly competitive. This essay concerns how people respond, as individuals and as groups, to real-world institutions. It is not about theoretical models.

Nor is it an attempt to explain all of society's problems in terms of some single concept, like individual responsibility. I would be mortified if people thought I was prescribing individual responsibility as a cure for all our social ills. Our society, like every other, is shot through with problems, and not all of them have solutions. As I write these words, a niece of mine is in labor. She is not married. She is seventeen. What would help her? What would help her younger sister to avoid making the same mistake? The first question is more urgent, but the second question is no less important.

In some people's eyes, the key question is whether my niece is at fault. But Robert Goodin believes (and I agree) that even if the hard life awaiting my niece is her own fault, that does not entail that she should be left to fend for herself. Similarly, even if the "system" is to blame, that does not entail that anyone has a duty to help. Who is to blame for her plight and who should take responsibility for her future are different questions. However we assign blame or credit, the question from a welfare perspective is, What makes people better off?

As Goodin translates it, that question means, How can we help people who cannot help themselves? Our form of social organization determines how bad it is to be left behind. Our task, therefore, is to change the system so as to make it less bad to be left behind.

I agree that institutions affect how bad it is to be left behind, but that is only part of the story. Institutions also affect whether people contribute to the tide and, thus, whether the tide leaves them behind. So, which institutions have a history of making people better off? Those that make being left behind less likely, or those that make it less bad? Those that lead people to contribute, or those that make it unnecessary to contribute?

From a static perspective, we see society as a snapshot, and what is wrong with the picture is that some people have unmet needs while others have plenty. The question defining the static perspective is, How do we get needed resources to needy people? How can we help those whom the system has left behind? From a more dynamic perspective, though, society is a process by which one snapshot evolves into another.[4] The question defining the dynamic perspective is, Which institutions make people less likely to need help in the first place?

From a static perspective, our task is to rearrange the resources visible in the snapshot, frame by frame. From a dynamic perspective, our task is to nurture the processes that produce the resources, and thereby produce better snapshots in the future. From a dynamic perspective, we might worry about the consequences of rearranging resources for purposes other than the purposes for which producers are producing them. When we worry about that, we appear from a static perspective to be willfully out of touch. We are talking about history or economic theory, perhaps, but not about the real world. The real world is the snapshot.

To people who see things from a purely static perspective, it will seem that those who take a dynamic perspective want people to suffer. Why else would people hesitate to rearrange resources? Those who see things from both perspectives, though, see a complicated dance of incentives, opportunities, evolving culture, and

---

[4] Coincidentally, Husock (1997) uses the same metaphor to describe a similar idea, as does Lynn Scarlett when she says, "This snapshot view also gives rise to a basic pessimism about technology and human action. Understandably, in a snapshot world view, technologies look like the problem rather than an evolving sequence of solutions" (1994, 252).

fragile personal values. They see that many things happen when we reshuffle resources, and that not all of them are good.

What should be our top priority – to clean up messes, or prevent them? Which is the key to reducing the amount of mess in the world? I am not against cleaning up messes, but I do want to say that if we focus on the first task and ignore the second, we miss the point of encouraging people to take responsibility for their own welfare. Encouraging people to take responsibility can help many of the people who need help right now, but that is not the main reason for such encouragement. The main reason is that when people take responsibility, they are less likely to need help in the first place.

When I refer to the static perspective as static, I mean no insult. I mean only to suggest that an exclusively static perspective is not enough. A static perspective looks at how things are, while a dynamic perspective looks at how things change. Each perspective is legitimate in its own way. The suffering we see from a static perspective is, after all, really there. Unfortunately, there are things we do not see from a static perspective. We do not see long-term progress. We do not see what causes long-term progress. Those things are abstract. They lack the visceral urgency of the crises of the day. But they are no less real.

If it is only from a static perspective that we fully appreciate the problems, it is only from a dynamic perspective that we fully appreciate what it takes to solve them.[5]

1.1.2 Individual versus Collective Responsibility: Not the Real Issue

I have been invited to defend individual responsibility and institutions that encourage it, but I have no problem with collective

---

[5] Robert Goodin (in section 2.3.2) draws an illuminating distinction between (backward looking) blame responsibility and (forward looking) task responsibility. Like Goodin, I focus on what he calls task responsibility. My distinction between static and dynamic perspectives can be thought of as a distinction between two ways of understanding our task responsibility.

responsibility per se. Individual versus collective responsibility is not the crucial distinction. More crucial is a distinction between what I call internalized and externalized responsibility. Economists say a decision involves a negative *externality* when someone other than the decision maker ends up bearing some of the decision's costs. A pulp mill dumping wastes into a river, leaving them to be dealt with by people downstream, is a classic example of a negative externality. The cost of cleaning up the mess is foisted upon people who played no part in causing it.

When I speak of responsibility being externalized, I have something similar in mind. Responsibility is externalized when people do not take responsibility: for messes they cause, for messes in which they find themselves. Responsibility is externalized when people regard the cleanup as someone else's problem. We can speak of responsibility being externalized whether the messes result from mistake, misfortune, or (in the case of the pulp mill) from business as usual. In contrast, responsibility is internalized when agents take responsibility: for their welfare, for their futures, for the consequences of their actions.[6]

The contrast between internalized and externalized responsibility does not neatly track the contrast between individual and collective responsibility. Collective responsibility can be a form of internalized responsibility. It can, in other words, be an example of people treating their welfare as their own responsibility. A group collectively internalizes responsibility when, but only when, members willingly take responsibility for themselves as a group. So, when family members willingly accept responsibility for each other, we can see them as internalizing responsibility even though the responsibility takes a collective form. To some extent, this is a semantic issue, but it points to a real difference: some people see their welfare as someone else's problem; other people see their welfare as their own problem.

---

[6] These different aspects of internalized responsibility sometimes amount to the same thing, but sometimes not. See section 1.3.2.3.

Someone could say redistributive taxation is a government's way of internalizing responsibility – in its eyes, those from whom it takes and those to whom it gives belong to the same group. That is not how I use the term, but I do not want to quibble over definitions. I introduce the idea of internalizing responsibility as one way of explaining what is going on in societies where people tend to prosper. In such societies, although people willingly take responsibility for themselves as individuals, they also willingly and reciprocally take responsibility for themselves as families, businesses, clubs, church groups, and so on. What strikes me about citizens of prosperous societies, then, is not their individualism so much as their willingness to take responsibility. It is that willingness to which the term 'internalization' is meant to point.

Collective responsibility as such is not a problem, but the urge to externalize responsibility is. Naturally, it would be comforting to know that if we lost our jobs tomorrow, strangers would be forced, against their will if necessary, to take care of us. So, why not say everyone has a guaranteed right to enjoy the kind of life-style that goes with being a productive member of society, whether or not one actually is a productive member? Edwin Baker claims, "If the practices of the society indicate that certain things are necessary in order to be a full member, then the community must assure the provision of these things to all who are expected to be part of the community."[7]

Baker leaps straight from the premise that some things are necessary to the conclusion that guaranteed provision of those things is necessary. That leap is a mistake. Our need for food, clothing, and shelter is beyond question; our need for guaranteed provision is not. Nor is guaranteed provision guaranteed to make people better off. After all, the guarantee does not mean the goods are free. What it means is someone else has to pay. It means people have to pay for other people's needs and other people's mistakes instead of their own.

---

[7] Baker 1974, 52.

1.1.3   Assigning Blame: Not the Real Issue

My brother Jim smoked two packs of cigarettes a day. He died of lung cancer at the age of thirty-nine. I sometimes think anyone who ever sold Jim a cigarette ought to be in jail, but Jim blamed himself. He did not need to guess at what role he played in his impending death, either. He knew beyond reasonable doubt. Untangling joint responsibility may be an intractable problem in theory. It can look that way to theorists. In practice, figuring out whom to blame is a matter of daily routine in any court of law.

But this essay is not about whom to blame. It is about institutional settings that make people more likely to take responsibility. *Holding* people responsible involves assigning blame or credit. When I speak of *taking* responsibility, I use the term in a different way. To take responsibility is to accept a cluster of challenges: to plan your future, to deal with your own mistakes as best you can, to deal with other people's mistakes as best you can, to make the best of your good luck, and your bad luck as well.

Internalizing responsibility, then, also is a cluster of things. In particular, it involves being committed to working for a living. (It need not involve working for wages. Homemakers and subsistence farmers work for a living.) It does not preclude cooperation or mutual aid, though. More generally, we internalize responsibility when we take responsibility for the future. We need not take credit for the past. We internalize responsibility when we take responsibility for making use of our opportunities. We need not take credit for the existence of those opportunities. We internalize responsibility when we see our problems as our problems; we need not see them as our fault.

Internalizing responsibility is not a matter of courts sorting out how much to blame Jim and how much to blame tobacco companies for Jim's death. It is more a matter of courts doing what they can (1) to make tobacco companies take a more proactive responsibility for the consequences of their actions, and (2) to make people like Jim do the same, so as to save people like Jim from tobacco companies, and also from themselves. In turn, citizens internalize responsibility when they face the world of tangled joint causation as it is, and do not rely on courts to save them from themselves.

Courts can be relevant to our question about what makes people better off, not by assigning blame so much as by leading people to take responsibility for their own choices. Holding drunk drivers accountable can make people think twice about drinking and driving. Holding polluters accountable can make pulp mills think twice about what they put in the river. We could say no one is to blame for anything, or everyone is to blame for everything. It would not affect the fundamental point. The upshot of the distinction between internalized and externalized responsibility is not that pulp mills are to blame for messes they cause, or that people downstream are to blame for messes in which they find themselves. The upshot is that people are better off when pulp mills take steps to avoid doing damage, and people are better off when people downstream take steps to avoid suffering damage.

How, then, can institutions help? It would be easy to oversimplify obstacles facing institutions that would lead people to internalize responsibility. The big oversimplification, though, lies in supposing we do not need to internalize responsibility – that a cure for poverty lies in taking wealth from those who create it and giving it to those who do not. Causation is indeed complex, so we should not be surprised if and when simply handing out other people's money fails to do much good.

Some people think social conditions partly determine whether people take responsibility. I agree. I have been stressing the point. I have heard it said that when people fail to take responsibility, it is not entirely their fault. And if it is not entirely their fault, then they should not be punished for it. Therefore, society – that is, other people who are not even partly at fault – ought to pay. That conclusion does not follow, but in any case, the real implication is hard to miss: if institutions determine whether people take responsibility, then we should favor institutions that lead people to take responsibility.[8]

1.1.3.1 Federal Deposit Insurance

Consider an example. It is hard to quarrel with America's Federal Deposit Insurance Corporation (FDIC). There was a time when depositors worried that if their bank went bankrupt, they would lose everything. The FDIC was created in 1934 to address this worry, which it did by guaranteeing that if a failed bank could not honor its commitments, the federal government would. The FDIC virtually eliminated panic-driven bank failures.

However, it did so by encouraging people to externalize responsibility. The FDIC guaranteed that the risk of depositing money at an insolvent savings and loan institution would be borne by taxpayers in general, not by particular depositors. Savings and loan institutions, in turn, no longer needed to worry that reckless lending policies would scare away depositors. Under the FDIC's umbrella, and empowered by a deregulation of interest rates, institutions began competing for deposits not by being safer than the competition – safety was a moot point – but by offering ever higher interest rates, thereby causing an epidemic of insolvency.

As described by Eugenie Short, a vice-president of the Federal Reserve Bank, "The FDIC charges a fixed premium for deposit insurance without regard to the riskiness of bank portfolios – an

---

[8] David Gauthier notes that a just society is not neutral among life plans. Where life plans are chosen, there is no injustice in declining to support a person whose plan involves not working. (These reflections are from my notes on Gauthier's presentation at the 1996 Wittgenstein Symposium.)

Robert Goodin (section 2.2.3) denies that people make detailed whole-life plans, but Gauthier presumably would say his point holds for the kinds of rudimentary plans (to get a job, to collect unemployment insurance) that people do in fact make. While I think Gauthier is right, my own argument does not depend on whether life plans are chosen. My concern is how to help, not whom to blame. However, to the extent that people do choose plans, the question of how to help people becomes a question of how to help people make better choices.

action that insulates banks from the full cost of incurring risk."[9] Federal deposit insurance "removes the incentive for depositors to monitor banks and withdraw deposits from banks that approach insolvency or assume increased asset risk, because the safety of deposits is guaranteed."[10] In fact, it "created an environment whereby depositors *sought out* the most insolvent institutions to earn higher yields on fully insured deposits."[11]

> Federally-insured depositors did not expect to incur financial losses on insured deposits and even sought to maintain deposits at insolvent institutions paying higher rates. . . . The higher rates offered by these insolvent institutions also pushed up the overall cost of deposits in local deposit markets as the solvent institutions bid up their own cost of funds to maintain their funding base. This competitive bidding process between solvent and insolvent financial institutions not only increased the cost of resolving the insolvent institutions, it also weakened the financial condition of the solvent banks and thrifts and may have contributed to additional financial failures.[12]

Hence, the crisis. People debate whether to blame deregulation or the FDIC itself. I consider that debate pointless. I am criticizing the combination: the effect of deregulating interest rates while leaving FDIC in place was to turn FDIC into a tool for externalizing responsibility for the cost of high-risk investments.[13]

Some sort of deregulation was necessary, though. The capping of interest rates had made savings and loan institutions unable to compete, leading to wild fluctuations in their reserves as changing money market and treasury bill rates (for example) led depositors to rush into or out of savings and loan institutions, thus creating the credit crunches for which the 1970s were famous.

---

[9] Short 1985, 13. Interestingly, this was written before America's savings and loan crisis.
[10] Short, Gunther, and Klemme 1991, 3.
[11] Short and Robinson, 1991, 128. Emphasis added.
[12] Ibid., 130.
[13] For a lucid analysis of the pros and cons of regulation and mixed economy institutions in general, see Ikeda 1996.

A different kind of deregulation – relaxing controls on interstate banking – enables banks to spread risk internally, insuring themselves against local crises. (Canada's Great Depression was as severe as America's, but no banks failed. There were no restrictions on interprovincial branch banking.) Relaxing controls on interstate banking would have put financial institutions in a better position to internalize responsibility. In contrast, relaxing controls on interest rates while leaving the FDIC in place put financial institutions in a better position to externalize responsibility. People were free to take risks in an environment where, if you lose, you lose someone else's money, not your own.

The example illustrates why we are tempted by externalized responsibility: by promising that people who make mistakes will not have to pay for them, externalized responsibility makes a sometimes frightening world feel safe. The same crisis illustrates externalization's typically high cost. More mistakes get made. Bigger mistakes get made. And someone has to pay.

1.1.4   How to Make Sure the Poor Are Left Behind

Some theorists look at those who are left behind, and all they see, to invoke another familiar metaphor, is the part of the glass that remains empty. My role in this book is to draw attention to the part of the glass that has been filled. That is the point of internalizing responsibility. The people who take responsibility are the people who fill the glass.

If the degree of internalization now in place has not filled the glass to the brim, some people conclude that internalization has failed. They say we need something else, usually something that, in my eyes, involves punching holes in the glass. Danziger, Haveman, and Plotnick estimate that every dollar in U.S. welfare transfers causes a twenty-three-cent reduction in the amount of labor that recipients contribute to the economy.[14] Is the number correct? I do not know, but I am confident that any institution that has such a result is not good for people. Not good for recipients.

---

[14] Danziger, Haveman, and Plotnick 1981, 1020.

Not good for their neighbors. My view is, if you want a full glass, then you want institutions that lead people to live and interact in ways that fill the glass.

President Clinton presumably wanted to help fill the glass in 1993 when he tried to appropriate $17 billion for a program he predicted would create five hundred thousand jobs. From a static perspective, it was an obvious response to problems visible in the current frame. Suppose Clinton's numbers were correct. That would amount to $34,000 for every job created. How many jobs would be created if that much money were left in the hands of those who produced it? Five hundred thousand? A million?

All we know for sure is that, when the appropriation was denied, the unemployment rate fell. By August 1996, it had fallen to 5.1 percent. The unemployment rate for African American males over age twenty fell to 8.1 percent.[15] No minority ever was more notoriously left behind than African Americans, yet their unemployment rate was lower than the *overall* unemployment rates of Germany (10 percent), Italy (12.2 percent), France (12.5 percent), and Spain (22.9 percent).[16] With no help from Mr. Clinton's plan to create five hundred thousand new jobs, the United States economy went on to create fifteen million.[17] It is easy to ignore the part of the glass that is full. When we ignore it, it does not occur to us to ask what fills it. In turn, it does not occur to us that the things we do to fill the empty part can undermine productive activities that fill the glass in the first place.

[15] *Time*, Sept. 16, 1996, p. 68.

[16] Grose 1996. There are several ways to explain (or explain away) these numbers. Grose says, "Laws in many European countries, including Germany, Italy, and France, make it all but impossible to fire people. So companies don't hire – they invest in equipment instead" (p. 2B). Gary Becker says the European picture is worse than the numbers suggest, for new jobs in Europe tend to be temporary or casual, owing to the difficulty of firing regular staff. Moreover, in Europe "those out of work for more than a year now account for one-third of the unemployed" (1996, 101).

[17] Between January 1993 and July 1997. In 1993, the unemployment rate was 7.5 percent. As of July 1997, it had dropped to 4.8 percent. Source: Bureau of Labor Statistics (on-line labor force statistics from the current population survey).

It is amazing that anyone could afford what average members of market societies can afford today. People in market societies view famine as an aberration, but it became unusual only recently, and only in some countries. People sometimes make an extraordinary claim about what market society can afford. They claim market society is so rich it can afford to become a non-market society – a society whose central government is licensed to distribute according to need. Or, if we cannot afford to convert the whole society to a nonmarket system, surely we can create enclaves within which people are sheltered from the imperative to produce something of value and can instead acquire money simply by needing it. Obviously, such enclaves can and do co-exist with market society, but not without cost. While people are sheltered from the tide (i.e., from the need to contribute to it), the tide is leaving them and their children behind. If the enclaves' inhabitants find themselves living like victims of a Third World economic disaster, and if their children are no more ready to participate in market society than suddenly free citizens of the former Soviet Union, what do we conclude? If we look only at the snapshot, it will seem obvious: we need bigger enclaves.

Robert Goodin has said that within a nation's population there is "much productive potential; but to bring out that productive potential, people must be healthy, educated, well fed, etc. The welfare state guarantees that such basic needs are met.... That the welfare state contributes in this way to economic efficiency is pretty well indisputable."[18] Is it true that children of welfare recipients are *guaranteed* to be healthy, educated, and well fed?

I wish it were true. William Ecenbarger spent five weeks in the Australian Outback. He came back with the story of Thomas Dutton.

> Over the past 40,000 years, some 1600 generations of Aborigines have lived in Australia.... But now Aborigines like Thomas Dutton are being subjected to something they may not

---

[18] Goodin 1988, 237.

outlast: a welfare system that creates dependency and destroys self-respect. . . . At 15 Thomas quit school, and five months later, on his 16th birthday, started collecting his new tax-free unemployment benefit and rent assistance – about $128 every two weeks. He automatically qualified, even though he had never worked. He spent most of the money to purchase as many hours of alcohol oblivion as he could. . . . During these years Wilcannia [Dutton's home town] deteriorated right along with Thomas Dutton. Technology in the wool industry reduced the need for shearers. People who preferred work to welfare moved to find jobs. Those content with the dole stayed on. . . . Between 1991 and 1995 the town saw 122 births and just three marriages. Thomas Dutton's sister, Vicky, had a son at 17 and immediately qualified for allowances totaling $283 every two weeks. Now 25, she spends her days drunk or wandering around Wilcannia begging for more money to buy booze. She has never had a job.[19]

None of us wants to live in a society where people are starving, but if we genuinely want to help our fellow citizens, we should stop to remind ourselves that the overwhelming majority of our fellow citizens are contributors. They are not being left behind. They do not need our help. We should try not to change that. Above all, we should avoid further disrupting the economic processes in virtue of which ordinary citizens of market societies do not need our help.

Welfare programs, though, sometimes seem highly disruptive. They seem not to encourage people to take responsibility. In the United States, out-of-wedlock births have risen by over 600 percent since 1960. They now comprise over 30 percent of the total. (Japan's illegitimacy rate, by comparison, is 1.1 percent.)[20] Thirty percent of out-of-wedlock births are to teenagers. Sixty percent are to women who were teenagers when they began bearing out-of-wedlock children.[21] Several studies suggest that

[19] Ecenbarger 1996, 169–73.
[20] Nechyba 1997.
[21] Tanner 1996, 70–1.

incentive structures of programs like Aid to Families with Dependent Children (AFDC) have made the problem worse.[22]

However, even if AFDC initially caused the problem, it does not follow that simply shutting down AFDC would make the problem disappear. The current problem is not merely a matter of perverse incentives but also a matter of transformed values and attitudes – a transformed sense of responsibility – and no one can think the transformation is easy even to understand, let alone undo.[23] We have experimented with externalized responsibility on a massive scale, without what scientists would consider an adequate experimental control.

In some cases, the experiments were self-conscious attempts to encourage dependency. There was a time when journalist Richard Elman could say, in all seriousness, "Perhaps when all our poor have been made dependent upon government and assured of stability and decency, liberty, and justice, we will be able to worry about how they work out their psychic destinies without seeming like hypocrites. In the meantime, data that the American poor are not yet dependent accumulates."[24] Elman concludes that "we of the rising middle class must somehow dispel our own myth that we are not dependent and do not wish to become dependent. We must try to create even more agencies of dependency."[25]

And so it was. When New York City Mayor John Lindsay appointed Mitchell Ginsberg as his social services commissioner,

> Ginsberg organized his staff to go out and recruit more people on to the welfare rolls. Using federal funds, they set up some 200 storefront centers in the city to recruit new welfare clients.... The new commissioner both raised payments and eliminated eligibility background checks – people qualified for welfare on their own say-so.... New York City's welfare population barely grew between 1945 and 1960. But between 1960 and 1965, it grew by more than 200,000 to a total of 538,000. It

---

[22] For example, Lundberg and Plotnick 1995.

[23] Nechyba 1997.

[24] Elman 1966, 198.

[25] Ibid., 300.

then ballooned to a staggering 1,165,000 in 1971 – larger than the total populations of 15 states and more than double the size of the state's second largest city, Buffalo. Amazingly, the explosion occurred amid a great economic boom and declining black male unemployment.[26]

As I said, we do not have an experimental control. We know only so much about what happens to people and to their children when they go on welfare. We do not know what would have become of them if they had relied on themselves and on each other instead. And we do not know what will happen if we throw them off welfare now, a few years after encouraging them to get on.[27] Intuitively, though, we do know that it is a mistake to rescue children from the prospect of growing up poor by putting them in a situation where they grow up not knowing what being productive (or feeling the self-respect that goes with it) would even be like. The cure is worse, much worse, than the disease.

Some people say welfare programs encourage (or even re-quire) people to drop out of the work force.[28] Is it true? Citing the aforementioned study by Danziger et al., and describing it as a "masterly synthesis," Robert Goodin says, "the major U.S. income transfer programs, all taken together, are probably responsible for a total reduction of work hours by recipients amounting to 4.8 percent of total work hours for all workers in the U.S."[29]

---

[26] Siegel 1996, 14, 16.

[27] In the United States, though, we are finding out. Escambia County, Florida, is the first in the nation to run up against time limits for receiving AFDC benefits. "More than 1,400 of the 2,894 welfare recipients subject to time limits have gotten full-time jobs. More than 700 others are working part-time. Average earnings are $5.21 an hour. Only 728 remain on welfare. The 95 recipients whose benefits have expired represent only 3% of the 2,894 faced with the program's time limits. And only 44 of them left without a job or a known source of income.... State officials say those who have been cut off from welfare without work refused to cooperate with the program. Their cases don't evoke much sympathy: Panels of citizens that review them have yet to stop the clock for someone who refused to comply with the program's work rules" (Wolf 1997a, 6).

[28] Mead 1986.

[29] Goodin 1985b, 233.

Some authors have inferred from this that welfare recipients are only 4.8 percent less likely to work. However, Danziger et al. say, "the percentage of reduction in work per transfer recipient implied by this estimate is substantially larger than 4.8 percent."[30] How large? Danziger et al. estimate that "AFDC reduces work effort of the average recipient by roughly 600 hours per year."[31] Since the average person works under 2,000 hours (i.e., fifty weeks full-time) per year, AFDC therefore reduces average work effort by over 30 percent. If the figure of 600 hours is anywhere near the truth, AFDC recipients are indeed dropping out.[32]

When adults drop out, they are less able and perhaps less willing to send their children a signal that taking responsibility for their own welfare is part of growing up. If parents do not send that signal, what will become of their children? The answer is that the financial gap between people who accept responsibility for themselves and people who do not cannot help but grow over time (and the gap in self-esteem will grow along with it). The only way to share fully in society's growing wealth is to participate fully in the process that makes wealth grow.

If we wanted to guarantee that the poor would be left behind, here would be the way to do it: teach them that their welfare is someone else's responsibility.

1.1.5   How to Minimize Suffering

Many people will say we can afford to help the most helpless of our fellow citizens. I see no reason to disagree. That is one of market society's virtues. Its members can afford to be activists. Obviously, charities are not a miracle cure for poverty. Just as

---

[30] Danziger et al. 1981, 998.

[31] Ibid., 997.

[32] Why do they drop out? There is no simple explanation, but Tanner, Moore, and Hartman (1995, 27) calculate that AFDC payments, together with food stamps and associated benefits, are the equivalent of a pretax hourly wage of $14.76 in New York, $12.45 in Philadelphia, $11.35 in Baltimore, and $10.91 in Detroit, based on a forty-hour workweek.

obviously, neither are government programs. So, after we decide to help the most helpless of our fellow citizens, we still have to look at the history of our ways of trying to help, and ask which ones help. Some organizations have a history of actually doing some good. Many do not.

We are left with two questions. First, which economic, political, and cultural institutions put people in a position to lead peaceful and productive lives and thereby turn their society into what is, in their own eyes, a "cooperative venture for mutual advantage"?[33] Second, how can institutions minimize the suffering of people who are unable to contribute to that venture?

To the first question, I would say an institution helps people to live peaceful and productive lives when it leads people to take responsibility for their own welfare. To the second, I would say that if we want to minimize suffering, we must do so within the context of the goal of leading people (as individuals or as a group) to take responsibility. We have to do it that way. Why? Because if we fail to lead people to take responsibility, we will not minimize suffering either.

If we want to make the prosperity that goes with participating in cooperative ventures more accessible to those who are not now participating, we must first admit that trying to make participation unnecessary is not the solution.

1.1.6   Responsibility and Welfare

I have come to believe that material progress has less to do with individual responsibility and more to do with internalized responsibility. Unfortunately, from a static perspective, where the only question is how to comfort those who suffer, internalizing responsibility seems beside the point. Thus, a static perspective naturally gravitates toward helping people in ways that externalize responsibility. That gravitation toward externalized responsibility,

---

[33] I borrow the phrase from John Rawls. I do not claim to be interpreting the phrase as Rawls would.

I believe, explains why current welfare policies have not been more successful. Crudely put, we are asking our institutions to guarantee that people will not need to fend for themselves (or each other) when we ought to be asking our institutions to make people willing and able to fend for themselves (and each other).

Most people agree that people taking responsibility for their welfare is a good thing. It is not merely a good thing, though; it is a good thing upon which much of what we regard as good depends. It contributes to material prosperity both for those who take responsibility and for those with whom they interact (especially their children). Perhaps more fundamentally, whether one takes responsibility affects the kind of person one becomes, not just how wealthy one becomes. If we compare those who take responsibility with those who do not, there is no mystery about which kind of person we would rather be, or which kind of person we would like our neighbors (or children) to be.[34]

Of course, individual responsibility is not a policy tool. It is not something legislators can decide to deploy. It evolves under hospitable social arrangements, and decays under hostile ones. When it is gone, it does not come back by decree. Still, institutions matter. The following chapters ask which institutions lead people to take responsibility for themselves in peaceful and productive ways, thereby contributing to the welfare of people in general. I contend that property rights are preeminent among institutions that lead people to take responsibility for their welfare. Property institutions are a continuously evolving response to emerging variations of the tragedy of the commons, a situation where unregulated access to a scarce or fragile resource makes people less able and less willing to take responsibility for maintaining it.[35] Private property is one response. Communal property is another.

---

[34] That deeper interest in self-construction is what psychotherapist Nathaniel Branden has in mind when he says, "Our interests are not served when as adults, we see ourselves as helpless victims, even though we might have been as children" (1996, 14). I explore how we choose ends with a view to self-construction in Schmidtz 1994.

[35] Hardin 1968.

They each have a history of solving problems, although neither is a panacea. Any society's prosperity depends on the ability of its culture and institutions to inculcate expectations of individual responsibility. Just as certainly, though, some ways of collectivizing responsibility are compatible with a culture of personal accountability and initiative. Some have a history of enabling people to take responsibility for themselves as a group.

1.2 Why Isn't Everyone Destitute?

THE EVOLUTION of property law is driven by an ongoing search for ways to internalize externalities: positive externalities associated with productive effort and negative externalities associated with misuse of commonly held resources. In theory, and sometimes in practice, responsibility is individualized and internalized over time. Increasingly, people pay for their own mistakes and misfortunes, and not for the mistakes and misfortunes of others.

It is this result that is most striking from a static perspective. It makes the whole idea of private property seem deeply offensive to some. The ideology surrounding private property is a celebration of strength, of will, of courage, of talent. That unflinchingly optimistic celebration of human excellence inspires some people and infuriates others. But neither the philosophy nor the historical reality is merely about praising human strengths. Each is also about giving people a chance to develop their strengths in the first place.

In some cases, though, people are born with no potential to support themselves. They have to hope to live in a society where their neighbors will be strong enough to carry those who cannot carry themselves. In other cases, people support themselves and even save for retirement in a market society but would be lost in a nonmarket setting. They do not need to be carried by neighbors, but they do need opportunities to trade for products they cannot make for themselves. Section 1.1.5 spoke of society as a cooperative venture for mutual advantage. To be a cooperative venture for mutual advantage, though, society must first be a setting in which mutually advantageous interaction is possible. In the parlance of game theorists, society must be a positive-sum game, for the sake of those who can support themselves through trade, and also for the sake of those who cannot.

So, what determines whether society is a positive-sum game? This chapter explains how property institutions convert negative-sum and zero-sum games into positive-sum games, setting the stage for society's flourishing as a cooperative venture. Institutions of property effect this conversion in virtue of constituting the human race's most pervasive and most successful experiment in internalized responsibility.

The term 'property rights' is used to refer to a bundle of rights that could include rights to sell, lend, bequeath, and so on. In what follows, I use the phrase to refer primarily to the right of owners to exclude nonowners. Private owners have the right to exclude nonowners, but the right to exclude is a feature of property rights in general rather than the defining feature of private ownership in particular. The National Park Service claims a right to exclude. Communes claim a right to exclude nonmembers. This section does not settle which kind or which mix of public and private property institutions is best. Instead, it asks how we could justify *any* institution that recognizes a right to exclude. My answer, in short, is that recognizing a right to exclude enables people to take responsibility for their own welfare and, in the process, to make a living in peace.

1.2.1 Original Appropriation: The Problem

The right to exclude presents a philosophical problem, though. Consider how full-blooded rights differ from mere liberties.[36] If I am at liberty to plant a garden, that means my planting a garden is permitted. That leaves open the possibility of you being at liberty to interfere with my gardening as you see fit. Thus, mere liberties

---

[36] See Hohfeld 1919.

are not full-blooded rights. When I *stake a claim* to a piece of land, though, I claim to be changing other people's liberties – cancelling them somehow – so that other people no longer are at liberty to use the land without my permission. To say I have a right to the land is to say I have a right to exclude.

From where could such rights have come? There must have been a time when no one had a right to exclude. Everyone had liberties regarding the land, but not rights. (Perhaps this does not seem obvious, but if no one owns the land, no one has a right to exclude. If no one has a right to exclude, everyone has liberties.) How, then, did we get from each person having a liberty to someone having an exclusive right to the land? What justifies *original appropriation*, that is, staking a claim to previously unowned resources?

To justify a claim to unowned land, people do not need to make as strong a case as would be needed, other things equal, to justify confiscating land already owned by someone else. Specifically, since there is no prior owner in original appropriation cases, there is no one from whom one can or needs to get consent.[37] What, then, must a person do? Locke's idea seems to have been that any residual (perhaps need-based) communal claim to the land could be met if a person could appropriate it without prejudice to other people, in other words, if a person could leave "enough and as good" for others. This so-called Lockean proviso can be interpreted in many ways, but an adequate interpretation

---

[37] Following Locke (1690/1960, section 25), some say we start out holding the earth in common, perhaps as a gift from God. But holding the earth in common does not mean we own it (in the sense of having a right to exclude). Holding is merely holding. Locke himself (section 25) distinguishes between holding the earth in common and owning it. See Simmons 1992, 232n. Locke is rebutting the absolute monarchist Robert Filmer, who fails to make this distinction and thus incoherently assumes that the situation preceding the land's initial acquisition is a situation in which people (as a group) already own it, and therefore already have a veto – a right to exclude. Filmer says that "if but one man in the world had dissented, the alteration had been unjust, because that man by the law of nature had a right to the common use of all things" (1652/1991, 234).

will note that this is its point: to license claims that can be made without making other people worse off.

We also should consider whether the "others" who are to be left with enough and as good include not just people currently on the scene but latecomers as well, including people not yet born. John Sanders asks, "What possible argument could at the same time require that the present generation have scruples about leaving enough and as good for one another, while shrugging off such concern for future generations?"[38] Most theorists accept the more demanding interpretation. It fits better with Locke's idea that the preservation of humankind (which includes future generations) is the ultimate criterion by which any use of resources is assessed. Aside from that, we surely have a more compelling defense of an appropriation when we can argue that there was enough left over not just for contemporaries but also for generations to come.

Of course, when we justify original appropriation, we do not in the process justify expropriation. Some say institutions that license expropriation make people better off; I think our histories of violent expropriation are ongoing tragedies for us all. Capitalist regimes have tainted histories. Communist regimes have tainted histories. Europeans took land from Native American tribes, and before that, those tribes took the same land from other tribes. We may regard those expropriations as the history of markets or of governments or of Christianity or simply as the history of the human race. It makes little difference. This essay discusses the history of property institutions, not because their history can justify them, but rather because their history shows how some of them enable people to internalize responsibility and thereby make themselves and the people around them better off.[39] Among such institutions are those that license original appropriation (as opposed to expropriation).

---

[38] Sanders 1987, 377.

[39] Regarding the difference between justifying an institution by looking at how it emerged versus looking at how it functions, see Schmidtz 1990.

Note also that original appropriation is not merely a theoretical issue. Charles Sabel has said that today, all appropriation is really expropriation from previous owners.[40] But Sabel is wrong. For one thing, property in land – what lawyers call "real" property – is not the only kind of property. Among the world's more valuable pieces of property are Microsoft software programs. A few years ago, they belonged to no one. (They did not yet exist.) Then Microsoft became their original owner. The example is not unique. People have just begun to stake claims to gene sequences. The legitimacy of those claims is a matter of hot debate. Therefore, original acquisition (and its justification) remains a contemporary issue. Indeed, it is more important than ever, since the property being discovered (or created) today is more valuable than land ever was.[41]

1.2.2   Original Appropriation: A Solution

Private property's critics often have claimed that justifying original appropriation is the key to justifying private property, frequently offering a version of Locke's proviso as the standard of justification. Part of the proviso's attraction for such critics was that it seemingly could not be met. Even today, philosophers generally conclude that the proviso is, at least in the case of land appropriation, logically impossible to satisfy, and thus that (private) property in land cannot possibly be justified along Lockean lines.

The way Judith Thomson puts it, if "the first labor-mixer must literally leave as much and as good for others who come along later, then no one can come to own anything, for there are only finitely many things in the world so that every taking leaves less for others."[42] To say the least, Thomson is not alone:

---

[40] In lectures at European University of Florence (December 15, 1995). See also Mautner 1982.

[41] For a balanced discussion of differences between real and intellectual property, and of different ways of protecting intellectual property, see Palmer 1990.

[42] Thomson 1990, 330.

> We leave enough and as good for others only when what we take is not scarce.[43]

> The Lockean Proviso, in the contemporary world of overpopulation and scarce resources, can almost never be met.[44]

> Every acquisition worsens the lot of others – and worsens their lot in relevant ways.[45]

> The condition that there be enough and as good left for others could not of course be literally satisfied by any system of private property rights.[46]

And so on. If we take something out of the cookie jar, we *must* be leaving less for others. This appears self-evident. It has to be right.

1.2.2.1   Appropriation Is Not a Zero-Sum Game

But it is not right. First, it is by no means impossible – certainly not logically impossible – for a taking to leave as much for others. Surely we can at least imagine a logically possible world of magic cookie jars in which, every time you take out one cookie, more and better cookies take its place.

Second, the logically possible world I just imagined is the sort of world we actually live in. Philosophers writing about original appropriation tend to speak as if people who arrive first are luckier than those who come later. The truth is, first appropriators begin the process of resource creation; latecomers get most of the benefits. Consider America's first permanent English settlement, the Jamestown colony of 1607. (Or, if you prefer, imagine the life-styles of the first people to cross the Bering Strait from Asia.) Was their situation so much better than ours? They never had to worry about being overcharged for car repairs. They never awoke in the middle of the night to the sound of noisy refrigerators, or leaky faucets, or flushing toilets. They never had to change a light

---

[43] Fried 1995, 230n.
[44] Held 1980, 6.
[45] Bogart 1985, 834.
[46] Sartorius 1984, 210.

bulb. They never agonized over the choice of long-distance telephone companies.

Philosophers are taught to say, in effect, that original appropriators got the good stuff for free. We have to pay for ugly leftovers. But in truth, original appropriation benefits latecomers far more than it benefits original appropriators. Original appropriation is a cornucopia of wealth, but mainly for latecomers. The people who got here first never dreamed of things we latecomers take for granted. The poorest among us have life expectancies exceeding theirs by several *decades*. This is not political theory. It is not economic rhetoric. It is fact.

Original appropriation diminishes the stock of what can be *originally appropriated*, at least in the case of land, but that is not the same thing as diminishing the stock of what can be *owned*.[47] On the contrary, in taking control of resources and thereby removing those particular resources from the stock of goods that can be acquired by original appropriation, people typically generate massive increases in the stock of goods that can be acquired by trade. The lesson is that appropriation typically is not a zero-sum game. It normally is a positive-sum game. As Locke himself stressed, it creates the possibility of mutual benefit on a massive scale.[48] It creates the possibility of society as a cooperative venture.

The argument is not merely that enough is produced in appropriation's aftermath to compensate latecomers who lost out in the race to appropriate. The argument is that the bare fact of being an original appropriator is not the prize. The prize is prosperity, and latecomers win big, courtesy of those who got here

---

[47]   Is it fair for latecomers to be excluded from acquiring property by rules allowing original appropriation? Sanders (1987, 385) notes that latecomers "are *not* excluded from acquiring property by these rules. They are, instead, excluded from being the first to own what has not been owned previously. Is *that* unfair?"

[48]   Or, at least, Locke estimates that 99 percent of the value of products of the earth is attributable to labor inputs (1690/1960, section 40, also 43). When we add this to the premise (implicit in section 35) that parceling the commons allows labor to multiply the products of the earth, we can infer that, in contemporary terms, appropriation is a positive-sum game.

first. If anyone had a right to be compensated, it would be the first appropriators.

1.2.2.2   The Commons before Appropriation Is Not Zero-Sum Either

The second point is that the commons before appropriation is not a zero-sum game either. Typically it is a negative-sum game. Let me tell two stories.[49] The first comes from the coral reefs of the Philippine and Tongan Islands. People once fished those reefs with lures and traps, but have recently caught on to a technique called bleach fishing, which involves dumping bleach into the reefs. Fish cannot breath sodium hypochlorite. Suffocated, they float to the surface where they are easy to collect.[50]

The problem is, the coral itself is composed of living animals. The coral suffocates along with the fish, and the dead reef is no longer a viable habitat. (Another technique, blast fishing, involves dynamiting the reefs. The concussion produces an easy harvest of stunned fish and dead coral.) You may say people ought to be more responsible. They ought to preserve the reefs for their children.

That would miss the point, which is that individual fishermen lack the option of saving the coral for their children. Individual fishermen obviously have the option of not destroying it them-selves, but what happens if they elect not to destroy it? What they *want* is for the reef to be left for their children; what is actually happening is that the reef is left for the next blast fisher down the line. If a fisherman wants to have anything at all to give his children, he must act quickly, destroying the reef and grabbing the fish himself. It does no good to tell fishermen to take respon-sibility. They are taking responsibility – for their children. Existing

---

[49] Regarding the first story, see Chesher 1985 and Gomez, Alcala, and San Diego 1981. Regarding the second story, I thank Peggy Fosdick at the National Aquarium in Baltimore for correspondence and documents. See also Fosdick and Fosdick 1994.

[50] Nash (1996) says fishermen currently pump 330,000 pounds of cyanide per year into Philippine reefs.

institutional arrangements do not empower them to take responsibility in a way that would save the reef.

Under the circumstances, they are at liberty not to destroy the reef themselves, but they are not at liberty to do what is necessary to save the reef for their children. To save the reef for their children, fishermen must have the power to restrict access to the reef. They must claim a right to exclude blast fishers. Whether they stake that claim as individuals or as a group is secondary, so long as they actually succeed in restricting access. But one way or another, they must claim and effectively exercise a right to restrict access.

The second story comes from the Cayman Islands. The Atlantic green turtle has long been prized as a source of meat and eggs. The turtles were a commonly held resource and were being harvested in an unsustainable way. In 1968, when by some estimates there were as few as three to five thousand left in the wild, a group of entrepreneurs and concerned scientists created Cayman Turtle Farm and began raising and selling captive-bred sea turtles. In the wild, as few as one-tenth of 1 percent of wild hatchlings survive to adulthood. Most are seized by predators before they can crawl from nest to sea. Cayman Farm, though, boosted the survival rate of captive-bred animals to well over 50 percent. At the peak of operations, they were rearing in excess of a hundred thousand turtles. They were releasing 1 percent of their hatchlings into the wild at the age of ten months, an age at which hatchlings had a decent chance of surviving to maturity.

In 1973, commerce in Atlantic green turtles was restricted by the Convention on International Trade in Endangered Species and, in the United States, by the Fish and Wildlife Service, the Department of Commerce, and the Department of the Interior. Under the newly created Endangered Species Act, the United States classified the Atlantic green turtle as an endangered species, but Cayman Farm's business was unaffected, at first, because regulations pertaining to commerce in Atlantic green turtles exempted commerce in captive-bred animals. In 1978, however, the regulations were published in their final form, and although exemptions were granted for trade in captive-bred animals of other species, no exemption was made for trade in turtles. The company could no longer do business in the United States. Even worse, the company no longer could ship its products through American ports, so it no longer had access via Miami to world markets. The farm exists today only to serve the population of the Cayman Islands themselves. The Atlantic green turtle's future is, once again, in doubt.

What do these stories tell us? The first tells us we do not need to justify failing to preserve the commons in its pristine, original, unappropriated form, because preserving the commons in pristine original form is not an option. The commons is not a time capsule. Leaving resources in the commons is not like putting resources in a time capsule as a legacy for future generations. In some cases, putting resources in a time capsule might be a good idea. However, the second story reminds us that there are ways to take what we find in the commons and preserve it – to put it in a time capsule – but that before we can put something in a time capsule, we have to appropriate it.[51]

1.2.2.3 Justifying the Game

Note a difference between justifying institutions that regulate appropriation and justifying particular acts of appropriation. Think of original appropriation as a game and of particular acts of appropriation as moves within that game. Even if the game itself is justified, a given move within the game may have nothing to recommend it. Indeed, we could say (for argument's sake) that any act of appropriation will seem arbitrary when viewed in isolation, and some will seem unconscionable. Even so, there can be compelling reasons to have an institutional framework that recognizes property claims on the basis of moves that would carry no moral weight in an institutional vacuum. Common law implicitly acknowledges morally weighty reasons for not requiring

---

[51] A private charity, The Nature Conservancy, is pursuing such a strategy. Although not itself an original appropriator, it has acquired over a billion dollars' worth of land in an effort to preserve natural ecosystems. Note that this includes habitats for endangered species that have no market value.

original appropriators to supply morally weighty reasons for their appropriations.[52] Particular acts of appropriation are justified not because they carry moral weight but rather because they are permitted moves within a game that carries moral weight.

Needless to say, the cornucopia of wealth generated by the appropriation and subsequent mobilization of resources is not an unambiguous benefit. The commerce made possible by original appropriation creates pollution, and other negative externalities as well. (See section 1.3.2.) Further, there may be people who attach no value to the increases in life expectancy and other benefits that accompany the appropriation of resources for productive use. Some people may prefer a steady-state system that indefinitely supports their life-styles as hunter-gatherers, untainted by the shoes and tents and safety matches of Western culture. If original appropriation forces such people to participate in a culture they want no part of, then from their point of view, the game does more harm than good.

Here are two things to keep in mind, though. First, as I said, the commons is not a time capsule. It does not preserve the status quo. For all kinds of reasons, quality of life could drop after appropriation. However, pressures that drive waves of people to appropriate are a lot more likely to compromise quality of life when those waves wash over an unregulated commons. In an unregulated commons, those who conserve pay the costs but do not get the benefits of conservation, while overusers get the benefits but do not pay the costs of overuse. Therefore, an unregulated commons is a prescription for overuse, not for conservation.

Second, the option of living the life of a hunter-gatherer has not entirely disappeared. It is not a comfortable life. It never was. But it remains an option. There are places in northern Canada and elsewhere where people can and do live that way. As a bonus, those who opt to live as hunter-gatherers retain the option of participating in Western culture on a drop-in basis during medical emergencies, to trade for supplies, and so on. Obviously, someone

---

[52] See Rose 1985.

might respond, "Even if the hunter-gatherer life is an option now, that option is disappearing as expanding populations equipped with advancing technologies claim the land for other purposes." Well, probably so. What does that prove? It proves that, in the world as it is, if hunter-gatherers want their children to have the option of living as hunter-gatherers, then they need to stake a claim to the territory on which they intend to preserve that option. They need to argue that they, as rightful owners, have a right to regulate access to it. If they want a steady-state civilization, they need to be aware that they will not find it in an unregulated commons. They need to argue that they have a right to exclude oil companies, for example, which would love to be able to treat northern Canada as an unregulated commons.[53]

If you say appropriation does not leave enough and as good for others, the reply should be, compared with what? Compared with the commons as it was? As it is? As it will be? Today, leaving resources *in the commons* does not leave enough and as good for others. The Lockean proviso, far from forbidding the appropriation of resources from the commons, actually requires appropriation under conditions of scarcity. Moreover, the more scarce that resources are, the more urgently the proviso requires that they be removed from the negative-sum game that is the unregulated commons.

I have made this point before.[54] A correspondent asked: "If we take the Proviso seriously – and assume it is actually enforced – then why would there be a tragedy of the commons?. . . If the Proviso precluded the taking of the property in the first place, then it doesn't seem as if the resource would be over-utilized." My point is that although the proviso *morally* precludes bleach fishing, the practice continues. Enforcement is a variable; it cannot be assumed. Real-world Tongan fishermen operate against a background of proviso violations, but a moral fisherman still faces the question of how to leave enough and as good for others. The

---

[53] See Tully 1994.
[54] Chapter 2 of Schmidtz 1991.

background of violations does not change the question, but it does change the answer. Specifically, when the burden of common use exceeds the resource's ability to renew itself, the proviso comes to require, not merely permit, people to appropriate the resource and regulate access to it. Even in an unregulated commons, *some* fishermen will practice self-restraint, but something has to happen to incline the *group* to practice self-restraint in cases where it has already shown it has no such inclination in an unregulated commons.

Removing goods from the commons stimulates increases in the stock of what can be owned and limits losses that occur in tragic commons. Appropriation replaces a negative-sum with a positive-sum game. Therein lies a justification for social structures enshrining a right to remove resources from the unregulated commons: when resources become scarce, we need to remove them if we want them to be there for our children. Or anyone else's.

1.2.3   What Is It Like to Be Poor?

This chapter defended appropriation of, and subsequent regulation of access to, scarce resources as a way of preserving (and creating) resources for the future. When resources are abundant, the Lockean proviso permits appropriation; when resources are scarce, the proviso requires appropriation. It is possible to appropriate without prejudice to future generations. Indeed, when resources are scarce, it is leaving them in the commons that is prejudicial to future generations.

But what about the present generation? Part of this chapter's point is that the present generation *is* a future generation. A variety of property institutions are internalizing responsibility and unleashing people's productive energies right now, not merely in the distant future. And that is why not everyone is destitute.

I noted that the welfare state by no means guarantees that children will be healthy, educated, and well fed. What is true, though, is that children in general are healthier, better educated, and better fed today (to the point of being taller on average) than children of a century ago. Our long-run prospects are improving.

Short-run trends are harder to discern. Some people think wages have stagnated since 1980, but U.S. Census Bureau statistics say otherwise.

> The Census Bureau keeps statistics separately for "families" and "unrelated individuals." Census Bureau figures show that between 1980 and 1989, real income for the middle quintile of families increased by 8.3%, while real income for the middle quintile of unrelated individuals increased by 16.3%.
>
> The CBO [Congressional Budget Office] manipulated this Census Bureau data by combining "families" and "unrelated individuals" into the single category of "families." Since demographic trends produced more rapid growth in the number of unrelated individuals in the 1980s, and since families headed by two adults on average have far higher incomes than unrelated individuals, combining these groups into a single category greatly depressed average "family" incomes. Thus, even though the incomes of middle-quintile families increased by 8.3% and the incomes of middle-quintile individuals increased by 16.3%, middle-quintile "families" in the CBO's sense saw their total incomes decline by 0.8% over the same period.[55]

If it is unclear how a group's income could drop as its component incomes rise by 8.3 and 16.3 percent, consider a simple illustration. Suppose family X's income is $1,000 and individual Y's is $100. Average income is $550. Later, family X's income rises to $1,080 while individual Y's rises to $116. Meanwhile, the extra money enables family X's daughter to leave home and live on her own, so there are now two individuals each earning $116. If we then average the three incomes, we get an average income of $437, an apparent $113 drop in average income even though everyone's income is in fact rising.

So, if even the Congressional Budget Office's numbers cannot be trusted, whom can we trust? Newspapers are full of statistics. I try to put some of them in perspective here, but we have to avoid being too impressed by numbers. Even a scrupulously honest treatment can mislead. For example, people who track

---

[55] Hinderaker and Johnson 1996, 35.

income trends correct for inflation, as they should, but they use the Consumer Price Index to measure inflation. If that measure is inaccurate, then the resulting adjustment for inflation will be increasingly misleading over time. Thus, Robert Samuelson suggests, "The notion that most people's incomes and living standards are stagnating is simply false. Not only is it contradicted by the outpouring of new consumer products and services. It is also contradicted by official statistics, which, once corrected for slight overstatement of inflation, show sizable gains."[56] In December 1996, a panel of five economists, commissioned by the Senate Finance Committee and chaired by Michael Boskin, concluded that the consumer price index overstates inflation by about 1.1 percent per year (perhaps as little as 0.8 percent; perhaps as much as 1.6 percent).[57] If Boskin's figure of 1.1 percent is correct, then "instead of the stagnation recorded in official statistics, a lower inflation measure would mean that *real* median family income grew from 1973 to 1995 by 36 percent."[58]

But suppose, for the sake of argument, that the bottom quintile's average income has not risen in thirty years. What would that mean? Would it mean a fifth of the population has incomes that were low to begin with and that have not risen in thirty years? Or would it mean a fifth of the population consists of youths barely out of high school who pump gas and work in fast-food restaurants, and whose wages are about what people their age were earning in the same jobs thirty years ago?

If the latter interpretation (corrected for overstated inflation as necessary) is closer to the truth, then what became of all those people who were young and poor thirty years ago? They are now about fifty years old. Are they still pumping gas? Or, if their place in the bottom quintile was inherited by people who are barely out of high school now, then where did they go as they grew older?

---

[56] Samuelson 1996, 32.
[57] Source: *Economist*, December 7, 1996, 25.
[58] Source: *U.S. News and World Report*, September 8, 1997, 104. Emphasis added.

The gap between the incomes of the rich and the poor seems to have widened over the past thirty years. What does it mean? Does it mean some people's incomes have always been high, other people's will always be low, and the gap has widened in real terms? Or does it mean people who are young and poor now have better opportunities than young people had thirty years ago – people are earning more as they age than their counterparts earned thirty years ago, thus producing a gap between poor twenty-year-olds and rich fifty-year-olds that is larger now than it was thirty years ago?

Thomas Nagel finds it "appalling that the most effective social systems we have been able to devise permit so many people to be born into conditions of harsh deprivation which crush their prospects for leading a decent life,"[59] but the Census Bureau found that 25.7 percent of those below the poverty line in 1987 were no longer below it *one year later*.[60] In absolute terms, "individuals in the lowest income quintile in 1975 saw, on average, a $25,322 rise in their real income over the 16 years from 1975 to 1991. Those in the highest income quintile had a $3,974 increase in real income, on average."[61] Note that the change is real, not nominal. (The change would be larger if we adjusted for inflation overstatement.)

If those numbers are correct, then we must be misinterpreting statistics that show a growing gap between incomes of the top and bottom quintiles. We see that gap as a growing gap between incomes of separate social classes, when in reality much of that gap is between young people just starting out and the same people as they reach their peak earning years. As of 1994, average household income is $16,407 when the head of the household is under 25. Average income rises to $34,051 for ages 25–34, to $46,217 for ages 35–44, and to $49,627 for ages 45–54.[62]

---

[59] Nagel 1991, 64.
[60] Reported by Schansberg 1996, 8.
[61] Census Bureau data, reported by Cox and Alm 1995, 8.
[62] Source: U.S. Department of Labor 1996, 8.

These numbers suggest that people move into higher income quintiles as they age. And indeed they do, as a general rule. The U.S. Treasury Department's Office of Tax Analysis found that of people in the bottom income quintile in 1979, 65 percent moved up two or more quintiles by 1988.[63] Is that finding unique? Not at all. Tracking a separate group of people occupying the lowest quintile in 1975, the Census Bureau saw 80.3 percent move up two or more quintiles by 1991.[64]

It is sometimes said that poverty rates are rising. The truth: poverty rates rise during recessions but the U.S. trend is downward. In 1929 the poverty rate was 40 percent.[65] In 1962 (the earliest year for which my Census Bureau sources give a number) the rate was 21 percent. In 1993, the rate was 15.1 percent. In 1994, 14.5 percent. In 1995, 13.8 percent.[66] If a long-term rise in poverty rates were to occur, it could mean people are getting poorer. Or it could mean people are getting older. The poverty rate is defined in terms of reported income. Other things equal, it should rise as more people retire and live on savings rather than earned income.[67]

Until recently, child poverty rates had been rising, which should not be surprising given that so many more children are being raised by single mothers. We would, however, expect statistics to exaggerate their poverty, for the welfare benefits upon which many of them depend are not included in the household's income. So, some people drop below the poverty line not because they are poorer but simply because they rely more on welfare benefits and less on (reported) earned income. (Here is another

---

[63] Reported by Schansberg 1996, 8.

[64] Reported by Cox and Alm 1995, 8.

[65] Levitan 1990, 5–6.

[66] Sources: U.S. Census Bureau 1996a, viii, xv, and Baugher and Lamison-White 1996, v.

[67] In 1970, 9.8 percent of the population was over sixty-five. In 1990, the figure was 12.5 percent. Moreover, people are retiring earlier. In 1967, 90 percent of men aged fifty-five to fifty-nine were in the labor force compared to 78 percent in 1993. Source: U.S. Census Bureau 1996c, table 2-1 and p. 4-1.

way in which statistics overstate the poverty of children raised by single mothers: when mothers live with men to whom they are not married, the man's income is not included in the household's income.)[68]

The idea of being in the bottom quintile conjures up images from the novels of Charles Dickens. What is it really like? In 1995, household income at the twentieth percentile was $14,400.[69] The poverty threshold in 1995 was $10,259 for a family of two.[70] So, statistically speaking, the income of a typical American graduate student is squarely within the bottom quintile, and is on the poverty line if the student has a nonworking spouse.[71] Of course, many graduate students get help from parents and thus do not live on reported income.[72] But that turns out to be pretty typical of people in the bottom income quintile. The U.S. Bureau of Labor Statistics reports that people in the bottom income quintile spend an average of $2.18 per dollar of reported before-tax earnings.[73] Their reported income is low, but half of what they spend comes from somewhere else.

In 1984, in households at or below the poverty line, 58.2 percent owned a washing machine, 12.5 percent owned a microwave oven, and 64.5 percent owned one or more cars. By 1994, the numbers had risen to 71.7, 60.0, and 71.8 percent,

---

[68] *The Economist*, citing a working paper by Christopher Jencks and Susan Mayer, says, "far from having increased by more than half, the child poverty rate is about the same as it was in 1969, and poor households are living a bit better. They have more space, with better plumbing; more than half have air conditioning; their children can see a doctor more often" (December 7, 1996, p. 28).

[69] U.S. Census Bureau 1996b, xii.

[70] Baugher and Lamison-White 1996, 1.

[71] Needless to say, not every poor person can afford the life-style of a typical graduate student. Indeed, it was a step up for me.

[72] I thank Jennifer Ryan for pointing this out. Many of my acquaintances had parental support as undergraduates. It had not occurred to me that this might be true of graduate students as well.

[73] Source: U.S. Department of Labor 1995, 14. The figure is for 1993. The on-line Consumer Expenditure Survey for 1995 reports that spending rose to $2.31 per dollar of reported before-tax earnings.

respectively.[74] This is not what we expect from an economy that is supposed to be leaving the poor behind.

According to the Bureau of Labor Statistics, 30 percent of those living in the bottom quintile own their homes *without a mortgage*.[75] It is no longer unusual for poor people to have access to flush toilets, hot running water, and electric light. It is not unusual for poor people to be able to hear the music of Mozart in their own homes. A century ago, these amenities and thousands of others would have been rare if not inconceivable for people in the bottom quintile. They are not inconceivable today, or even unusual. People in the bottom quintile are spectacularly well off compared with those who occupied the bottom quintile (or the top quintile) a century ago. We can see that by comparing representative graduate students, janitors, and especially housewives.[76] (People think life was simpler then, but I doubt my grandmothers would have agreed. Consider what was involved in the family's weekly bath night: water from a well, heat from a wood-burning stove, and soap from the fat of butchered farm animals.) In 1900, average life expectancy was 47.3 years in the United States. By 1990, it had risen to 75.4 years.[77]

There are people, though, who find it offensive to compare snapshots of today with snapshots of a century ago. To some, the fact that life in market society is vastly better than it was a century ago is beside the point. Therefore, my focus on processes that made life better will seem irrelevant. The only things that matter to them are problems they see in snapshots of today – the part of the glass not yet filled. No doubt, we all have much to learn. The dynamic aspect of poverty discussed in this section is only part of a larger picture, but it too often is the part that

---

[74] Source: Census Bureau data, as reported by Cox and Alm 1995, 22.

[75] Source: U.S. Department of Labor 1995, 14. My original source was Bartlett 1995.

[76] Geddes and Lueck 1997 discuss how far women have come in legal, cultural, and economic terms.

[77] Census Bureau data, reported by Hardie 1995, A3. This rise occurred despite the fact that the United States has a relatively poor record of reducing infant mortality.

goes unmentioned by reporters who have neither the training nor the incentive to understand current events from a dynamic perspective. That is why I stress it as much as I do.

People who take a static perspective sometimes think those who see things differently are indifferent to suffering. In some cases they may be right. People who take a dynamic perspective sometimes think those who see things differently do not care about the damage they do in their zeal to prove their hearts are in the right place. In some cases they too may be right. The world and what to do about it look very different from the two perspectives, which partly explains why debates about welfare policy can be so emotional. It is hard to resist attributing the worst motives to those who see things differently: racism, sexism, envy, whatever. We are tempted to do this not because we have evidence of such motives, but rather because, when it comes to human suffering, it is hard to imagine how decent people could have priorities radically unlike our own. I wish it were otherwise.

1.3   Responsibility and Community

S ORTING OUT individual contributions to cooperative ventures
is a classic problem facing any attempt to distribute equitably
the benefits of a communal enterprise. People being what they
are, some see themselves as doing more than their share. In their
eyes, other people are shirking. So they cut back. A co-worker
sees them cutting back, she too cuts back in response, and the
downward spiral has begun.

The problem is universal. Different forms of social organization
embody different solutions. Some solutions are better than others. Large private firms face the same problem – how to identify
and properly reward individual contributions. Finding answers
that everyone can live with is not always easy, but it is not always difficult, either. The degree of ambiguity attaching to individual contributions depends on the nature of the institutional
framework.

When ambiguity becomes a big problem, people invest in forms
of social or corporate organization that make it easier to evaluate
and quantify individual contributions. Private firms come up with
answers accurate enough to meet their needs, if and when they
perceive a need. Firms that become too big and cumbersome to
monitor properly the connection between contribution and compensation tend to break up into smaller units with better internal
accounting. Taking the costs and benefits of continued association into account, and not expecting perfection, employers and
employees reach an understanding they can live with, or else
they part company. The theoretical indeterminacy surrounding

the question of how to distribute the fruits of cooperation is never completely resolved in practice, and does not need to be. People learn to cooperate in ventures that remain mutually advantageous despite the indeterminacy.

Private firms handle the problem better than communes do, if we judge by what private firms produce compared with what communes produce. In no case, though, must the problem be fatal. However insuperable the problem may seem to theorists, the fact remains that people are better off when they go ahead and solve the problem as the need arises, theoretical difficulties notwithstanding.

Sometimes the lack of accounting is not a problem. Parents try to raise children who will have rewarding careers. Many of the benefits of their labors are dispersed as positive externalities, enjoyed but not paid for by future employers. Employers in turn train employees. The benefits eventually are dispersed as positive externalities enjoyed but not paid for by subsequent employers. Every parent and every employer benefits from previous contributions by other parents and employers. Money does not change hands, accounts are never settled, but everyone ends up better off.[78]

It is sometimes said that every invention is the result of thousands of people helping to produce the kind of society in which that invention becomes possible. Who would deny it? That is the nature of the tide. In a market society, we set sail on a tide already rising on the strength of other people's contributions.

We can admit that Thomas Edison's contributions were the result of thousands of people creating the tide of progress that put Edison in a position to do what he did. We can wonder what that means: should we honor those who did contribute, or take their money and give it to those who did not? We need not wonder,

---

[78] Some say money ought to change hands. They say governments should commodify child rearing by paying parents for being parents. (I trust it is obvious that paying them would involve raising their taxes and then giving their money back minus administrative costs.) My own view is that child rearing is roughly the last thing in the world that should be commodified.

though, whether to blame the unemployed (for avoiding work) or the government (for regulations that create so-called structural unemployment). In the end, what matters is this: however opaque individual contributions to social outcomes are in theory, a theory cannot stop people who take responsibility from making themselves and those around them better off. And it cannot stop people who fail to take responsibility from making themselves and those around them worse off.

Private property enables people (and gives them an incentive) to take responsibility for conserving scarce resources. It preserves resources under a wide variety of circumstances. It is the preeminent vehicle for turning negative-sum commons into positive-sum property regimes. However, it is not the only way. Evidently, it is not always the best way, either. Public property is ubiquitous, and it is not only rapacious governments and mad ideologues who create it. Sometimes it evolves spontaneously as a response to real problems, enabling people to remove a resource from an unregulated commons and take responsibility for its management. Like private property, public and communal property can enable people to internalize responsibility and thereby positively contribute to social welfare. This section discusses research by Harold Demsetz, Robert Ellickson, and Carol Rose, showing how various property institutions help to ensure that enough and as good is left for future generations.

1.3.1   The Unregulated Commons

An unregulated commons need not be as disastrous as the ones described in the previous chapter. An unregulated commons will work well enough so long as the level of use remains within the land's carrying capacity.[79] As use nears carrying capacity, however, there will be pressure to shift to a more exclusive regime. As an example of an unregulated commons evolving into something

---

[79] A resource's carrying capacity is the level of use the resource can sustain. See Hardin 1977.

else as increasing traffic began to exceed carrying capacity, consider Harold Demsetz's account of how property institutions evolved among indigenous tribes of the Labrador peninsula.[80] As Demsetz tells the story, the region's people had, for generations, treated the land as an open-access commons. The human population was small. There was plenty to eat. Responsibility for maintaining the resource was externalized, but it did not matter, because the pattern of exploitation was within the land's carrying capacity.[81] The resource maintained itself. In that situation, the Lockean proviso, as interpreted in section 1.2, was satisfied. Original appropriation would have been permissible, other things equal, but it was not required.

With the advent of the fur trade, though, the scale of hunting and trapping activity increased sharply. The population of game animals began to dwindle. The unregulated commons had worked for a while, but now the tribes were facing a classic tragedy. The benefits of exploiting the resource were internalized but the costs were not, and the arrangement was no longer viable. Clans began to mark out family plots. The game animals in question were small animals like beaver and otter that tend not to migrate from one plot to another. Thus, marking out plots of land effectively privatized small game as well as the land itself. In sum, the tribes converted the commons in nonmigratory fur-bearing game to family parcels when the fur trade began to spur a rising demand that exceeded the land's carrying capacity.

---

[80] Demsetz 1967. Demsetz has been criticized. "The essence of all the criticism is that Demsetz ignores how value-laden might be the processes that lead from common to private ownership," according to Dukeminier and Krier 1993, 61. Their overview, however, is favorable on the whole, and they cite several works (p. 62) that generally corroborate Demsetz's account.

[81] This was not true everywhere. I have seen places where tribes hunted bison by stampeding whole herds over the edge of a cliff. So I accept Dukeminier and Krier's warning against forming "an unduly romantic image of Native American culture prior to the arrival of 'civilization.' There is considerable evidence that some American Indian tribes, rather than being natural ecologists who lived in respectful harmony with the land, exploited the environment ruthlessly by overhunting and extensive burning of forests" (1993, 62).

When demand began to exceed carrying capacity, that was when the proviso came not only to permit but to require original appropriation.

One other nuance of the privatization of fur-bearing game: although the fur was privatized, the meat was not. There was still plenty of meat to go around, so tribal law allowed trespass on another clan's land to hunt for meat. Trespassers could kill a beaver and take the meat, but had to leave the pelt displayed in a prominent place to signal that they had eaten and had respected the clan's right to the pelt. The new customs went to the heart of the matter, privatizing what had to be privatized, leaving intact liberties that people had always enjoyed with respect to other resources where unrestricted access had not yet become a problem.

1.3.1.1 The Communal Alternative

We can contrast the unregulated or open-access commons with communes. A commune (following Ellickson)[82] is a restricted-access commons. In a commune, property is owned by the group rather than by individual members. People as a group claim and exercise a right to exclude. Typically, communes draw a sharp distinction between members and nonmembers, and regulate access accordingly. Public property tends to restrict access by time of day or year. Some activities are permitted; others are prohibited.

Ellickson has come to believe that a broad campaign to abolish either the kind of individual responsibility embodied in private property or the kind of collective responsibility embodied in public and communal property would be ludicrous. Each kind of property serves social welfare in its own way. Likewise, every ownership regime has its own externality problems.[83] Communal management leads to overconsumption and to shirking on maintenance and improvements, because people receive only a

---

[82] Ellickson 1993. This section discusses Ellickson's article in some detail. While I take little credit for the ideas in the next few pages, any errors are presumably mine.

[83] Ibid., 1326.

fraction of the value of their labor, and bear only a fraction of the costs of their consumption. To minimize these disincentives, a commune must intensively monitor people's production and consumption activities.

In practice, communal regimes can lead to indiscriminate dumping of wastes, ranging from piles of unwashed dishes to ecological disasters that threaten whole continents. Privately managed parcels also can lead to indiscriminate dumping of wastes and to various other uses that ignore spillover effects on neighbors. One advantage of private property is that owners can buy each other out and reshuffle their holdings in such a way as to minimize the extent to which their activities bother each other. But it does not always work out so nicely, and the reshuffling itself can be a waste. There are transaction costs. Thus, one plausible social goal would be to combine private and public property in a way that reduces the sum of transaction costs and the cost of externalities.

1.3.2   Local versus Remote Externalities

Is it generally better to convert an unregulated commons to smaller private parcels or to manage it as a commune with power to exclude nonmembers? It depends on what kind of activities people tend to engage in. Ellickson separates activities into three categories: small (e.g., cultivating a tomato plant), medium (e.g., damming part of a river to create a pond for ducks), and large (e.g., using an industrial smokestack to disperse noxious fumes).[84] The distinction is not meant to be sharp. As one might expect, it is a matter of degree. It concerns the relative size of the area over which externalities are worth worrying about. The effects of small events are confined to one's own property. Medium events affect people in the immediate neighborhood. Their external effects are localized. Large events affect people who are more remote. Ellickson says private regimes are clearly superior as methods for

---

[84] Ibid., 1325.

minimizing the costs of small and medium events. When it comes to large events, though, there is no easy answer to the question of which mix of private and public property is best.

1.3.2.1   Small Events

Small events are not much of a problem for private regimes. When land is parceled out, the effects of small events are internalized.[85] Neighbors do not care much when we pick tomatoes on our own land; they care a great deal when we pick tomatoes on the communal plot. In the former case, we are minding our own business; in the latter, we are minding theirs. Ellickson credits that point to Demsetz, adding that much of the internalization process has to do with changing monitoring costs. Private owners need only monitor border crossings, whereas communal owners need to monitor people's movements in much more elaborate and intrusive ways. As Ellickson puts it, "detecting the presence of a trespasser is much less demanding than evaluating the conduct of a person who is privileged to be where he is."[86] Guard dogs and motion detectors can detect trespassers; detecting shirkers is not so easy. Compared with the situation in private regimes, monitoring costs associated with small events in communes are prohibitive. It is not that private parcels do not require monitoring – they do. But the cost of monitoring small events is lower, and the kind of monitoring that has to be done is less intrusive. In short, "when land uses have no spillover effects, individual ownership directly and precisely punishes land misuse and rewards productive labor."[87]

1.3.2.2   Medium Events

In contrast, the effects of medium events tend to spill over onto one's neighbors, and thus can be a source of friction. Nevertheless, privatization has the advantage of limiting the number of

---

[85] Ibid., 1327.
[86] Ibid.
[87] Ibid.

people having to be consulted about how to deal with the externality, which reduces transaction costs. Instead of consulting the entire community of communal owners, each at liberty with respect to the affected area, one consults a handful of people who own parcels in the immediate area of the medium event. Regarding medium events, then, a virtue of privatization is that it reduces the number of people with whom one needs to negotiate or coordinate one's effort.[88]

Regarding medium events, Ellickson mentions two further benefits of privatization. First, privatization increases the extent to which interactions are of a repeating character. It tends to put people in long-term, face-to-face, binary relations with neighbors. It thereby increases the extent to which people's dealings are with familiar and friendly faces, which is valuable in its own right and also insofar as it puts the resolution of externality problems from medium events in the hands of persons who are most likely to have ongoing relationships and thus be most motivated to cooperate.[89] Second, privatization puts decisions in the hands of people most familiar with local circumstances. There will be disputes, of course, and there is no guarantee that familiar faces will be friendly faces. (Those who want friendly neighbors sometimes need to change neighborhoods.) Still, in a private regime, disputes arising from medium events tend to be left in the hands of people in the immediate vicinity, who tend to have a better understanding of local conditions and thus are in a better position to devise resolutions without harmful unintended consequences. They are in a better position to foresee the costs and benefits of a medium event.

1.3.2.3 Large Events

Large events involve far-flung externalities among people who do not have face-to-face relationships. The difficulties in detecting such externalities, tracing them to their source, and holding

---

[88] Demsetz 1967, 356–7.
[89] Ellickson 1993, 1331.

people accountable for them are difficulties for any kind of property regime. There is no general answer to the question of which regime best deals with them.[90] Taking responsibility, as characterized in section 1.1.3, is a multifaceted thing. It involves taking responsibility for our own welfare and for the consequences of our own actions. Sometimes, though, those are two different things. When actions have negative externalities, tending to our own welfare may require tending to the consequences of other people's actions, and tending to the consequences of our actions may require tending to how our actions affect other people's welfare. It is no easy task to devise institutions that encourage pulp mills to take responsibility for their actions while simultaneously encouraging people downstream to take responsibility for their welfare, and thus to avoid being harmed by negative externalities.

Private regimes respond to negative externalities in various ways, through contract law, tort law, regulatory statutes (nuisance laws, zoning restrictions), and a matrix of conventions about neighborliness. All such responses are imperfect. One alternative is to return the land to the commons, and that too is imperfect.

A large event will fall into one of two categories. Releasing toxic wastes into the atmosphere, for example, may violate existing legal rights or community norms. Or such laws or norms may not yet be in place. Most of the problems arise when existing customs or laws fail to settle who (in effect) has the right of way. That is not a problem with the parceling of land per se but rather with the fact that key resources like air and waterways remain in a largely unregulated commons.

So, privatization exists in different degrees and takes different forms. Different forms have different incentive properties. They internalize responsibility in different ways and to different degrees. Simply parceling out land or sea is not always enough to stabilize possession of the resources that make land or sea valuable in the first place. Suppose, for example, that a resource, such

---

[90] Ibid., 1335.

as fish or game, is known to migrate from one parcel to another. In that case, owners have an incentive to grab as much of the migrating resource as they can whenever it passes through their own territory. Thus, simply dividing fishing grounds into parcels may not be enough to put fishermen in a position to avoid collectively exceeding sustainable yields. It depends on the extent to which the sought-after fish migrate from one parcel to another, and on conventions that are continuously evolving to help neighbors deal with the inadequacy of their fences (or other ways of marking off territory).

We could multiply examples. Temporal parceling of time-share condominiums, for example, is an open invitation to shirk responsibility for cleaning up; the mess one leaves is someone else's problem. Clearly, not all forms of privatization are equally good at internalizing responsibility. Privatization per se is not a panacea, and not all forms of privatization are equal.

There are obvious difficulties with how private property regimes handle large events. The nature and extent of the difficulties will depend on the details. So, for purposes of comparison, Ellickson looked at how communal regimes handle large events.

1.3.3 Jamestown and Other Communes

The Jamestown colony is North America's first permanent English settlement. It begins in 1607 as a commune, sponsored by the London-based Virginia Company. Land is held and managed collectively. The colony's charter guarantees to each settler an equal share of the collective product regardless of the amount of work personally contributed.[91] Of the original group of 104 settlers, two-thirds die of starvation and disease before their first winter. New shiploads replenish the population, but the winter of 1609 cuts the population from 500 to 60. In 1611, visiting Governor Thomas Dale finds living skeletons bowling in the streets, waiting for someone else to plant the crops. Their main food source

---

[91] Ibid., 1336.

consists of wild animals such as turtles and raccoons,[92] which settlers can hunt and eat by dark of night before neighbors can demand equal shares. In 1614, Governor Dale has seen enough. He assigns three-acre plots to individual settlers, which reportedly increases productivity sevenfold. The colony converts the rest of its landholdings to private parcels in 1619.

Why go communal in the first place? Are there advantages to communal regimes? One advantage is obvious. Communal regimes can help people spread risks under conditions where risks are substantial and where alternative risk-spreading mechanisms, like insurance, are unavailable. But as communities build up capital reserves to the point where they can offer insurance, they tend to privatize, for insurance lets them secure a measure of risk spreading without having to endure the externalizing of responsibility involved in the communal regime.

A communal regime might also be an effective response to economies of scale in large-scale public works that are crucial in getting a community started. To build a fort, man its walls, dig wells, and so on, a communal economy is an obvious choice as a way of mobilizing the teams of workers needed to execute these urgent tasks. But again, as these tasks are completed and the welfare of the community increasingly comes to depend on small events, the communal regime gives way to private parcels. At Jamestown, Plymouth, the Amana colonies, and Salt Lake, formerly communal settlers "understandably would switch to private land tenure, the system that most cheaply induces individuals to undertake small and medium events that are socially useful."[93] (The legend of Salt Lake says the sudden improvement in the fortunes of once-starving Mormons occurred in 1848 when God sent sea gulls to save them from plagues of locusts, at the same time as they coincidentally were switching to private plots. Similarly, the Jamestown tragedy sometimes is attributed to harsh natural conditions, as if those conditions suddenly changed in

---

[92] As reported by CNN News, September 13, 1996, on the occasion of the excavation of the original Jamestown fort.
[93] Ellickson 1993, 1342–3.

1614, multiplying productivity sevenfold while Governor Dale coincidentally was cutting the land into parcels.)

Of course, the tendency toward decentralized and individual-ized forms of management is only a (strong) tendency and, in any case, there are trade-offs. For example, what would be a small event on a larger parcel becomes a medium event under more crowded conditions. Loud music is an innocuous small event on a ranch but an irritating medium event in an apartment complex. Changes in technology or population density affect the scope or incidence of externalities. The historical trend, though, is that as people become aware of and concerned about a medium or large event, some of them seek ways of reducing the extent to which the event's cost is externalized. Social evolution is partly a pro-cess of perceiving new externalities and devising institutions to internalize them.

Historically, the benefits of communal management have not been enough to keep communes together indefinitely. Perhaps the most enduring and successful communes in human memory are the agricultural settlements of the Hutterites, dating in Europe back to the sixteenth century. There are now around twenty-eight thousand people living in such communities. Hutterites believe in a fairly strict sharing of assets. They forbid the possession of radio or television sets, to give one example of how strictly they control contact with the outside world.[94]

Hutterite communities have three special things going for them: a *population cap*: when a settlement reaches a population of 120, a portion of the community must leave to start a new community, a process that helps them retain a close-knit society; *communal dining and worship*: people congregate several times a day, which facilitates a rapid exchange of information about individual be-havior and a ready avenue for supplying feedback to those whose behavior deviates from the norm; a *ban on birth control*: the av-erage woman bears nine children, which more than offsets what

---

[94] There were several Hutterite colonies near my home town. We almost never saw them except on Saturdays selling eggs at the farmers' market, where they were conspicuous because of their customary black clothing.

little emigration there is.[95] We might add that Hutterite culture and education leave people ill-prepared to live in anything other than a Hutterite society, which surely accounts in part for the low emigration rate.

Ellickson also discusses kibbutzim and other less pure and less enduring examples of communal property regimes.[96] But the most pervasive example of communal ownership in America, Ellickson says, is the family household. American suburbia consists of family communes nested within a network of open-access roadways.[97] Family homes tacitly recognize limits to how far we can go in converting common holdings to individual parcels. Consider your living room. You could fully privatize it, having one household member own it while others pay user fees. The fees could be used to pay family members or outside help to keep it clean. In some respects, it would be better that way. The average communal living room today, for example, is notably subject to overgrazing and shirking on maintenance. Yet we put up with it. No one charges user fees to household members. Seeing the living room degraded by communal use may be irritating, but it is better than treating it as one person's private domain.

Some institutions succeed while embodying a form of ownership that is essentially collective. History indicates, though, that members of successful communes take responsibility for themselves as a group, and they internalize the rewards that come with that collective responsibility. In particular, they reserve the right to exclude nonmembers. A successful commune does not run itself as an open-access commons.

1.3.4   Governance by Custom

Many commons (such as our living rooms) are regulated by custom rather than by government, so saying there is a role for

---

[95] Ellickson 1993, 1347–60.

[96] Israel's kibbutzim have existed since 1909. The percentage of Israel's Jewish population living in kibbutzim has declined from its peak of 7.9 percent in 1948 to 3.6 percent by 1986 (ibid., 1347).

[97] Ibid., 1395.

common property and saying there is a role for government management of common property are two different things. As Ellickson notes, "Group ownership does not necessarily imply government ownership, of course. The sorry environmental records of federal land agencies and Communist regimes are a sharp reminder that governments are often particularly inept managers of large tracts."[98] Carol Rose tells of how, in the nineteenth century, public property often was thought to be owned by society at large. The idea of public property often was taken to imply no particular role for government beyond whatever enforcement role is implied by private property. Society's right to such property was held to precede and supersede any claim made by government. Rose says, "Implicit in these older doctrines is the notion that, even if a property should be open to the public, it does not follow that public rights should necessarily vest in an active governmental manager."[99] Sometimes, the rights were understood to be held by an "unorganized public" rather than by a "governmentally organized public."[100]

Along the same lines, open-field agricultural practices of medieval times gave peasants exclusive cropping rights to scattered thin strips of arable land in each of the village fields. The strips were private only during the growing season, after which the land reverted to the commons for the duration of the grazing season. (The communal arrangement allowed people to take turns tending the communal herd rather than spend their entire day tending their own small herds. It also saved them from the expense of fencing their small parcels.) Private ownership during the growing season internalized responsibility for producing crops. Then, during the grazing season, customary use of the commons was hedged with restrictions that prohibited activities inconsistent with the land's ability to recover.[101] In particular, the custom of "stinting" allowed the villagers to own livestock only in proportion to the relative size of their (growing

---

[98] Ibid., 1335.
[99] Rose 1986, 720.
[100] Ibid., 736.
[101] Ibid., 743.

season) landholdings. Governance by custom enabled people to avoid commons tragedies.[102]

Custom is a form of management unlike exclusive ownership by either individuals or governments. Custom is a self-managing system for according property rights.[103] For example, custom governs the kind of rights claims you establish by taking a place in line at a supermarket checkout counter. Rose believes common concerns often are best handled by decentralized, piecemeal, and self-managing customs that tend to arise as needed at the local level. So, to the previous section's conclusion that a successful commune does not run itself as an open-access commons, we can add that a successful commune does not entrust its governance to a distant bureaucracy.

1.3.5 The Hutterite Secret

Section 1.2 argued that the original appropriation of (and subsequent regulation of access to) scarce resources is justifiable as a mechanism for preserving opportunities for future generations. There are various means of exclusive control, though. Some internalize responsibility better than others, and how well they do so depends on the context. My argument does not presume there is one form of exclusive control that uniquely serves this purpose. Is individual responsibility better than communal responsibility? That depends on what kind of activities are most prevalent in a community at any given time. It also depends on the extent to which communal responsibility implies control by a distant bureaucracy rather than by local custom. I tried to explain why individualizing responsibility often is the best way of internalizing responsibility, and also why it is not the only way. The next chapter pursues the point further, exploring how mutual

---

[102] See Ostrom, Gardner, and Walker 1994, for more examples. Of course, no one thinks governance by custom automatically solves commons problems. Custom works when local users can restrict outsider access and monitor insider behavior, but those conditions are not always met, and tragedies like those discussed in section 1.2.2.2 continue to occur.

[103] Rose 1986, 742.

aid societies collectivize responsibility (1) without externalizing it, and (2) without relinquishing local control.

As mentioned earlier, I have heard people say Jamestown failed because it faced such harsh natural conditions. But communal (and noncommunal) settlements typically face harsh natural conditions. Jamestown had to deal with summer in Virginia. Hutterites dealt with winter on the Canadian prairie. It is revealing, not misleading, to compare Jamestown with settlements that faced harsher conditions more successfully. It also is fair to compare the two Jamestowns: the one immediately before and the one immediately following Governor Dale's mandated internalization of responsibility. What distinguished the first Jamestown from the second was not the harshness of its natural setting but rather the thoroughness with which it externalized responsibility.

Sociologist Michael Hechter considers group solidarity to be a function of the extent to which members depend on the group and the extent to which the group can monitor and enforce compliance with expectations that members will contribute to the group rather than free-ride upon it.[104] On this analysis, it is unsurprising that Hutterite communal society has been so successful. Members are extremely dependent, since their upbringing leaves them unprepared to live in a non-Hutterite culture. Monitoring is intense. Feedback is immediate. But if that is the secret of Hutterite success, why did Jamestown fail? They too were extremely dependent on each other. They too had nowhere else to go. Monitoring was equally unproblematic. Everyone knew who was planting crops (no one) and who was bowling (everyone). What was the problem?

The problem lay in the guarantee embedded in the Jamestown colony's charter. Jamestown's charter entitled people to an equal share regardless of personal contribution, which is to say it entitled people to externalize responsibility. In that respect, Jamestown was the antithesis of Hutterite society. Therein lies the key to one society's prosperity and another society's destitution.

---

[104] Hechter 1983, 21.

1.4 Mutual Aid

A MERICA'S First Lady, Hillary Clinton, lately has been reminding us of an old saying, "it takes a village to raise a child." I believe the saying, but I am not sure Mrs. Clinton understands that a welfare check is not a village. A village is a place where neighbors rely on themselves and on each other, and raise their children to do the same. Governments lull us into thinking that the only alternative to individual responsibility is government responsibility; villages teach us that we have another option.

We need another option, too. It would be a fallacy to assume that those who criticize need-based redistribution by government do not care about need. Presumably, some of them care about need but think need-based distribution by a central bureaucracy is not what people need.[105] When we address problems of poverty by turning some portion of the productive capacity of individuals into a common-pool asset and then giving welfare agencies access to it, the recipe has all the ingredients of a tragic commons. Eventually, one would expect, the common-pool asset will be exhausted. The problems will be worse than before.

Some people think we can end poverty through redistribution, and that ending poverty would be well worth any marginal reduction in overall productivity. Thus, after noting Danziger et al.'s calculation (see section 1.1.4) that welfare programs reduce total

---

[105] For examples, see Arnold 1994 and Boettke 1993.

work hours in the United States by as little as 4.8 percent, Robert Goodin concludes, "it is clear that the effects of social welfare programs along the lines of those in the U.S. have only a marginal impact on economic efficiency."[106]

Really? Consider this: if the annual growth rate of America's gross domestic product (GDP) had been 1 percentage point lower between 1870 and 1990, America's per capita GDP would be less than one-third its current level, which would put it on a par with Mexico.[107] From a dynamic perspective, marginal impacts matter. They add up, quietly, between the snapshots.

Meanwhile, spending on welfare programs by the U.S. government is now over 5 percent of GDP.[108] Thus, if (as Danziger et al. report) welfare recipients contribute over twenty cents less to the economy for every dollar of welfare benefits, that by itself implies a reduction of per capita GDP of over 1 percent.

Spending on Social Security consumes an additional 5 percent of GDP, and is projected to double over the next decade.[109] Martin Feldstein, Harvard economist and former chairman of the President's Council of Economic Advisers, has investigated "the extent to which an unfunded social security system causes a decline in national capital income and economic welfare" compared with a private or funded program.[110] (In a funded program, taxes go into a trust fund to be invested at market rates of return, unlike the current system in which social security taxes are spent as soon as received.) Feldstein concludes that even "conservative assumptions imply a combined annual loss of more than four percent of GDP as long as the current system lasts" and that the young and the poor are among those hurt most.[111] Four percent, when an

---

[106] Goodin 1988, 235.

[107] Pitsch 1995, 7. Pitsch cites Harvard economist Robert J. Barro as his source. I verified with a pocket calculator that if real per capita GDP had grown by 0.75 percent annually between 1870 and 1990, it would have grown from $2,224 to $5,452. Adding an extra 1 percent per year to the per capita GDP left us instead with a per capita GDP of $17,835.

[108] Source: Tanner 1996, 57.

[109] Source: Church and Lacayo 1995, 28.

[110] Feldstein 1996, 6.

[111] Ibid., 13.

annual loss of 1 percent is more than enough, in the long run, to blow the bottom out of the glass.

I say this without presuming for a moment that GDP captures everything that goes into helping people prosper.[112] Nevertheless, no one honestly can think slower GDP growth would be good for the poor. Every year, hundreds of thousands of Mexicans risk their lives seeking to enter the United States. They come not because America is a worse place for the poor, nor because America is a better place for the rich. They come because America is a better place for the poor, even from the perspective of an illegal immigrant. And it is better not because of programs that cut per capita GDP growth, but despite them.

Goodin thinks state-administered redistribution is superior to market society when it comes to meeting needs of the poor, at least in the short term.[113] He observes, "What a straightforward redistribution would accomplish in an instant, supply-side policies would accomplish only in due course."[114] Goodin has a point. In terms of a proverbial metaphor, giving someone a fish accomplishes in an instant what teaching the person to fish accomplishes only in due course. The other side of the coin is that giving someone a fish helps for only an instant too. The nice thing about policies that lead people to take responsibility for themselves is that what they accomplish tends to stay accomplished. We certainly want to know what constitutes "due course." However, it misconceives the nature of market society to think its relatively poor members have no choice but to sit around waiting for wealth to "trickle down." In the nineteenth century, poor people found

---

[112] For example, a parent's investment in educating children is not directly measured by GDP, although the investment eventually does show up in the GDP as children enter the work force.

[113] In section 2.2.5, Robert Goodin says those who vilify welfare dependency need some analysis of why depending on welfare programs is worse than depending on family and markets. If I were to join that debate, my analysis would be straightforward. I would ask, Empirically speaking, what makes for a more peaceful and prosperous community: depending on programs or depending on family and markets?

[114] Goodin 1988, 271.

health care unaffordable. They did not passively wait for the long term. This chapter explains how they got together and solved the problem.

1.4.1 Friendly Societies in a Sometimes Hostile World

In his 1996 State of the Union Address, President Bill Clinton said we cannot go back to the time when people were left to fend for themselves. What time was that? Mr. Clinton did not say. Perhaps he was talking about the time before Roosevelt's New Deal. Were people left to fend for themselves? If so, what happened? Did they roll over and die? Should we assume people starved to death (because there were no welfare programs to feed them)? Should we assume people flourished in the manner of Robinson Crusoe (because there were no welfare programs to corrupt them)? Or should we find out what happened?

Perhaps Mr. Clinton is right: perhaps those days are gone forever. Perhaps no one knows for sure. What is more certain is that it is a false dichotomy to suppose the only alternative to the welfare state is everyone having to fend for himself. Francis Fukuyama says, "the United States has never been the individualistic society that most Americans believe it to be; rather, it has always possessed a rich network of voluntary associations and community structures to which individuals have subordinated their narrow interests."[115] Institutions of collective responsibility per se are nothing new.

They seem to have taken a new shape, though. Collective responsibility once manifested itself almost exclusively in family-based and community-based norms. Those norms sustained neighborhoods and a rich network of mutual aid and thus helped people to prosper. People took responsibility for themselves and for their neighbors. Although the charitable sector remains enormous, at least in the United States, people have come to associate the concept of collective responsibility with a distant bureaucracy.

---

[115] Fukuyama 1995, 29.

It has been externalized. Too many people have come to think of their welfare, and also their neighbors' welfare, as the government's problem.

Conservatives often accuse welfare states of eroding norms of individual responsibility. That may not be the worst of it. The more damaging consequence may lie in how welfare states warp our sense of collective responsibility. David Green says that, in recent times, "socialists have not seen the good person as someone who gave his own time and energy in the service of others, but as the individual who demanded action by the state at the expense of other taxpayers."[116] In many countries, though, there once flourished organizations known as friendly societies. According to Green, these societies historically shared with trade unions an older kind, a self-help kind, of socialist philosophy.[117]

> Through the trade unions workers would win the wages necessary to sustain a decent existence, and through the friendly societies they would organize their own welfare services – social insurance, medical care, even housing loans. The profit motive, too, was to be supplanted: in the factory by the mutuality of the workers' co-op; and in retailing by the co-op store. Not all of these working-class hopes were realized, but the friendly societies, the trade unions, and the co-op stores were successful and offered a fraternal alternative to the sometimes cold world of commercial calculation. Particularly striking is the success of the friendly societies, whose social insurance and primary medical care schemes had attracted at least three-quarters of manual workers well before the end of the nineteenth century. Until the 1911 National Insurance Act every neighborhood of every town was dotted with friendly society branches, each with their own doctor, who had usually been elected by a vote of all the members assembled in the branch meeting.[118]

How *expensive* was participation in such societies? Access to club medical care was inexpensive to the point of being an outrage

---

[116] Green 1993, 3.
[117] Green 1985, 1, 4–5.
[118] Ibid., 1.

to the organized medical profession. David Beito writes that, in America in 1900, a lodge member "could acquire a physician's care for about $2 a year; approximately a day's wage for a laborer at the time."[119] Green and Cromwell report that, in Australia in the 1830s and 1840s, fees charged by private doctors were sometimes over ten shillings per visit – well beyond the means of most people. By 1869, friendly societies had emerged, providing medical service at a rate of ten shillings per *year* for members, plus an additional ten shillings per year for a member's wife and children. (Members were all men back then. Active recruitment of female members began a decade or two later, followed by the emergence of friendly societies catering exclusively to women.) To win election to a post as club doctor, would-be club doctors submitted to questioning by the assembled members regarding their training and experience. Candidates offered competitive rates and perks such as free house visits within three or four miles of the lodge.[120]

Health care is more expensive today, of course. Higher prices presumably have much to do with the real cost of late twentieth-century medical technology. On the other hand, technological advance hardly entails rising prices. As already mentioned, prices dropped during the period when friendly societies were emerging. In fact, the explosion in health care costs began not with some technological innovation but rather with the 1911 National Insurance Act. The act gave panels staffed by representatives of insurance companies and doctors' unions the authority to regulate fees paid by friendly societies. As a result, fees more than doubled within two years.[121]

How *widespread* was participation in friendly societies? Beito reports that according to surveys taken in 1919, 93.5 percent of African American households in Chicago had at least one insured member. In Philadelphia that same year, 98 percent of African American families had at least one insured member.[122] In

[119] Beito 1997a, 580.
[120] Green and Cromwell 1984, 76–80.
[121] Green 1985, 113.
[122] Beito 1990, 718–19.

England, Green estimates that by 1911 "at least 9 million of the 12 million originally included in the National Insurance scheme were already members of friendly societies offering medical care."[123]

How *adequate* was the care provided by such societies? Green reports disputes between the societies and the organized medical profession over the societies' refusal to exclude wealthy members; means testing was contrary to the principle that all joined on equal terms.[124] Evidently, so many wealthy members were using the service that their business was worth fighting over. The care must have been quite good – good enough to attract the wealthy. Part of its attraction was that lodge doctors were pioneers in preventive medicine. For doctors on yearly contracts, effective prevention was one cost-cutting measure that would be praised rather than punished at the lodge's annual meeting. All told, health care inside the friendly societies was not only cheaper but probably of higher quality than that available outside the societies, especially to people of modest means (although competition with friendly societies eventually did force regular fees for service down to levels that most people could afford).[125]

For what it is worth, friendly societies were a remedy for exploitation as well. When there are multiple providers of relevantly similar services, people who dislike terms offered by one provider can look elsewhere, which minimizes their dependence on and consequent vulnerability to any particular provider. No particular provider or coalition of providers was in a position to dictate terms to clients. The plethora of friendly societies, together with voluntary hospitals and provident dispensaries,[126] decentralized

---

[123] Green 1985, 95.

[124] Ibid., 19–21.

[125] In the early 1900s, spokespersons for the International Order of Foresters "repeatedly contrasted the death rate of members (6.66 per 1,000) with that of the same age group in the general population (9.30)" (Beito 1997a, 585). Again, though, I would caution against being too impressed by numbers. Presumably, the mortality gap was due in part to superior health care within the lodge, but also in part to lodge prohibitions of high-risk vices such as drunkenness.

[126] Unlike voluntary hospitals, provident dispensaries charged "a low annual contribution, felt to be within the means of the very poor, and the balance was supplied by the honourary members" (Green 1993, 73).

collective responsibility for medical care without turning it into a strictly individual responsibility. Individually and collectively, they gave people a range of choices at prices that almost anyone, even then, could afford. (A royal commission assigned to investigate whether the poor were systematically deterred from joining friendly societies found that, in 1901–2, "registered friendly society membership was highest in rural areas where wages were lowest.")[127]

They served as a welfare safety net, too. In 1855, for example, the Grand Lodge of Maryland provided aid to nine hundred orphans of deceased members.[128] The following, gleaned by Beito from the 1916 minutes of the Ladies Friends of Faith, seems to have been typical.

> At nearly every meeting, the society heard at least one plea from a member unable to pay because of unemployment or poor health. One of the most desperate of these concerned a woman who was "out of doors, and had no money." In such cases, the society was generally ready to extend help. It allowed twenty-four members extra time to pay off their debts, while it passed the hat for ten others. Not once did the Ladies Friends of Faith reject any of these appeals outright.[129]

Lodges were able to contain costs and minimize abuse apparently because the safety nets were administered, and paid for, by neighbors.[130]

So, what happened? Several factors contributed to the friendly societies' decline. First, as taxes rose, employer-provided tax-free benefit packages became an increasingly attractive form of compensation compared with taxable wages. Also, during periods of wage and price controls, employers sweetened benefit packages as an alternative to straightforward wage hikes. As those packages became common, they made some friendly society services redundant. There was less reason for workers to pay society dues for services already provided through employers.

---

[127] Ibid., 68.
[128] Beito 1997b, 33.
[129] Beito 1997a, 575.
[130] Hechter 1987, 117.

Meanwhile, professional medical associations hated the friendly societies, correctly believing that friendly societies gave medical consumers the bargaining power they needed to undermine price collusion by doctors. By the early 1900s, medical associations had become a powerful political force, especially when they joined forces with for-profit insurance companies (which also viewed friendly societies as an obstacle to higher profits). Together, they were an active and highly visible cause of the friendly societies' decline. In England, they played a major role in amending early drafts of the 1911 National Insurance Act so that the final legislation would do maximum harm to friendly societies.

Two features of the act are crucial. First, the act established price floors that made it illegal for friendly societies to offer health care at lower prices. Second, the act compelled male workers earning less than a certain income to purchase government medical insurance, thereby making it more difficult if not pointless to pay friendly society dues – which the price floors had made more expensive – on top of compulsory fees for government services. (Interestingly, in some respects, the act hardly even pretended to be providing national insurance. For example, the act made no provision for the care of widows and orphans, because insurance companies felt such provision would make it harder to sell life insurance.)[131]

Similar forces were at work in the United States. David Beito reports that medical associations warned members that if they worked for lodges, they faced forfeiture of membership or, just as seriously, a boycott by other medical providers. "In 1913, for example, members of the medical society in Port Jervis, New York, vowed that if any physician took a lodge contract they would 'refuse to consult with him or assist him in any way or in any emergency whatever.' In this instance, and many others, boycotts extended to patients as well. One method of enforcement was to pressure hospitals to close their doors to members of the guilty lodge."[132]

[131] Green 1993, 99.
[132] Beito 1997a, 592.

Their decline notwithstanding, friendly societies seem to have had many of the features that we wish our health care system had today: the ability to contain costs, to provide clients with an effective voice, to provide state-of-the-art service with a personal touch, and to reach all segments of society effectively. They also provided services like old-age pensions, unemployment insurance, life insurance, workmen's compensation, and day care, at the same time serving as a form of community association.

1.4.2   Could Friendly Societies Work Today?

Is it realistic to think friendly societies in the twenty-first century could emulate their earlier success? Realistically, they could never be like they were, simply because they would be responding to needs that are not the same as the needs of nineteenth-century lodge members. Also, in their time, they were a kind of direct democracy; doctors were directly accountable to annual member assemblies. If members were not satisfied, doctors were not reelected. That feature may or may not be reproducible today. Today such organizations might become more like health maintenance organizations, where doctors are directly accountable to insurance companies or boards of directors rather than to the collective voice of clients. (Health maintenance organizations are new, of course. They will continue to evolve. In time, some may become more like friendly societies.) Or the cost of malpractice insurance may rise until it rules out low-cost medical care regardless of delivery mechanism.[133] We do not know. Times change. The future is bound to surprise us. No matter what we do, there will be an element of risk.

A nice thing about the friendly societies, though, is that they are not a thought experiment. They are not a utopian dream. As recently as the 1960s, fraternal hospitals in rural Mississippi provided state-of-the-art medical coverage. Adults paid thirty dollars per year. The yearly fee for children was four dollars. At one

---

[133] I thank Thomas Pogge for insightful reflections on how friendly societies might fare today.

hospital, run by the Knights and Daughters of Tabor (an African American fraternal society), that same fee covered thirty-one days of hospitalization, major and minor surgery, basic examinations, routine tests, and drugs. There were extra fees of two dollars for an electrocardiogram, four dollars for an x-ray, and fifteen dollars for a normal childbirth.[134]

Although that recent experience is encouraging, it does not change the basic fact that conditions essential to an institution's history of success may no longer be operative, and we may not realize that until after we try and fail to replicate its success in another time and place.[135] We have to live with that uncertainty, and we should not ignore it.

We should not blow it out of proportion, either. I do not know how to make a toaster. Not many people do. But that uncertainty is no reason to stop people from making toasters, or from inventing better ones. Nor is it a reason to ignore alternatives to government-funded or government-provided health care, social security, and even unemployment insurance, especially when those alternatives have been tried with success. Those who have never seen unemployment insurance provided by anything other than a government naturally have difficulty imagining how it would work. Indeed, it can be hard to understand the workings of things we see and use every day. In a discussion of "ways in which markets would *necessarily* fail,"[136] Robert Goodin argues that if participation in a private insurance program were voluntary,

> then better-than-average risks would opt out of the scheme (preferring to self-insure) and only bad risks would be left in it. Premiums would have to rise to cover the above-average level of claims from those now left in the pool. As they did, more and more people would find it to their advantage to opt out. Eventually, only the very worst risks would remain in the pool,

[134] Beito 1996.
[135] Friendly societies would have an advantage today that they lacked a century ago, namely modern actuarial and accounting techniques.
[136] Goodin 1988, 155. Emphasis in original.

and the whole scheme would collapse. To remedy the problem of adverse selection, insurance must be made compulsory.[137]

The argument leaves us with an interesting puzzle. The argument implies that ordinary life insurance is economically impossible. How, then, do insurance companies do such a brisk business despite the logic of adverse selection? Perhaps the truth is simple: like other businesses, they offer a valuable product at an affordable price. Their coverage is worth more to those who are at greater risk, of course, and perhaps those customers pay more too. (One gets a discount for being a nonsmoker, for example.) Insurance companies do not avoid customers who are at greater risk, so long as someone is willing to pay what the product is worth. Such institutions may well leave us, at least temporarily, with a residual population of people who want the product but cannot afford it. (A century ago, most people could not afford to listen to Mozart in their living rooms, either. Who would have predicted that the problem would turn out to be temporary?) When the demand is there, however, organizations like mutual aid societies and mutual insurance companies tend to emerge to meet it at an affordable price, sometimes by means that once would have been almost inconceivable.

Of course, as a matter of policy, governments are free to decide that it is not in their interest to sit back and wait for miracles to occur. We should keep in mind, though, that when a government jumps in to fill what appears to be a vacuum, it sometimes is crowding out the processes that actually fill the glass.

According to Michael B. Rappaport, Metropolitan Life of New York for twenty years sought the repeal of state laws prohibiting the sale of unemployment insurance. In 1919, a bill that would have legalized private unemployment insurance was rejected by the State Senate as the entering wedge of socialism. (Indeed, perhaps that is what it was, although the socialism in question was the older, self-help kind.) The bill passed the Senate in 1924 but the State Assembly rejected it on the ground that it would

---

[137] Ibid., 158.

give labor unions an advantage in collective bargaining. The bill passed both houses in 1931 but was vetoed by then governor and presidential candidate Franklin Roosevelt because it would have stolen the spotlight from his plan to create federal unemployment insurance.[138] Rappaport concludes that Metropolitan Life would have made money. But could a private unemployment insurer handle a large-scale economic depression? An independent reviewer assessing Metropolitan Life's ability to deliver the product concluded that even in the depths of the Great Depression the company would not have run a deficit.[139] It may be hard to imagine how such institutions could work, but especially when they have worked in the past, potted a priori arguments that they are impossible will not do. Theorists cannot match the creativity of people on the ground needing to solve real problems.

Friendly societies have a history of collectivizing responsibility with success. Individual medical savings accounts and private pension plans are currently being studied as ways of helping people to internalize and individualize responsibility for their health care and their retirement.[140] Friendly societies are a distinct alternative. They were an alternative to private insurance, not a kind of private insurance. They were a supplement to self-reliance, not a kind of self-reliance. They enabled people to take responsibility for themselves as a group and to govern themselves at the local level rather than be governed by a distant bureaucracy. Friendly societies have a history of enabling people to internalize responsibility in a collective form.[141]

---

[138] Rappaport 1992, 67–8.

[139] Marquis James, as quoted in Rappaport 1992, 71.

[140] For example, see Worsham 1996 and Shapiro 1997.

[141] Lawrence Mead (in conversation) acknowledges that friendly societies were effective providers of health care to the poor, but questions whether welfare recipients today are competent to do what poor people did a century ago. If Mead is right, we are left with a question of how to instill competence. One might start by observing that we are not born competent. We acquire competence in a given activity through practice. Our culture helps us become competent partly by making it clear that we are expected to become competent.

1.4.3   The Possibility of Political Disarmament

Many people, spanning the political spectrum, report that the overall quality of life of the poor, or at least the nonworking poor, began to decline when welfare programs were created to help them, even as life got better for the rest of society. Why? The decline, if there was a decline, coincided with the programs' success in externalizing responsibility for the welfare of the nonworking poor. Should we conclude that the decline was *caused* by the externalization?

What would have happened without the programs? What if per capita GDP had grown an additional 1 percent – each year – for the past thirty years? How much better would that have been for those whom the current system has left poor and jobless?

We will never know. Patrick Moynihan is among the welfare state's most ardent defenders. In the United States, he was one of its architects. Yet he says, "the negative income tax experiments of the 1970s appeared to produce an increase in family breakup. That pattern of counterintuitive findings first appeared in the 1960s. . . . To this day I can't decide whether we are dealing here with an artifact of methodology or a much larger and more intractable fact of social programs." Moynihan quotes similar confessions by other experts.[142]

Another long-respected defender of the welfare state, Susan Mayer, recently said that on the most realistic assumptions available, "we can calculate that *doubling* low-income families' income would reduce the overall high school dropout rate from 17.3 to 16.1 percent, and increase the mean years of education from 12.80 years to 12.83 years. Male idleness would increase, and the percentage of young women who become single mothers would hardly change. From this we can conclude that any realistic income redistribution strategy is likely to have a relatively small impact on the overall incidence of social problems."[143] She

[142]   Moynihan 1996, 33–6.
[143]   Mayer 1997, 145. Emphasis added.

concludes that "although children's opportunities are unequal, income inequality is not the primary reason."[144]

Greg Duncan and Jeanne Brooks-Gunn are likewise recognized and respected supporters of the welfare state, but their claims on its behalf are similarly circumspect. Their recent anthology indicates that family income during a child's preschool years is statistically correlated to some measures of the child's ability and achievement, but the correlation fades after children begin school. They also caution against jumping to conclusions about why income matters. (For example, insofar as it is simply income itself that matters, income transfers can help. But insofar as income matters because of the ethos that goes with earned income, income transfers can do more harm than good.) Duncan and Brooks-Gunn say much good is done by targeted programs (e.g., those that provide immunizations, nutritional supplements, and early childhood education), but when it comes to cash assistance, they summarize the findings of their anthology's thirty-five contributing authors by saying, "In no case did the evidence here suggest that income transfers alone would produce a dramatic improvement in the physical health, mental health, or in behavioral development of children."[145]

So, uncertainty and disappointment about the welfare state's performance are widespread. Yet I know from experience that some people do not want to hear about alternatives. Why? Perhaps the alternatives repudiate some people's tacit assumption that the poor are incompetent. Robert Goodin says, "state officials are probably better informed as regards questions of what are the best means to people's chosen ends. It may also be true that they are better informed even as regards questions of what people's ends really are – or will be."[146] Admittedly, friendly societies did not leave people on their own when it came to selecting medical providers. Indeed, when members assembled to interview

---

[144] Ibid., 156.
[145] Duncan and Brooks-Gunn 1997, 608.
[146] Goodin 1988, 241.

candidate providers, they had better opportunities to collect, share, and discuss information than anyone has today. But societies did operate on the assumption that people were competent. At the time, the assumption was a self-fulfilling prophecy. Members made it their business to become competent. There is no guarantee that the same thing would happen today. There was no guarantee a century ago either.

Friendly societies also leave unaddressed an issue that concerns some egalitarians: even if the poor could afford adequate health care, those with more money could afford better care. I do not share this concern, but those who do may want to recall that friendly societies welcomed rich and poor members on equal terms and that many rich people accepted the offer. It is also worth recalling how a price mechanism works in a world of production. In a world without production, increased demand drives up price, thereby crowding out poorer consumers. In a world of production, increased demand drives up supply while economies of scale drive down price, unless trade barriers stop would-be providers from entering the market. And friendly societies did increase effective demand. They created a massively effective demand for low-cost service. The United Kingdom's National Insurance Act dissipated that demand. The effective demand for low-cost health care was gone and, thus, so was low-cost health care.

Here is another source of antagonism toward friendly societies. For some people, sharing is intrinsically desirable, and understandably so. It is a form of community. Theda Skocpol defends the welfare state and is skeptical about mutual aid societies on the grounds that the former institution has woven into it a pattern of sharing (to use Skocpol's apt phrase) while the latter does not.[147] I think exactly the opposite. What is woven into the welfare state is literally a pattern of transfer, not a pattern of sharing. It is mutual aid societies, not welfare state programs, that were knit together by a pattern of sharing. I doubt Skocpol believes that when welfare programs move in, fraternal feelings flourish.

---

[147] In conversation.

I doubt she believes authentic community spirit was dead before decades of expanding welfare programs brought it back to life. Perhaps some people believed it a few decades ago. As far as I know, no one believes it today.

Fraternal feeling is possible in small groups, but when we try to regiment altruism on a national scale, the possibility of community is precisely what we give up.[148] If there ever was a time when it was plausible to think of the welfare state as an institutional expression of fraternity, that time has passed. The welfare state's actual operation provides more occasion for mutual recrimination than for fraternal feeling. It turns people into faceless strangers, not neighbors. Taxpayers and welfare recipients might have more respect for each other if they ever talked to each other, but welfare programs deliberately minimize such contact.

By giving people a right to extract benefits from productive ventures without contributing to them, welfare programs turn individual production into a commons problem. Commons problems have a history of turning people against each other, turning them into what communitarians call "social atoms."[149] Experiments in communal ownership tend to end in poverty and alienation: poverty, because such experiments remain prone to commons tragedies; alienation, because the tragedies are caused by individual overconsumption and underproduction. When people are forced to pay, day after day, for each other's real or perceived overconsumption and underproduction, they end up not liking each other very much.[150]

If we want a system that nurtures fraternal feeling, we have to start by acknowledging that compulsory deductions from paychecks do nothing of the kind. Rightly or wrongly, taxpayers often feel victimized by the welfare state. Rightly or wrongly, beneficiaries often feel the same way. Both sides find it unfathomable that

---

[148] I thank James Buchanan for this point.

[149] For example, see Taylor 1985.

[150] This dynamic is observable even in communes with only two members. Years ago, I read that the most-cited reason for divorce in Canada (more than all others combined) was enmity over management of pooled finances.

people on the other side would feel like victims. In sum, when the welfare state externalizes responsibility, it does the opposite of engendering a sense of community. If communitarians are right to say Western society has been atomized, then surely one of the causes has been the state's penchant for making itself (rather than the community) the primary focus of public life.

What we need are ways of bringing people together that are (in their own eyes) in their common interest, so that they may come together willingly. We must look for ways of enabling people to live peaceful and productive lives, pursuing their own projects in such a way as to make themselves better off by making the people around them better off. The belief that government should strive to be an impartial referee, enforcing rules that enable people to pursue their own plans in peace, is no longer widely shared. It has been supplanted by a belief that the government should be a player rather than a referee. It sounds like a good idea in principle; government has all that power, so why not use it to make sure the right side wins? In practice, though, when the power of government is up for grabs in a game that no longer has a referee, people have little choice but to fight over it, creating nothing of value in the process.

In contrast, voluntarily assumed responsibility, whether individual or collective, reduces the extent to which people represent threats to each other. By enabling people to help themselves and each other without first needing to fight for political power, voluntarily accepted responsibility becomes a form of political disarmament. As with literal disarmament, it is a recipe for peace and prosperity.

1.4.4   Babies Born Destitute

We all understand that babies are born into poverty every day, and that it is not their fault. Does that change the picture? Not at all. On the contrary, the same arrangements that prevent people from becoming destitute are equally necessary to prevent their babies from being born destitute. So, what sort of arrangements help instill a general ethos of personal responsibility, thereby helping people, and thus their babies, from falling into poverty in the first place?

The system that minimizes destitution is the system by which a person's income is contingent on producing something that other people value. No amount of compassion for people with crippling handicaps can change that fact. No theory about dependency or exploitation or the defects of labor markets can change it. We can wonder whether children of unwed teenagers would be worse off without AFDC. We can doubt they even would have been born without AFDC. We can admit that AFDC is doing both harm and good, and that we do not know how much harm and how much good. After all the theories and policy proposals are on the table, though, the fact remains that from a welfare perspective there is no substitute for systems that induce people to contribute: that is, systems in which income is contingent on producing something that other people value. If we want to help people, we will have to build on that system, not tear it down.

Mutual aid societies preserve that contingency while enabling people collectively to spread risk and amplify their knowledge and bargaining power, thereby increasing their ability to negotiate favorable prices for basic services. In the process, they not only catch the tide; they contribute to it. As with other market processes, people do get something for virtually nothing, but they still have to be part of the tide. For better or worse, they still have to contribute.

Some will say only a central government can guarantee that handicapped people will never be left behind, but no one reasonably can expect a central government actually to deliver on such a guarantee. No matter what assistance the government tries to offer, there will be people who fail to receive it, and among them will be some of those who need it most. Is that the government's fault? Again, fault is beside the point. The point is that the alternatives should be assessed in terms of what they deliver, not what they promise. Every system leaves people behind, even Jamestown, whose charter guaranteed that no one would be left behind. Experiments in collective responsibility hardly ever fail quite as spectacularly as Jamestown did. They hardly ever guarantee as much as Jamestown did. They hardly ever externalize responsibility to quite that extent.

What do we want from a welfare safety net? Is it enough for an economic system to help people become so prosperous that they can afford to carry those who truly cannot carry themselves, or must there be a guarantee that those who cannot carry themselves will be carried by someone else? Should we look at the actual history of charity and mutual aid, or is the bare lack of a guarantee sufficient grounds for denying that charity and mutual aid can serve as a safety net? If there has to be a guarantee, is it enough *officially* to guarantee that no one will ever have to carry himself in times of trouble, or should we insist on some level of actual performance as well? But what if we have to choose between official guarantees and actual performance? What then?

Can a welfare safety net be packaged in such a way that people would willingly pay for it, thereby internalizing responsibility in a collective sense? The answer is that such schemes are possible; in fact, they have a long history. The history of friendly societies is a history of people producing and paying for their own guarantees as a group. Friendly societies never were perfect, and never would be, but in many countries they have a history of doing what a welfare safety net is supposed to do, and doing it increasingly well over time as they evolved in response to consumer demand. They were not trying to make some people better off at other people's expense. They internalized rather than externalized responsibility. In the process, they made people better off.

1.5 But Is It Just?

FRIENDLY SOCIETIES internalized responsibility. They survived mainly as cooperative ventures for mutual advantage.[151] That troubles some people, because for them the point of collectivizing responsibility is to externalize it: to break the link between contributing to a cooperative venture and sharing in its benefits. Why? Sometimes externalization is endorsed because it is expected to have good consequences; more often, it is endorsed despite the consequences. It is endorsed as a matter of justice.

Name an institution and someone will endorse it – while someone else condemns it – as a matter of justice. Is there any way to sort out what really merits endorsement as a matter of justice? What would it take to show that internalizing responsibility is unjust?

1.5.1 The Concept of Justice

What is justice? We probably all agree on the basic concept. Although we argue about what justice requires, the very fact that we are arguing presupposes some common understanding. Specifically, if we argue about what is just, we will understand ourselves to be arguing about what people are due. Accordingly, there is such a thing as a general concept of justice. In the most general

---

[151] Advantage need not be construed in egoistic terms, though. For some, being able to express fraternal impulses was one of membership's advantages.

terms, justice is about people getting what is coming to them. Justice is, analytically, a matter of people getting their due.

We begin to disagree when it comes to specifying exactly what people are due. Following Rawls, we may distinguish between the basic *concept* of justice – that people ought to get their due – and particular *conceptions* of what people are due.[152] We have different conceptions of what people are due, and part of our problem is that the basic concept of justice lacks the internal resources to settle which of them is correct. We cannot settle whether justice is about getting what we need rather than what we earn, for example, merely by analyzing the term 'due'. We must look elsewhere. In the end, the grounding of particular conceptions of justice turns on something other than considerations internal to the basic concept, because the basic concept underdetermines the applicability of particular conceptions. That is one reason why we argue, and why we cannot settle which of our conceptions of what people are due is more in keeping with the basic concept of justice.

A second reason is that different conceptions of the general concept are appropriate for different contexts. John Rawls says justice is the first virtue of social institutions.[153] However, the idea that justice is a virtue does not imply that a given person's conception of justice is a virtue. Nor does it imply that any given conception of justice is a virtue in every context. For example, in a case of child neglect, we could argue that the child's due is partly determined by the child's needs. In contrast, if a century ago we had been discussing whether women should be allowed to vote, it would have been irrelevant to question whether women *need* to vote, because what women were due in that context was a recognition of their equality as citizens rather than a recognition of their needs.

Could any particular conception of justice plausibly be considered the first virtue of social institutions? Evidently, many people think so, for it is not uncommon in political philosophy to

[152]   Rawls 1971, 5.
[153]   Ibid., 3.

represent some hypothetical original position as *the* position from which one derives principles of justice. A theorist makes claims about what the right kind of agent would choose in that situation, then infers that those hypothetical choices constitute principles of justice for other situations. The result: theorists end up applying a particular conception – the one they find intuitively right in (what they consider) paradigmatic circumstances – to a broader range of circumstances than is warranted.

I doubt that any conception of justice accurately specifies the whole of what is involved in giving people their due. Moral life is too complex for any single, simple principle to identify concretely what everyone is due regardless of context. Justice, the first virtue of social institutions, is a cluster concept.

1.5.2   When, If Ever, Does Equal Respect Mandate Equalization?

If justice is a cluster concept, and if the nature of a person's due depends on the context, that may explain why people disagree, and why they need not disagree as much as they do. This section looks at some of the contexts that ground our egalitarian intuitions, and some that do not. Among our most powerful intuitions is the idea that a just regime accords its citizens equal respect. Equal respect is a citizen's due. But what connects the idea that we command equal respect to the idea that we command equal shares?

Bruce Ackerman imagines that you and he come upon a garden. You see two apples on a tree and swallow them in one gulp while an amazed Ackerman looks on. Ackerman asks you, Shouldn't I have gotten one of those apples?[154] Should he? Why? (Why only one?) What, then, grounds our admittedly compelling intuition that Ackerman should get (exactly) one apple? Ackerman himself elects not to appeal to need.[155] He seems instead to presume that, as a brute fact, equal shares is a moral

[154] Ackerman 1983.
[155] Ibid., 62.

default; it is what we automatically go to if we cannot justify anything else. Is he right?

It depends. When we arrive all at once, equal shares has the virtue of not requiring further debate about who gets the bigger share. Equal shares is easier. We all walk away with more than we had, and no one has reason to envy anyone else's share. When we arrive all at once, equal shares really does show equal respect to the parties involved. When we arrive all at once, equal shares is a cooperative, mutually advantageous, and mutually respectful departure from that particular status quo. Justice is a cluster concept, as I said, and Ackerman is right to think that equal shares is part of it.

If there is a difficulty in generalizing from Ackerman's thought experiment, it is because we do not begin life by dividing a sack of apples that somehow, on its own, made its way to the bargaining table. Instead, we start with resources that some people have helped to produce and others have not, which are already possessed and in use by some people as others arrive on the scene. Contractarian frameworks like Ackerman's depict everyone as getting to the bargaining table at the same time; it is of fundamental importance that the world is not like that.

Why do property regimes around the world and throughout history consistently operate on a principle of first possession rather than equal shares? The reason, I suppose, is that in the real world people arrive at different times. When people arrive at different times, equal shares no longer has the intuitive salience it had in the case of simultaneous arrival. When someone else has gotten there first and is peacefully trying to put his or her discovery to use, then trying to grab a piece of the action, even if only an equal piece of the action, is not a peaceful act.[156] It is not a respectful act. A rule of first possession lets people live in communities without having to view newcomers as a threat; a rule of equal shares does not. If we were to regard every newcomer as having a

---

[156] It should go without saying that territoriality is not a cultural artifact. Throughout the animal kingdom, trespass upon staked-out territory is viewed as a potentially mortal insult.

claim to an equal share of our holdings, the arrival of newcomers would be intrinsically threatening. (Even now, people who see the world in zero-sum terms tend to despise immigrants.)

The rule of equal shares is not analytically part of the cluster concept we call justice. It does have a role to play in translating the concept into practice; that is, there are times when an equal share really is a citizen's due. However, it would be a mistake to think a commitment to treat people with equal respect entails any *general* commitment to make sure they have equal shares. Equal shares could be a principle of just distribution among people who invested equally in the good being distributed, and yet be manifestly unjust when some people have helped to produce the good and others have not.

1.5.2.1   Equal Opportunity

William Galston says, "The world's fastest sprinter doesn't deserve his natural endowment of speed, but surely he deserves to win the race established to measure and honor this excellence."[157] Perhaps. In any case, Galston's point reminds us that, in a race, the reason why contestants should have equal opportunity is that the race otherwise fails to perform its function, which is to measure a particular excellence. Do we have the same rationale for equal opportunity in market society as a whole? Only if measuring excellence (measuring, not fostering) is the purpose of society as a whole, and it is not. When a system's purpose is to enable people to cooperate for mutual advantage, or simply to prosper, it usually will be more to the point to be creating and improving opportunities rather than equalizing them.

Section 1.2.2.2 noted that the outcomes of particular races may well be morally arbitrary. What is justified is the game itself, not the moves within the game. An economic system's purpose is not to protect winners against those who cross the finish line a minute too late. Nor is its purpose to ensure that contestants have an equal chance of reaching the finish line first. Its purpose is to

---

[157] Galston 1991, 197.

give people reason and opportunity to race for the finish line and thereby participate in, contribute to, and ultimately create society as a cooperative venture for mutual advantage. To the extent that the racing itself serves a worthy purpose, and to the extent that rewarding winners serves the purpose of inducing people to race, it is not arbitrary to reward those who win, even in cases where people win partly on the strength of arbitrary luck. Equal opportunity surely is part of the cluster concept we call justice, but it is a limited part.

As mentioned in this essay's opening pages, we tend to see human commerce as a zero-sum game. The job market, in particular, typically is regarded as a zero-sum game. Every job taken is seen as a job removed from a fixed stock, thereby reducing opportunities for everyone else.[158] We all know from experience that the person who loses the race feels a sense of loss. Nevertheless, the racing makes the economy productive, and that is where the prizes (including the jobs) come from in the end. When people get jobs and begin to produce new wealth, they also seek opportunities to spend it, in the process creating opportunities for others to earn a living by meeting the new demand.

This is an optimistic scenario, to be sure. At its most giddy extreme, it might be taken to imply that a market economy can create tens of thousands of new jobs every month. We would laugh at such optimism except for the fact that monthly news reports tell us this is exactly what market economies do. More pessimistic Marxist scenarios, which assume the stock of jobs in a market economy is fixed over time, are simply (albeit wildly) false. Thomas Edison did not "succeed only on condition that others fail." He did not take someone else's job; on the contrary, he created millions of opportunities for others to earn a better living. On a humbler scale, ordinary working men and women do

---

[158] The premise that the job market is a zero-sum game drives Van Parijs's (1991) argument that everyone has a right to an unconditional basic income and thus, in effect, to collect retirement benefits at the age of eighteen. In Van Parijs's view, benefits are justified as a reward not for a lifetime of work but rather for a lifetime of not working, and thus not taking jobs from those who want them.

the same thing. Their work creates new capital, and new capital means new opportunities.

1.5.3   Consequences Matter

How would we know whether a given set of background institutions is just? How can we adjudicate among rival conceptions of justice? I have argued that we cannot answer that question merely by appealing to the basic concept. Because we cannot assess a conception's appropriateness in terms of the basic concept alone, we have no choice but to take something else into account.

What then should we take into account? I agree with Rawls when he says, "other things equal, one conception of justice is preferable to another when its broader consequences are more desirable."[159] Rawls's proposal has the virtue of not begging the question. One can care about whether an institution enables people to live decent lives without presupposing any particular conception of justice. If and when we have no other way of settling whether institutional practice and social norms ought to conform to a given conception of justice, we can ask, If we try to make institutional practice and social norms conform to that conception rather than another, will it help people live peaceful and productive lives? Or will it put us at each other's throats? If abiding by an institution's rules would not help us to avoid or resolve conflict and, more generally, it would not help us to live peaceful and productive lives, it becomes hard to imagine any grounds for believing that justice requires us to abide by those rules. If institutionalizing one conception of what people are due leads to prosperity while an alternative leads to destitution, then we have good reason to endorse the former conception and reject the latter.

Philosophers may note that none of this presupposes any particular theory of the good, beyond the idea that prosperity is preferable to destitution. Nor does it assume the good is prior to the right.[160] Rawls himself insists that the right is prior to the

---

[159] Ibid., 6.
[160] I develop a theory of the good and discuss when the right is prior to the good, and when it is not, in part II of Schmidtz 1995.

good, despite acknowledging the relevance of consequences. Put it this way: if we want to evaluate the soundness of a house's foundation, we can do so without presuming that there is something more foundational than the foundation. We evaluate a foundation by asking what kind of house can be built on it. Ultimately, we ask, what kind of life will its occupants be able to live? Similarly, we evaluate an institution and the conception of justice it embodies by asking what kind of society is emerging (or predictably will emerge) in response to that institution. Such an evaluation does not presume that considerations of utility are more foundational than considerations of justice. Conduciveness to prosperity is not a conception of justice, but we have no choice but to consider things like conduciveness to prosperity if we are to have any basis for evaluating competing proposals to implement particular conceptions of justice.[161]

How do we know what leads to prosperity and what to destitution? We can learn a lot by looking at history. Robert Goodin says, "Working within the constraints set by natural scarcity, the greatest practical obstacle to achieving as much justice as resources permit is, and always has been, the supposition that each of us should cultivate his own garden."[162] However, Jamestown's charter (see section 1.3.3) did not suppose each of us should cultivate his own garden. It supposed the opposite. Colonists abided by the charter, and it killed them. Meanwhile, people in other colonies were tending their own gardens, and thriving.

If our policies ignore the fact that people tend their own gardens when given a chance, and that no one has the power simply to decide that people will tend other people's gardens rather than their own, then our policies will have bad, perhaps even fatal, consequences. We have to look at how institutions (and the conceptions of justice they embody) affect actual behavior, because it is by affecting behavior that institutions have consequences.

---

[161] We do well, though, to follow Fred D. Miller's Aristotelian distinction between overall advantage (the good of most members) and mutual advantage (the good of each member) and to construe the latter as more relevant to the question of what each person is due (1995, 205–24).

[162] Goodin 1985b, 1.

Institutions serve the common good by inducing behavior that serves the common good, which they do by inducing people to tend their gardens in ways that serve the common good.

None of this presupposes that people are selfish. Whatever people care about, the fact remains that letting people invest in causes they care about tends to increase a society's resource base, whereas forcing people to invest in causes they do not care about tends to decrease society's resource base. It discourages people from creating resources in the first place.

To be sure, what people care about is sensitive to social context, and we should applaud institutions that encourage people to care for each other. But telling people that they are required to tend someone else's garden rather than their own does not encourage people to care for each other. It does the opposite. It encourages spite. The people of Jamestown reached the point where they would rather die, bowling in the street, than tend the gardens of their free-riding neighbors, and die they did.

1.5.4   Escaping the Status Quo

If we seek to approximate society as a cooperative venture for mutual advantage in the real world, we need to start by asking what would be mutually advantageous starting from here. Like it or not, where we start from is relevant when deciding where we should try to go. No one thinks the status quo is or ever will be fair, but sooner or later people need to ask what would make for a better future. Starting from where we are, how can we launch cooperative ventures for mutual advantage? We could ignore the status quo and immerse ourselves in our favorite thought experiment – the one in which imaginary bargainers consent to our favorite social experiment – but an arrangement that is hypothetically a cooperative venture for mutual advantage is no substitute for the real thing. The practical question is how to make society a truly cooperative venture, rather than how to remake it in the shape of some theorist's conception of what a hypothetical bargainer would agree to.

In an actual negotiation, when no agreement to change the status quo is reached, what we are left with is the status quo, not an idealized state of nature and not equal shares. For example, if Americans cannot agree on how to change their Social Security system, they will be left not with an idealized state of nature but with the status quo: a government careening toward bankruptcy. Does this beg the question by assuming the status quo is morally just? Absolutely not. Whether or not the status quo is just, it is the status quo, and we need to deal with it. In an ideal world, we would never have created unfunded retirement systems, but that does not mean we can simply abolish them now.

Fairly drastic action, however, is inevitable. Social Security tax revenues currently exceed annual payouts, but in the 1990s, the federal government has been borrowing and spending the excess, which it lists as off-budget spending in order to disguise the real magnitude of current operating deficits. Thus, the Social Security Trust Fund is a mirage; the money has already been spent. On top of that, the demographics are shifting. "In 1950 there were 16 workers paying taxes for every retiree collecting benefits. Now three workers support each pensioner. . . . By the year 2030, there will be only two workers to support each pensioner."[163] That is what I mean by "careening toward bankruptcy." Our politicians have been foisting the cost of current consumption on future generations, and have treated the future as someone else's problem. But the future has arrived. Big mistakes have been made, and someone has to pay.

What can we do? Van Parijs says everyone has a right to an unconditional basic income. In essence, his proposal is that we lower to eighteen the age when a person can retire and collect Social Security benefits.[164] It would be more realistic, though, to raise the age when people qualify for Social Security benefits. Slowly phasing out the unfunded system by raising the age of eligibility

---

[163] Church and Lacayo 1995, 28.
[164] Van Parijs 1991.

six months each year, for example, would make currently retired people more secure. Their benefits would be unaffected
and they would no longer need to worry about the system going
bankrupt. They unequivocally would be better off. People near
retirement would benefit for the same reason. They would wait a
bit longer, but would not face bankruptcy. (Further compensation
could come in many forms. For example, individual retirement
accounts could be made tax-free, not merely tax-deferred. And
the age when people begin to draw on fully funded individual
retirement accounts could be left where it is.)

People not near retirement would benefit (1) because they
have nothing to lose – they already know that the system will
collapse before they become eligible for benefits – and (2) because their Social Security taxes could gradually be lowered or
diverted to individual retirement accounts.[165] Nearly everyone,
then, could be made better off. To be sure, my proposal would be
unfair to young people. They would remain liable for trillions of
dollars in unfunded obligations that the system has already in-
curred. But they would be better off. Their prospects are far worse
under the status quo.

Of course, proposals regarding welfare reform must answer
for the effects they have in the short run as well as the long run.
People frequently say that, although they support welfare reform
in principle, it is not right to punish children just for the sake
of the system's long-term viability. I completely agree. If welfare
reform has any point at all, the point is to stop multiplying the
burdens we currently are foisting on the next generation. For
welfare and Social Security reform to be politically and morally
viable, it will have to improve the prospects of people (including
children) as they are and as they could be.[166]

---

[165] Shapiro (1997) and Ferrara (1997) discuss ways of managing the transition
to a financially solvent system anchored by individual retirement accounts.

[166] In the United States, "welfare rolls have dropped by 22%, from 14.4 million
in March 1994 to 11.2 million in March 1997" as a result of welfare reform
measures and a booming economy (Wolf 1997b, 3). What happened to the
three million who left welfare? Most are employed, according to officials
quoted by Wolf (and they must be; overall unemployment fell during that
period, from 6.9 to 4.8 percent). The long-term effects remain to be seen.

When people are willing to carry on from where they are in a peaceful and constructive way, society will be a cooperative venture for mutual advantage. If people instead say, "It is too convenient for you suddenly to be preaching the gospel of win-win. We had our turn being losers. We want you to know how it feels," then society will not be a cooperative venture. It will not be mutually advantageous. It will not be much of a society.

I acknowledge – in fact, I insist – that there is injustice in the status quo, and that mutually advantageous departures from the status quo do not always make amends for prior injustice. (It is hard to imagine what could make amends for injustices done to aboriginal peoples around the globe.) The fact remains that society as a genuinely cooperative venture for mutual advantage gets off the ground only when people are willing to proceed from where they are. Without that willingness to proceed, we are not going to make the world a better place. We will not make it a more just place either.

1.5.4.1 An Alternative View

If I seem to be belaboring the obvious when I say cooperative ventures have to begin as departures from the status quo, then consider an alternative view that may be more common among political philosophers. Although it is natural to say partners in cooperative ventures should be rewarded for their contributions, Thomas Nagel says people's contributions are so unequal that "the defense of equality requires that rewards *not* depend on productive contribution."[167] Nagel says the right way to look at it is to compare two kinds of regimes: one guarantees equal shares; the other guarantees a minimally decent share, a basic income.[168] If we imagine two parties (one of them relatively disadvantaged) negotiating the choice of regimes, we will conclude that "each of the two systems being compared provides one of the parties with benefits above the minimum at the expense of the other."[169] In a system that guarantees only a decent minimum standard of

---

[167] Nagel 1991, 99.
[168] Ibid., 80–4.
[169] Ibid., 81.

living (thereby failing to guarantee equal shares), losers "are being asked to accept a low standard of living on the ground that it would be an intolerable burden on the winners further to reduce their after tax income."[170] Nagel continues:

> We are responsible, through the institutions which require our support, for the things they could have prevented as well as for the things they actually cause. That is why the worse off, under the guaranteed minimum, are being asked to sacrifice for the benefit of the better off, just as surely as the better off are asked to sacrifice for the sake of the worse off under an egalitarian system. If sacrifice is measured by comparison with possible alternatives rather than by comparison with the status quo, the situations of possible winners and possible losers are symmetrical.[171]

Nagel's view seems to be that there are only two possible alternatives and, incredibly, the status quo is not one of them. Thus, when we transfer money from one person to another so as to provide the recipient with a basic income, we are to see the recipient as the one who loses money in the process, because we can imagine larger sums being transferred under the equal shares alternative. (Evidently, when we imagine an equal shares regime, we are not supposed to wonder whether anyone would bother to plant crops.)

No one disputes Nagel's philosophical brilliance, but Nagel's way of looking at things in this case is not an auspicious basis from which to launch cooperative ventures for mutual advantage. Sacrifice involves actually giving something up. When people provide me with an unearned income, my receiving that income is not a sacrifice, and I do not turn it into a sacrifice merely by declaring that in my mind the only "possible alternative" consists of people giving me more.

Whether we like it or not, the fact remains that those who consider it a sacrifice to be made better off relative to the status

---

[170] Ibid., 82.
[171] Ibid., 84.

quo, and who hold out for being made better off relative to an imaginary baseline, will be left behind. We do them no favor when we teach them to think in such self-destructive terms.

1.5.5   Real Self-Esteem

We start out relying on resources that (some of) the people around us have helped to produce. As we grow up, we accept increasing responsibility for our own welfare and, eventually, for each other's welfare as well. What about those whose handicaps are completely incapacitating? Is it fine to leave them behind?

I do not think it is. But, I argued, there are other questions we need to answer first. Which basic structures help and encourage people to develop their capacity to contribute to cooperative ventures? What are the welfare implications of encouraging people to think that developing their capacity is someone else's responsibility? (What happens to their children when we encourage them to think that way?) Which system puts us in a position to help those whose handicaps are incapacitating? We should also ask which system creates career paths that enable handicapped people to contribute, because whether a handicap is incapacitating can depend on the social context. Every system wastes human capital, but market society, wasteful though it may be, is vastly better than the alternatives at minimizing the significance of physical limitations. It has given us eyeglasses, motor transportation, and, more fundamentally, a radical division of labor that enables people to earn a living by working at a desk. Increasingly, people can work around handicaps, child-rearing responsibilities, and so on. Opportunities are not equal, and never will be, but they are improving.

The same institutions that enable people to cooperate for mutual advantage also enable people to experience the dignity and self-affirmation that go with being part of such relations. Although I have said little about the issue in this essay, it should at least be mentioned that what is at stake is people's form of life, not just their quality of life. We think the life of a noncontributor is a bad life, and what repels us about the prospect of living such a life is not what we would get; it is what we would be. There is something noble in a system that enables us to live as contributors to a community of contributors. Being in a position to trade on equal terms – to benefit others as much as they benefit us – is a kind of equality, an important kind, indeed a key ingredient of self-esteem. Thomas Nagel speaks of how, "in the grossly unequal world in which we live, the primary significance of the impersonal [i.e., radical egalitarian] standpoint for those at the bottom of the social heap is that it compounds their personal wretchedness with a perception that they do not really count."[172] But it would be a mistake of fact to think poor people need to be reassured by philosophy professors that they count. It is likewise a mistake of fact to think poor people need to be reassured that, although they do not deserve anything, neither does anyone else.

What actually serves as a basis for self-esteem among working people is neither a sense of unearned and abstract equivalence, nor an assurance that their welfare is someone else's job, but rather a concrete sense of being willing and able to take responsibility for themselves, for their families, for their futures, and – to a more limited extent – for their neighbors as well. Self-esteem among working people is primarily based not on equality but on *efficacy*, on being willing and able to meet life's challenges. We do untold damage when we set up programs that make recipients less willing (and their children correspondingly less able) to meet life's challenges in peaceful and productive ways.

1.5.6 The Bottom Line

What explains market society's unparalleled success in helping people to prosper? The key, I have argued, lies in background institutions, especially property institutions, that lead people to take responsibility for their own welfare. Such institutions help to internalize responsibility, and it is internalized responsibility (rather than individual responsibility per se) that makes people better off. Institutions that lead people to take responsibility for

---

[172] Ibid., 19.

themselves as a group also help to internalize responsibility, albeit in a collective form. They too can make people better off.

That way of understanding how individual responsibility contributes to the welfare of people in general is not the only way, but I find it instructive. It helps explain how the institution of private property contributes, when it does. It helps explain how communal ownership contributes, when it does, and why it fails, when it fails. It helps explain why some organizations that facilitate collective risk sharing have been successful, and why welfare programs have been so much less successful than we once hoped and expected. The welfare state would have made people better off if it had led neighbors to rely on each other and on themselves, but it seems to have done the opposite.

I have spoken in favor of internalized responsibility, but what I really favor is whatever helps people to pursue their projects in peaceful and productive ways. It is people living peaceful and productive lives, and the institutional structures that encourage them, that make people better off in the long run. And what helps poor people's children in the long run is the same thing that helps poor people in the short run – internalized responsibility, and the synergistic combination of self-reliance and spontaneous mutual support that goes with it.[173]

I have not settled which conceptions of justice are appropriate to which circumstances. Equal shares is appropriate to some circumstances, equal opportunity to others, and first possession to many others. But whatever we say about the parts of the cluster, we clearly have good reason to endorse a known prescription for prosperity in preference to a known prescription for destitution, and it is unlikely that any reason could be good enough to justify going the other way. Do we have a known prescription for

---

[173] Some people want to say self-reliance in a social setting is a contradiction. As the term is ordinarily used, though, a person can be self-reliant without being a hermit. As I use the term, social beings are self-reliant insofar as they rely upon their ability to produce and to return value for value to those with whom they transact. On this conception, the bare fact of drawing a salary does not make a person self-reliant, and the bare fact of being a housewife does not preclude being self-reliant.

prosperity? Yes, we do. There is no such thing as a conception of justice whose institutional implementation is guaranteed to create a tide that lifts all boats, but the internalization of responsibility that evolves in a market society does in fact create a tide that comes closer than any known alternative to lifting all boats.

What market society does not do is guarantee a right to enjoy a comfortable life as a noncontributor. There is a lot of room for improvement in the market societies we live in today, but real improvement lies in better preparing people for life as responsible adults, not in making responsible adulthood unnecessary.

2 Social Welfare as a Collective Social Responsibility

Robert E. Goodin

2.1 The Policy Context

S OME philosophical debates cannot be fully appreciated out-side their larger social contexts. On the face of it, it is hard to see how there can be much argument over the desirability of people's taking responsibility for the well-being of themselves and their families. We ordinarily do so more or less automatically and unreflectively. We almost invariably agree that it is good that we should do so.

But that of course is not what the argument is about.[1] Un-questionably, behaving responsibly is a virtue. Those who take responsibility for the welfare of themselves and their families, particularly when times are tough, unquestionably deserve high praise. The question is merely what to do about people who are unable or unwilling to assume responsibility in this way.

Clearly, those who abnegate responsibility for the welfare of themselves and their families have behaved badly – if they rea-sonably and realistically could have done otherwise. But ques-tions of who could have done what, and how we (or even they) could ever tell, are far from transparent. Many of the more vexing issues here are less factual than counterfactual, posing "what if?" questions that are by nature inherently indeterminate.

Furthermore, statements about your personal responsibilities are first and foremost statements about what *you* should do.

[1] Nor is the public debate about "responsibility for self" – whether or not one really can choose one's own values and preferences – which poses deep philo-sophical issues of free will versus determinism. On that, see Taylor 1976; Scanlon 1988; Frankfurt 1988; Schoeman 1987; and, for an attempt to bring some of that literature to bear on welfare dependency debates, Arneson 1997.

Nothing necessarily follows from those propositions as to what others should do, if you fail to do what you should have done. Sometimes others should make you do it; other times it seems better for them simply to do it for you or do something else altogether in the place of what you were supposed to have done; still other times it seems better for them to do something that will put you in a better position to do it for yourself subsequently. It is simply impossible to read off of statements about what *you* should do any automatic conclusions about what, failing that, *we* should do.

This conjunction of counterfactual speculations and indeterminate action implications makes issues of "personal responsibility for welfare" politically hot and philosophically contentious. That, rather than any dispute over root moral intuitions in the baseline cases, is what is at issue in these disputes. The question is not whether to praise those individuals who are shouldering responsibility for themselves and their families. The question is instead what we collectively should do, as a matter of public policy, when individuals fail to live up to that ideal. Simply reiterating the ideal cannot, in and of itself, resolve that question.

2.1.1   What's the Problem?

From the demise of the old Poor Law through the rise of New Age Democrats, social welfare policy has long been seen as posing problems of personal responsibility versus public dependency. In proto-Victorian debates over Poor Law reform, the question was what to do with the "able-bodied poor" – whether to provide them with "out-door relief" (particularly in the form of a monetary dole) or whether to subject them to the punitive "in-door" regimes of the poorhouse or the workhouse.[2] (Earlier methods

---

[2] The cannonical text is the *Report from His Majesty's Commission for Enquiring into the Administration and Practical Operation of the Poor Law* (Blomfield et al. 1834), reprinted in part as *The Poor Law report of 1834* (Checkland and Checkland 1974); see esp. pp. 82–113, 124–7 of that latter edition, to which all subsequent references will refer. Similar attacks on the old Poor Law are found, most famously, in T. R. Malthus, *Essay on the principle of population* (1803/1992), esp. bk. 3, chaps. 5–7, and bk. 4, esp. chap. 8; and Alexis de Tocqueville's 1835 "Address to the Royal Academy of Cherbourg" (Tocqueville 1835/1983). For further background, see Blaug 1963; Rothschild 1996; de Swaan 1988; and Himmelfarb 1984, 1994a, 1994b.

of dealing with "sturdy beggars" were, of course, more punitive still.)[3] In our own day "welfare mothers" have come to symbolize the problem of public dependency[4] – and regimes not so very dissimilar to Victorian workhouses have been canvassed, at least on the further fringes of the policy community, among possible solutions.[5]

The able-bodied poor of old had "only themselves to blame" for their poverty. Being able-bodied, they were presumably perfectly capable of providing for themselves. If they failed to do so, instead becoming a charge on the public, then they did so of their own volition. The problem with welfare mothers today is

---

[3] Lopping off ears, branding, public execution, and such like (Checkland and Checkland 1974, 72–81).

[4] Fraser and Gordon 1994; Young 1995; Lewis 1995. It is an interesting question why welfare mothers with the clear encumbrances of family responsibilities have come to be assimilated to the "able-bodied poor" of old, who had no excuse for not working for a living, rather than widows and orphans who were traditionally regarded as the "deserving poor" not expected to earn their own keep on the labor market. Welfare reforms (such as the 1996 U.S. act: U.S. Congress 1996) make concessions for mothers of very young children, but all those with children over age two are expected to find paid employment. To do so, however, they must pay someone else to take care of their own children, in a child-care analogue of fisherwives taking in each other's laundry. It is unclear that this makes any great sense, economically or sociologically, and can perhaps best be understood as a matter of purely punitive moralism (Kittay 1995, 1996).

[5] Such policy proposals recur from time to time. The particular documents that will serve as my principal foils are the House Republicans' *Contract with America* (1994) and an earlier "consensus report" of the Working Seminar on the Family and American Welfare Policy convened by the American Enterprise Institute, *A community of self-reliance: The new consensus on family and welfare* (Novak et al. 1987). While these politically prominent statements are endorsed by a large number of prominent people, and thus cannot be discounted as the idiosyncratic scribbling of some academic without influence, these too will soon become "yesterday's news." My recurrent references to Malthus and the 1834 Poor Law reforms are meant to show that these are just recent manifestations of arguments that have been recurring for some time, however, and can reasonably be expected to recur again in some form or another. For critiques of that contemporary discourse, see Gans 1995; Gilbert 1995; Handler and Hasenfeld 1991, esp. chap. 5; and, for a carefully researched, empirically grounded critique of the *Contract with America*'s proposals, Weaver and Dickens 1995.

similarly said to arise largely from recklessness and fecklessness.[6]
It is to a large extent the sheer irresponsibility of "children having
children" – together with the even greater irresponsibility of the
often older men who sire them and then abandon them – that
causes both the children and their mothers to become, in effect,
wards of the state.[7]

While welfare mothers constitute the clearest analogues in
contemporary debates to the able-bodied poor of old, broadly the
same complaints are lodged against the "underclass" more generally. Abandoning the American dream, the estranged poor have,
it is said, simply ceased trying to make anything of themselves,
wallowing instead in a culture of poverty and depending on public
relief rather than their own initiative for their very subsistence.[8]

In both cases the remedy is said to lie in inculcating a stronger
sense of personal responsibility in people, encouraging individuals to take charge of their own lives. Listen, for example, to
Margaret Thatcher speaking of the "Victorian values" which she
had hoped to reinstill: "We were taught to work jolly hard. We
were taught to prove yourself; we were taught self-reliance; we
were taught to live within our income. You were taught that
cleanliness is next to godliness. You were taught self-respect. You
were taught always to give a hand to your neighbour. You were
taught tremendous pride in your country. All of these things are
Victorian values. They are also perennial values."[9] Or, again, listen

---

[6] Or from young women being taken advantage of by (often literally) rapacious
   men, or from deficiencies in their upbringing, leading to a lack of religious
   values or moral strength.

[7] As President Clinton himself asserted from the Reverend Martin Luther King's
   last pulpit; the relevant passage from his speech is reprinted in Himmelfarb
   1994a, chap. 1. Similar themes figure largely in the catalog of "findings" concerning "out-of-wedlock pregnancy" that the U.S. Congress (1996, sec. 101)
   claims motivated the Personal Responsibility and Work Opportunity Reconciliation Act of 1996.

[8] Mead 1992. Although that is the way the idea has been widely received in
   policy circles, the careful scholars responsible for coining the phrase have a
   much more nuanced understanding of the phenomenon. See esp. Wilson 1987,
   1991; Hochschild 1991, 1995; and Gans 1995.

[9] Quoted in Himmelfarb 1994a, 4.

to Ronald Reagan's 1986 State of the Union Message, invoking Franklin Roosevelt's image of welfare as "a narcotic, a subtle destroyer of the human spirit" and insisting that "the success of welfare should be judged by how many of its recipients become independent of welfare."[10]

In recent years, the heady rhetoric of "personal responsibility" has more often associated with the meaner fringes of the political right.[11] But historically, values of personal responsibility, self-reliance, and self-sufficiency have long enjoyed widespread support. "The Lord helps those who help themselves" is a *Poor Richard*–style motto familiar to readers of Aesop.[12] Goals of self-reliance have been written into the preambles of virtually every major piece of social welfare legislation for a century or more.[13] Thus, contrary to claims of the New Right, there is nothing especially "new" about the consensus around values of self-reliance, as such.[14]

What is new is the particular ways in which those values have recently been operationalized and mobilized, both in the New Right's attacks on the welfare state and in New Age Democrats' responses to them. Under the guise of a "Personal Responsibility Act," the House Republicans' 1994 *Contract with America*

---

[10] Quoted in Goodin 1988, 335. A decade later, the Republican-controlled U.S. House of Representatives' (1996, 2186) report endorsing the Personal Responsibility and Work Opportunity Reconciliation Act of 1996 reiterated, "The welfare system contradicts fundamental American values that ought to be encouraged and rewarded: work, family, personal responsibility and self-sufficiency."

[11] Block et al. 1987.

[12] Aesop n.d./1960. Its most famous manifestation in American culture, perhaps, is Ralph Waldo Emerson's 1841 essay on "Self-Reliance." The British equivalent, Samuel Smiles's *Self-Help* (1859), literally opens with this line; this book, a runaway best seller in its time (being multiply reprinted and selling over a quarter million copies by the end of the century), has most recently been reprinted by the Institute of Economic Affairs, with a glowing foreword by its former director, Lord Harris of High Cross (Smiles 1859/1996).

[13] Most recently, in the U.S. Family Support Act of 1988, on which see Bane and Ellwood 1994. For precursors in the United States and abroad, see Goodin 1988, chap. 12.

[14] Cf. Novak et al. 1987, 94.

proposed to withdraw Aid to Families with Dependent Children (AFDC) from many most in need of it.[15] Having vetoed one version of that legislation, the Democratic president promptly issued an administrative order itself implementing most "personal responsibility" provisions of the bill.[16] Three months later, at a press conference announcing he would sign a lightly revised version of the original bill – originally introduced as the "Welfare Reform Act of 1996," but tellingly retitled in its passage through Congress the "Personal Responsibility and Work Opportunity Reconciliation Act of 1996" – President Clinton proudly proclaimed:

> A long time ago I concluded that the current welfare system undermines the basic values of work, responsibility and family, trapping generation after generation in dependency and hurting the very people it was designed to help.... When I ran for president four years ago, I pledged to end welfare as we know it ... – to transform a ... system that traps too many people in a cycle of dependence to one that emphasizes work and independence; to give people on welfare a chance to draw a paycheck, not a welfare check. [This legislation] gives us a better chance to give those on welfare what we want for all families in America, the opportunity to succeed at home and at work. For those reasons I will sign it into law.[17]

---

[15] House Republicans 1994, 9–10, 17, 65–77. The original proposals, only partly reflected in the final legislation, would have denied AFDC to any unwed mother who is under eighteen (who being young and less skilled is presumably less likely than others to be able to find paid employment); or who has another child while on AFDC (and who presumably therefore needs more help, not less, with child rearing); or who, except in cases of rape or incest, refuses to name the child's father (who presumably cannot be counted on for help in raising the child, either); or who has been on AFDC for five years (and who therefore has minimal chances of finding paid employment). While defended in terms of providing massive disincentives to taking the welfare option, the irony is that the harsher those deterrents (and hence the more they succeed in deterring those who have it within their power to avoid them), the more those who are left suffering the penalties are those who do not in any way deserve them. See further section 2.5.1.

[16] Vobejda 1996.

[17] Clinton 1996a, 2216; see similarly 1996b. For further details of the legislation and politicking surrounding it, see Katz 1996a, 1996b, and U.S. Congress 1996.

For the welfare mothers who were the clearest targets of welfare reformers, "personal responsibility" and "taking charge of
their own lives" seem primarily matters of getting control over
their own fertility – not necessarily by means of abortion, which
would be widely regarded as evading responsibility yet again, but
rather through prudent contraceptive practices or (better yet)
through sexual abstinence. For the underclass more generally,
taking control of one's life is seen to be principally a matter of securing paid employment through the assistance of "workfare."[18]
State-subsidized employment and training schemes of that form
constitute, in the classic phrase, a "hand up, not a handout";[19]
they make "welfare [what it] was meant to be,... a second chance,
not a way of life."[20]

While welfare mothers and the estranged poor serve as light-
ning rods for the rhetoric of personal responsibility, such rhetoric
strikes elsewhere as well, particularly in the area of public health.
Many ailments are ones that people help bring upon themselves
through their own life-style choices and consumption behavior.
People's smoking contributes to cancers in their lungs. Their rich
diets and sedentary life-styles contribute to their obesity and consequent coronaries. Their unsafe sexual practices render them
vulnerable to sexually transmitted diseases. Their experimentation with drugs of dependency leads to their addictions. And so
on. In all these ways, we can sheet home to individuals themselves at least some measure of personal responsibility for their
own health problems.[21]

It is an open question what, in policy terms, follows from such
observations. Some say that such people have "only themselves to

---

[18] Bane and Ellwood 1994, esp. chap. 4; Handler and Hasenfeld 1991, esp.
   chap. 5; King 1995, esp. chap. 5.
[19] In language borrowed directly from the House Republicans' *Contract with
   America* (1994, 65), "A helping hand, not a handout" was the title of the in-
   troductory section of the House Report (U.S. House of Representatives 1996,
   2184) on the Personal Responsibility and Work Opportunity Reconciliation
   Act of 1996. See similarly the manifesto for the New U.K. Labour Party (Commission on Social Justice 1994, 8).
[20] Clinton 1996, 2216.
[21] Wikler 1987, 1978.

blame" for their health problems, and they have no right to foist the costs onto others who have neither contributed to causing them nor consented to paying for them[22] – just as, in welfare debates, it is said that welfare mothers have no right to foist onto the rest of us the costs of children they knew they could not afford.[23] For my own part, clearly I shun those particular conclusions, for reasons to be elaborated here. Still, it must certainly be agreed that had people behaved "more responsibly" in all of those ways from the outset many health and welfare problems would simply not have arisen.

2.1.2   Some Blunt Facts about Social Policy

Shortly I shall turn to more arid matters of logic and analysis, as befits a book of philosophy. Before passing to those topics, however, it is important to set straight some facts about the policy environment in which those arguments arise.

Notwithstanding the heated public discourse surrounding welfare mothers, they are relatively small beer in terms of overall public expenditure. Leave aside the comparative costs of aircraft carriers. Even just as a proportion of U.S. social welfare expenditures, spending on welfare mothers accounts for a small fraction of the total. Much the largest part of social welfare expenditure goes to the elderly. AFDC spending in 1993 was running at some $22.6 billion – a not inconsiderable sum, but one that pales in significance when compared with federal outlays on Social Security ($304.6 billion) or even on Medicare ($130.6 billion).[24] Outlays on AFDC constitute just over a tenth of all federal spending on means-tested income support; they are about half the size of federal expenditures on workers' compensation; they are about on a par with federal spending on food stamps and the national school

---

[22] Such seems to be the view of, for example, Tollison and Wagner (1988, chap. 4). Wikler (1987, 336–44) canvasses these views, while himself adopting a much more nuanced version.

[23] Gauthier 1997.

[24] U.S. Census Bureau 1995, tables 612, 522, pp. 388, 337, respectively.

lunch program.[25] Counting federal, state, and local outlays altogether, spending on education would swamp all those more specifically social welfare programs many times over.

Although aid to education and the elderly costs far more, no one seems to complain of the dependency those programs engender. There may be many reasons. One, perhaps, is that dependencies in those realms are at least sometimes socially constructed ones, imposed by laws and practices (e.g., about who is allowed, encouraged, and expected to work for a living) which we as a community collectively adopt and foist upon young and old.[26] Another reason, paradoxically, may be that since neither Social Security nor Medicare nor state schooling is means-tested, most recipients neither especially need nor particularly depend on it: so maybe those programs actually engender little or no dependency, anyway.[27]

In terms of the wider public discourse, however, I suspect the real reason those other programs occasion so little comment lies elsewhere. Underlying the discourse on welfare dependency are certain perceptions, typically tacit and almost invariably undefended, about natural and appropriate stages of human development. Associated with those are certain perceptions about the natural and appropriate place of women, and of the natural and appropriate role of families and communities. Dependencies associated with those ostensibly "natural and appropriate" aspects of social life are not so much excused as simply overlooked, treated as if they did not constitute dependencies at all. These silences and elisions give rise to the moralized definition of dependency, the nature and problems of which will be discussed more fully in section 2.2.5.

---

[25] Ibid., tables 587, 613, pp. 376, 389 respectively.

[26] Titmuss 1958. His prime examples are "workforce exclusions" mandated by child-labor laws and compulsory retirement laws respectively. Legislative reforms have rendered the latter example otiose in most jurisdictions, but the general point remains nonetheless valid.

[27] It is of course another question why it should be so much more acceptable to receive public money when you do not need it than when you do. But let us merely note that paradox and then let it pass.

Fevered critiques of welfare dependency mislead in other respects as well. Also contrary to impressions created by that discourse, most recipients do not actually depend on public assistance very heavily or for very long. Most of the people who go
onto welfare rolls stay there for a relatively short time. Typically
some particular life crisis – illness or injury, loss of a partner or of a
job – precipitates a financial crisis. Public assistance serves to tide
people over, and once the crisis has passed, most people get back
on their own feet again within a couple of years. That is broadly
characteristic of public assistance recipients in general.[28] It is also
true, if only slightly less so, of welfare mothers in particular.[29]

Short-stay welfare clients are not, of course, those upon whom
critics fixate.[30] Program administrators and taxpayers alike are
inevitably more concerned with the minority of claimants who
stay on welfare rolls year in and year out, or who keep cycling
on and off welfare rolls. Furthermore, it is also perfectly true that
those long-term clients also constitute the bulk of the welfare case
load at any given time. That might seem paradoxical, in light of
what has just been said about turnover rates and the duration of
the average welfare spell. But consider the analogy of a hospital.
Suppose a new hospital admits 100 people every day – 99 for day
surgery, and 1 for chronic care stretching over a year. On the
hospital's first anniversary, the hospital's residents will number

---

[28] Duncan (1984, 75) reports that although 25 percent of the U.S. population
received welfare income sometime over the decade 1969–78, only 8.3 percent
received it for five years or more and only 2 percent for all ten years. Looking
at those depending heavily on welfare payments (i.e., for more than half their
family's income), both those percentages drop by roughly two-thirds.

[29] According to Bane and Ellwood (1994, 28), "half of all spells [of AFDC re-
ceipt] last less than two years; only 14 percent last ten years or more"; it is
also true, however, that, being more vulnerable to economic shocks, welfare
mothers cycle back onto welfare rolls more frequently than do others. See
further Moffitt 1992, 24–7, and Weaver and Dickens 1995, 36–4, and the
many sources cited therein.

[30] Indeed, notice how the more socially approved term "client" comes most
naturally in speaking of them. There is a suggestion that we start talking
of "welfare participants," instead of "welfare recipients," the hope being that
changes in langauge might cause rather than be caused by changes in attitudes.
Would that it were so easy.

465 (99 in the day ward, admitted just that day, together with 366 in the long-stay wards, admitted at the rate of one-a-day throughout the year). But were all the hospital's ex-patients to return for the hospital's first birthday celebrations, caterers would have to accommodate the other 36,135 former short-stay patients (365 times 99) treated over the course of the year, in addition to the 465 still resident on the day itself.[31]

No one denies the importance of trying to figure out why some linger on welfare or return time and again to it. No one denies the importance of trying to think if there is any other way of delivering social assistance that would be more useful to them in carving out an independent life for themselves. (There may or may not be, of course: think again of the analogy to a hospital's chronic-care patients.)[32] But judging programs by whom they have helped, it must be said that most of the people helped by social assistance – even AFDC – are people who depend on that assistance only briefly before getting back on their own feet again.

In searching for ways to reduce the dependency of long-term welfare recipients, we ought also to be wary of collateral damage that policy reforms might cause to the short-term recipients who make up the bulk of the case load over time. Some reforms might benefit both groups, of course. But given the preponderance of short-term and perfectly appropriate users among the clients of most social welfare programs, any reforms that simply "crack down" on recipients across the board have far more scope for harming appropriate users than for weeding out inappropriate ones.[33]

---

[31] See Bane and Ellwood 1994, 29–30.

[32] Evidence that even moderately large changes in AFDC policy parameters makes moderately small differences to overall AFDC case load suggests that that may be an apt model (Bane and Ellwood 1994, 191, 122). One option might be lump sum capital infusions for worthwhile projects that might make recipients subsequently self-supporting, as proposed by the minister of social security in a former Labor government in Australia (Baldwin 1995).

[33] We must, in more formal terms, weigh the risks of "false negatives" (wrongful denial of benefits) versus "false positives" (wrongful granting of benefits) (Goodin 1985a).

Thus, for example, it seems morally reckless to adopt the iron-clad rule, embodied in the 1996 Welfare Reform Act, that would cut off AFDC (which it renames Temporary Assistance for Needy Families) to mothers after two continuous years (or five years, in total) on the program. Most of them, as I have said, do manage to get off AFDC rolls within two years; but many of them are still leading a pretty precarious existence, and some 35 percent of them find that some crisis erupts (a child gets sick, their car breaks down, their partner leaves or dies) and they lose their job or other source of income and need to resume claiming AFDC. Most of them do not end up claiming AFDC for more than five years in total, over the course of their whole lives; but some 39 percent do, some 22 percent for ten years or more.[34] Some of those recidivists have only themselves to blame, perhaps, and deserve whatever harsh treatment the new regime proposes to mete out. But there are so very many of them that that is unlikely to be true of them all. An ironclad rule, cutting off benefits to everyone who exceeds the time limits, is bound to harm many who in no way deserve it. Maybe no other rule would work better to discriminate between deserving and undeserving. But if so, maybe we really ought stop worrying about punishing the undeserving and think more of the deserving upon whom such restrictive policies would inflict such undeserved suffering.

Finally, let us probe the ostensible "irresponsibility" of the much-maligned welfare mothers themselves. Scrutinize their choices to see wherein exactly their irresponsibility lies. Once a woman has fallen pregnant, deciding to go through with the pregnancy rather than terminating it seems (at least in one clear sense) to be the more "responsible" course of action.[35] Once she has given birth, deciding to raise the child herself rather than putting it up for adoption again seems (again, in at least one clear sense) the more "responsible" choice at that fork of the decision tree. And those who criticize welfare mothers for irresponsibly choosing to

---

[34] Bane and Ellwood 1994, 38–9.
[35] Petchesky 1981. The discourse of young women contemplating an abortion is replete with the language of "responsibility" on both sides of the question, judging from the reports of Gilligan and Belenky (1980).

stay at home with their children, at government expense, regard it as the height of "responsible mothering" for wealthier mothers to stay at home with their children, at their husbands' expense.[36] Welfare mothers may well be doing the right thing for the wrong reasons, or it may be irresponsible of them to accept responsibility while lacking the resources to discharge it effectively. But on the face of it, each of those choices seems in at least one clear sense to betoken a more rather than less responsible cast of character.

Welfare mothers' "irresponsibility" seems to be confined almost literally to the moment of conception.[37] They irresponsibly "got themselves pregnant" – with the aid of equally or more irresponsible partners, whom welfare reformers quite rightly have in their child-support sights as well. And the "irresponsibility" of getting themselves pregnant lies, here, in their doing so knowing that they neither have nor have any realistic prospect of securing either a husband or an income capable of sustaining themselves and their child. In getting themselves pregnant in these circumstances, they are abdicating personal responsibility for themselves and their child and counting on the state to support them.[38]

Issues of reproductive responsibility have undoubtedly become more complicated with the advent of new medical and legal possibilities. Now that contraceptive technologies are readily available, it is easy to suppose that any woman who fails to use them and gets pregnant in consequence has "only herself to blame" – forgetting that those options might not be nearly so readily available (economically, medically, and sociologically) to young women in the

---

[36] Conservative critic George Gilder (1987) himself emphasizes this point in criticizing the American Enterprise Institute report (Novak et al. 1987).

[37] Luker 1996. Certainly illegitimacy rates figure centrally in the rhetoric of writers like Charles Murray (1984, 1994, 1995).

[38] In Malthus's (1803/1992, bk. 3, chap. vi) version of this argument, the complaint was lodged against the man, enabled by the Poor Laws to "marry with little or no prospect of being able to support a family without parish assistance," with the resulting "obvious tendency . . . to increase population." While such a procreational focus has long lain at the core of objections to generous social provision, the empirical evidence clearly indicates that, once we have controlled for other relevant factors, there is no statistically significant link between levels of welfare benefits and illegitimate birth rates. See Moffitt 1992, 27–34, and the many other studies cited therein.

ghetto.[39] Now that women have the option of a safe, legal, socially accepted abortion, it is easy to suppose that if a woman decides not to abort and to have the child against the father's wishes, then the responsibility is hers rather than his[40] – forgetting how hard and morally ambiguous a choice abortion is for a woman.[41]

I do not for a moment to question the value of the gains these legal and medical advances have brought in securing a great many women control over their own reproductive lives. At the same time, however, we should also recognize how those same developments have also made it easier than it used to be – in many ways, easier than it still should be – for others (be they irresponsible men or richer women) to blame those in the ghetto who "get themselves pregnant."

Be all that as it may, though, if merely having "got themselves pregnant" is the welfare mothers' besetting sin, the punishment entailed by a more punitive welfare regime hardly seems to fit the crime. Many at all times and in all social classes experience unplanned pregnancies; although always awkward, few of them occasion so much grief as welfare reformers would impose upon welfare mothers in the name of "personal responsibility." Many at all times and in all social classes deviously plan pregnancies to "trap their man" or to "get out of their father's house." Although many subsequently have occasion to regret that choice, few find quite such reason to regret it as some welfare reformers would apparently wish to give welfare mothers.[42]

---

[39] Kittay 1996.

[40] Certainly such logic seems, rightly or wrongly, to have altered the balance of bargaining advantage within unwed couples (Akerlof, Yellen, and Katz 1996).

[41] Not to mention how dubious is the "last clear chance" principle of responsibility to which the man would here be appealing (Hart and Honoré 1985, 219–25).

[42] Part of what animates these arguments might be a view that unplanned pregnancies pose more of a problem for women with fewer resources (which is undoubtedly true), and that women with fewer resources therefore have more of an obligation morally to protect against them. But it is not clear why that should follow, morally (as opposed to merely prudentially: except for those who would elevate prudence to a morality of its own, or who would reduce morality to mere prudence).

Finally, suppose mothers who have gotten pregnant, knowing full well that they cannot themselves afford to care for the ensuing child, really have behaved wickedly. Suppose a child should indeed be seen as a pure consumption good from the mother's point of view, and the costs to the community of state support in rearing it as an uncovenanted externality.[43] Suppose in that sense welfare mothers really are free riders (or worse), taking unfair advantage of our collective reluctance to let poor babies starve.[44]

Even if we stipulate welfare mothers have behaved badly in bringing those children into the world, what follows? A firm scolding, no doubt, and strong exhortations to do better. But beyond that, what follows from the simple fact of their immorality for *our* subsequent actions and choices? Once the children are here, does anyone seriously suggest that it is morally permissible for us to allow them to starve? Would anyone seriously suggest that it is morally appropriate to starve those mothers, as a lesson to others? Does anyone seriously suggest that welfare mothers ought, as a condition of receiving welfare, be sterilized to prevent them from having further children while on welfare? Well, maybe Reverend Malthus did, and maybe a few on the further fringes of politics still do. But for most of us, surely, the force of such questions must be almost purely rhetorical.

Is there then *nothing* we can expect of welfare mothers, in return for the public assistance that they receive? Not sexual abstinence? Not a sincere effort to find a job? Not even a word of thanks? Well (to affect the gentrified tones of Georgian romances, as seems to befit the topic), it would be "damnably decent" of them if they did all of those things; they would be vaguely "rotters" if they did not. But, again, do we really think we should make our assistance to them literally *conditional* on any such

---

[43] Pronatalist social welfare policies, characteristic of Sweden and France, regard them very differently, of course (Myrdal 1940; Tilton 1990).

[44] This, in exaggerated form, is the position of Gauthier (1997); the notion of "fairness" at work, though, is common enough (Rawls 1958). Arneson (1997) shows how such notions of reciprocity might underlie much of the public welfare dependency debate.

performances? Which is to ask, Do we really think it would be right to withdraw the social safety net from any of them who, for whatever reason, did not meet our conditions? Again, some on the further fringes of politics may say yea to such a proposition. But most surely recognize that it is in the nature of safety nets and last resorts that, in order to perform their residual safety net function at all, they simply must be unconditional in form.

Philosophical problems of population policy are notoriously vexed. We have neither settled judgments nor even any particularly solid intuitions as to how to decide how many people there should be or what we may legitimately do to influence people's procreation patterns.[45] Many of our difficulties in framing an appropriate moral response to procreation among welfare mothers undoubtedly stem, in part, from those more general philosophical perplexities surrounding population policy in general. What is puzzling is simply why people who are so properly circumspect in their approach to world population problems should so confidently endorse punitive measures for coping with irresponsible procreation among welfare mothers domestically.

All that is mainly by way of saying that arguments against the welfare state couched in high-minded terms of "personal responsibility" are often, quite simply, arguments in bad faith. The proverbial visitor from Mars would find the rhetorical vilification of welfare mothers and such like utterly mystifying in light of analogies such as I have just been drawing. The first crucial fact required to help the penny to drop for our friend from Mars is, quite simply, the fact of race. Welfare mothers are (in the popular perception, even more than in the statistical reality) predominantly black; and long-term welfare recipients are even more disproportionately black, yet again. It is the blackness of their skin rather than of their character that marks them out for such very special treatment in the political rhetoric of the New Right.

The second crucial fact is, of course, that of gender. Welfare mothers are, by definition, mothers. Policies aimed at relieving poverty among women have long taken a decidedly second

---

[45] Parfit 1984, pt. 4; Dasgupta 1993, chap. 13; Sen 1996, 1035–61.

place – less generously funded, more tightly scrutinized – than corresponding programs aimed at aiding men, be they former workers or former soldiers.[46] The effects of this long-standing prejudice have simply become magnified with the "feminization of poverty" occasioned by the rising numbers of single mothers.

Thus, there is a risk of treating arguments in favor of "personal responsibility for social welfare" with more respect than they deserve. Equally, though, there is a risk of treating them with less. Some proponents of more personal responsibility – my coauthor of this volume, together with a great many sincere social reformers, clearly among them – are perfectly sincere, guided by argument and reason rather than blinded by bigotry. Out of respect to those who deploy such arguments in good faith, I proceed to discuss those arguments on their merits. It is, however, a courtesy which many others clearly do not in the least deserve.

---

[46] Nelson 1990; Sapiro 1990; Skocpol 1992; Gordon 1994.

2.2   Some Key Words in Context

S EVERAL key words recur like mantras throughout contemporary social policy debates. A crucial first step in appraising
those debates philosophically is to examine those terms in context. This is not a matter of standing back from the debates, analyzing concepts from the high plane of philosophical abstraction.
Instead, it is a matter of examining "words in use," registering the
ways those particular terms are deployed in those particular debates. The aim is not linguistic legislation, stipulating how these
words "should" be used. The exercise is instead more akin to social ethnography, examining the way words actually are used for
clues to the social theories and practices lying behind them.

The key words meriting particular attention in this regard are
those of "dependency" and "reliance" (which are used more or
less interchangeably in these debates) and of "the self." (The notion of "responsibility" is discussed separately in section 2.3.) I
offer a few remarks upon each of those terms in isolation, but
it is their conjunction and interaction that matters most in these
connections.

2.2.1   Dependency, Reliance, and Social Welfare

For a concise, general definition of the notions of "dependency"
and "reliance," the following will suffice:

  X is "dependent" (or "relies") on Y for Z insofar as:
  (1) X *receives* Z from Y.

(2) X *needs* Z in order to protect some vital interests.
(3) Y is X's *only source* of supply of Z.[47]

Much might be said in elaboration of this definition.[48] But at that level of generality the definition of dependency seems not to be in much dispute. That is roughly what is meant by virtually all parties to debates over welfare dependency, over "dependencia" in economic development, over growing "interdependence" within the New World Order, and so on.[49]

There is, however, one peculiarity about the notion of "dependency" as it figures in social welfare debates. There, the term seems to have uniformly negative connotations, whereas in a great many other contexts the notion carries either no such connotations or anyway much more mixed ones. In everyday life, we depend on gravity to keep our feet on the ground and on other drivers to keep to their side of the road. We do so in both cases without much occasion for comment and none for regret. Similarly, we depend on family and friends for moral support, on banks to safeguard our money, on police to secure our streets, on the armed forces to defend our borders, on teachers to educate

---

[47] Adapted from Goodin 1985b, 195–6.
[48] Probably only two other things are crucial for present purposes. One is that two further features, together with those other three, are required to make the X's dependency "exploitable" by Y. Those are:
    (4) Y exercises *discretionary control* over the distribution of Z.
    (5) The balance of power between X and Y is *asymmetrical*, in that Y is more dependent on X for needed resources than X is on Y.
The exploitation and manipulation of other people's dependencies is discussed more fully in section 2.2.2.
    Second, notice that although it is more convenient to phrase these conditions in "absolute" terms, dependency and reliance can and typically will be relative, more-or-less things. (The balance of power can be more or less asymmetrical; X's need for the resource can be greater or smaller; Y can be more or less X's only source of supply.) Thus, strictly speaking, we might want to say that a middle-income Briton "is [pretty heavily] reliant" upon the National Health Service for the kidney transplant he or she needs, even though he or she may have some options of a fairly farfetched or unattractive sort (e.g., going to India and finding an impoverished donor there willing to sell a spare kidney).
[49] See Goodin 1985b, chap. 7, and the further references therein.

our children. Whenever dependencies such as those are remarked upon, it is in tones of appreciation rather than of regret.

Such examples clearly suggest that whatever it is that makes welfare dependency so uniformly objectionable, it is something somehow peculiar to the social welfare debates here in view. There seems to be nothing about dependency as such that makes it necessarily objectionable. There seems to be nothing wrong with taking certain things (about either the external world, or even our social environment) for granted, framing our own action plans on the basis of assumptions about contingencies that are not within our own power to control.

If dependency is not invariably bad, how then can we differentiate objectionable dependencies (e.g., on public welfare) from innocuous ones (e.g., on gravity's tug or other people's driving)? I shall canvass various possibilities. But none proves wholly satisfactory until we frankly admit the distinctly moralized character of the criteria here in view, which (as I shall show in section 2.2.5) poses problems of its own.

One way of differentiating among dependencies would be to say that unobjectionable dependencies are somehow *natural* in a way that objectionable ones are not. Something like that certainly seems to be suggested in welfare debates by the way in which "natural" dependencies (e.g., within families) occasion no critical comment but "unnatural" ones (e.g., upon the state) do.

As a general analysis of what differentiates objectionable dependencies from unobjectionable ones, however, that will not do. Among the various dependencies we find unobjectionable, only the force of gravity might be deemed natural in some straightforward sense. None of the forces at work in any of the other cited examples can be unambiguously so characterized. Which side of the road we drive on is utterly conventional, and not at all natural: we socially create those conventions; we enact and enforce driving laws to underwrite them. Banks too are creatures of company law, and the security of our deposits in them is a function of the law of contracts and of trusts and of various more specific enactments. Even the affection of family and friends for one another, natural though it may be in itself, manifests itself differently from place to place and time to time: what exactly we can "count on" by way of material assistance from family and friends clearly depends heavily on social conventions. It is simply not true that all of those morally unobjectionable dependencies can all somehow be seen as "natural" ones.

A second way of trying to frame the distinction between objectionable and unobjectionable dependencies, almost inverse to the last, might point to the crucial difference between voluntary dependencies and involuntary ones. It is one thing to depend on someone or something, of your own volition – for friends and lovers voluntarily to put themselves "in one another's power," trusting and depending on one another of their own free choice.[50] It is quite another thing – and something much worse – to *have* to trust and depend upon particular others without having any choice in the matter.[51]

This distinction, too, picks up a perfectly familiar use of the term "dependency" within social policy and administration. On tax forms and social security applications, "dependents" refers to people like underaged minors, the blind, and disabled. Dependents, in that sense, are indeed people who are necessarily dependent on others for assistance and support.

The dependency of tax-form dependents is not what arouses the ire of opponents of welfare dependency, however. The young and the disabled represent what used to be tactlessly termed the "impotent poor." They have always been explicitly exempted from the wrath of opponents of welfare dependency. That wrath is focused instead on the "able-bodied poor," who being "able bodied" could well earn their own living if only they tried. What is objectionable about their dependency is precisely that they depend on others when they do not have to do so. Their dependency is a voluntary dependency – and, exactly opposite to the analysis here in view, all the worse for that fact.

In general, there seems to be no important moral distinction to be drawn among dependencies in terms of the voluntariness of

---

[50]   Wilson 1978; Blum 1980; Badhwar 1993.

[51]   The natural dependencies that the previous analysis celebrated would be involuntary in ways that this analysis denigrates – which is what makes this analysis almost the inverse of the last.

the dependency relationship. The earlier examples of innocuous dependencies (on gravity, or on others to keep to their side of the road) seem to testify to that fact. For all intents and purposes, we have no choice but to depend on natural forces like gravity and social forces like the rules of the road.[52] Yet we reckon ourselves none the worse morally (if occasionally perhaps a little worse off materially) in consequence of those dependencies.

A third way of trying to frame the distinction between acceptable and objectionable dependencies might be in terms of the dependability of the things being depended upon. It would be obviously reckless to rely on something that is obviously unreliable; and that sense of sheer imprudence may explicate at least some of our objections to dependency in general. Skating on transparently thin ice or investing in obviously insecure banks amounts to putting yourself at the mercy of things that cannot be reasonably relied upon to produce the desired results. The combination of those facts – that you are at the mercy of external forces (if things start to go wrong, there is nothing much you can do to rescue yourself), and that there is no good reason to trust those forces to work to your advantage – constitutes a powerful objection to the practice. Trusting people and things, facts and forces that are unworthy of trust is an error of judgment, which, if persisted in, perhaps betokens a flaw of character as well.

True though that all may be as applied to thin ice and shady characters, it seems at first blush an odd way to couch the objections here in view to welfare dependency. But something like that is, perhaps, lurking in the background. There is a certain sort of sturdy individualist who preaches self-reliance precisely on the grounds that "big government" cannot be trusted ("the social security trust fund is bankrupt" and so on). In contrast, "family is family" and "friends will always be there for you." Or so the theory goes.

---

[52] Perhaps it is just barely conceivable that we might be able to lead our lives without depending on those things: we could wear moon boots everywhere we went, perhaps, and travel about only at times the roads are sure to be empty. But a life lived like that would be utterly unlike life as we know it. While there may be no logical necessity in depending on these things, the practical necessity is enormous.

Still, on closer inspection, this analysis of depending only on what is dependable does not really capture the nuances of the welfare debates here in view, either. For one thing, opponents of welfare dependency systematically oppose reliance on others and systematically urge "self-reliance" instead. But when others are more able or informed or experienced than you are yourself, counting on them might be a better way of "getting reliably good results" than relying on your own feeble efforts. There, the self-reliance that opponents of welfare dependency champion is the more unreliable course of action.

Furthermore, if the objection to dependency lay merely in depending on the undependable, then one perfectly good solution would be to make those things upon which people rely (such as welfare benefits) more reliable. In various other contexts, that seems to be our preferred response. In personal relationships, we think it is good that people should be trustworthy, and if they betray our trust, the fault is said to be theirs for betraying our trust rather than ours for relying on it. So too are the responsibilities of public officials often characterized as a "public trust," and the responsibilities of professionals toward their clients and of firms toward their employees and customers as "fiduciary" ones.[53] Indeed, a whole panoply of economic relations (within firms, as well as among firms) have come to be analyzed as "relational contracts" establishing a framework of "trust" within which parties can negotiate subsequent issues as they arise.[54] In all these various circumstances, the right solution to problems of having relied on people who subsequently proved unreliable clearly would be to make the others more trustworthy rather than to become ourselves less trusting.

So too in the social welfare realm, perhaps. It may well be that the unreliable, undependable, erratic nature of social assistance – rather than any flaw in the character of potential recipients of that assistance – poses the real problem to which we should be seeking a solution. That has long been a theme of "welfare rights"

---

[53]   Goodin 1985b, 52–70.
[54]   Kreps 1990; Williamson 1985; Williamson and Winter 1991.

activists, keen to make social assistance a minimally discretionary matter of fundamental social entitlement.

Clearly, however, that is not the preferred solution among those who rail against welfare dependency. What they want is for people to be more self-reliant, to stand on their own feet – which in these quarters would be regarded as being antithetical to their welfare benefits being put on a more secure footing. What we are trying to do here, remember, is to map the discourse of those who oppose social welfare on grounds of dependency. If so, then it is no good to offer an analysis that has as one of its principal implications that the benefits upon which the poor depend should be made more secure.

At the end of all this, we are still left asking critics of welfare dependency, What's the problem? As we have seen, the problem cannot be that people rely on external forces (whether *natural* or *social*). The problem cannot be that people rely on external forces on which they *have to* rely. The problem cannot be that people rely on external forces which are *intrinsically unreliable*.

We are left with the simple conclusion that the objection to welfare dependency is instead that people are relying on things on which *morally* they ought not rely. What crucially differentiates unobjectionable dependencies from objectionable ones, in the view of critics of welfare dependency, seems just to be the moral appropriateness of relying on some things (such as family and friends, social conventions, and natural forces) compared with the moral inappropriateness of relying on others (such as public assistance, at least when you do not have to).[55]

---

[55] Note in passing that there is probably an analogously moralized analysis of what constitutes "having to" rely on public assistance at work here. Modal language suggests a strong sense of "impossible to do otherwise." But it is simply not the case that there is no possible world in which the people in question do not rely on public assistance. There is one possible world, for example, in which the impotent poor starve rather than relying on such assistance (it is no less possible a world for their not being in it, after all). There is one possible world in which welfare mothers' children die of neglect while they are out working. And so on. "Have to" does not really mean "impossible not to" but rather "should not (or should not be expected to) do otherwise," with the "should" there signaling a shift from modality to morality as the operative criteria.

2.2.2 Dependency from the Dependent's Perspective

I shall return in due course (in section 2.2.5) to the problems that arise from moralizing the definition of dependency in that way. First, however, let us note that there is no analogous puzzle about what is wrong with dependency from the dependents' point of view. The problem, from their perspective, is that they "have no options."[56] Others who are in control of the resources that one needs can exploit their arbitrary discretionary power over the supply of those resources to manipulate anyone who is dependent on them. If their discretion is unfettered, they can make their largesse conditional on whatever performances from dependents that they care to insist upon: singing the praise of God in the soup kitchen, the humiliating doffing of caps, or whatever.[57]

It is always possible, of course, that those who enjoy such asymmetrical power might exercise it generously and benevolently, setting either no conditions or anyway only perfectly reasonable ones on the exercise of their discretionary largesse. But then again, they might not. They are in a position to demand virtually anything of those dependent on them for needed resources, and those dependent on them have virtually no choice but to comply with whatever conditions they set. That is the problem of dependency, from the point of view of dependents. That is the virtue of "welfare rights" and other nondiscretionary forms of social entitlement, from the point of view of those wanting to solve the problems of dependency thus construed.[58]

---

[56] Or anyway not many, or no very good ones.

[57] Goodin 1985b, chap. 7; Gibson 1985. Note that even the Poor Law of 1834 (4 & 5 Wm 4, C 76, § 19) specifically prohibits compelling workhouse inmates to attend any religious services contrary to their religious beliefs. More typical of the period, perhaps, is Malthus's praise of the power of private charity to "purify and exalt" both benefactor and beneficiary (1803/1992, bk. 4, chap. 10, p. 284).

[58] Goodin 1988, chap. 7. Nondiscretionary categorical benefits pose much the same problem: an administrator's discretion is then merely shifted to the determination of whether a given claimant falls into the category of people entitled to benefit (as was noted, already, by Malthus [1803/1992, bk. 4, chap. 10, p. 284]). The solution to that problem is, obviously, nondiscretionary, noncategorical welfare rights – which is to say, unconditional payment of "basic income" (Goodin 1995, chap. 14; Atkinson 1995b, 1996).

In its early years, Aid to Families with Dependent Children displayed precisely those failings. In those early years, cohabitation constituted grounds for disqualification from receipt of AFDC. Welfare administrators conducted "midnight searches" looking, literally or figuratively, for a "man under the bed." Welfare recipients resented the intrusive searches and arbitrary administrative judgments involved. But having no other source of income, they had no choice but to submit to whatever arbitrary practices that those charged with the highly discretionary administration of the program chose to impose.

That led in turn to calls for welfare programs like AFDC to be put on a rights-based "entitlement" footing, depriving administrators of such arbitrary discretionary powers.[59] Over the next two decades, AFDC went far in that direction. Cohabitation rules were relaxed and administrative discretions limited. Far from being the weakest link in the social safety net, AFDC came to be seen as one of its stronger ones. Almost uniquely among social welfare programs, AFDC had come to underwrite women's capacity to establish an "autonomous household": a household of their own, independent of the arbitrary will of fathers or husbands. Those keen on "regulating the poor" in general and on enforcing patriarchy in particular will certainly object.[60] So too, perhaps, might others who take a more paternalistic interest in the welfare of poor unwed mothers and, especially, of their children. But from the perspective not only of feminists but also, more importantly, of dependents themselves ("dependents," here, in the tax-form sense), depending on minimally discretionary AFDC payments was highly liberating compared to the alternatives of depending on highly discretionary distributions from parents or partners.[61]

Welfare dependents and conservative critics more generally have systematically different perspectives on the problem of "welfare dependency." From the dependents' point of view, the

---

[59] Reich 1963; Handler 1979.

[60] For critical accounts of these perspectives, see Piven and Cloward 1971 and Pateman 1988.

[61] Orloff 1993; see also Young 1995 and Fraser 1994.

problem is that they have *no option* but to rely on assistance from a single source, on whatever terms that assistance is offered. From the conservative critics' point of view, the problem is that welfare dependents come to have *no will* of their own. They passively, placidly take what they are given. Rather than trying to find other options for themselves, they simply rely on the assistance of others on whatever terms it is offered.[62]

The behavioral manifestation is the same, either way. The estranged poor are depressed and dispirited and (for the most part) passive and quiescent. How best to interpret that phenomenon is the question. Where the conservative critic sees a failure of will, the welfare dependent sees an absence of realistic alternatives.

Which is the more apt characterization of the situation is, of course, largely a matter of empirical investigation. I will make no attempt here to weigh all the empirical evidence that would be required to resolve that issue. Let me just observe in passing, however, that there is indeed plenty of evidence for supposing that, for most welfare mothers in most urban ghettos, opportunities for jobs that would pay enough to make them worthwhile are indeed scarce.[63] For most welfare mothers, it is hardly crazy to say that, realistically, they have virtually no alternatives.

Of course, some of the particularly lucky or particularly enterprising among them do manage to find gainful employment in regular labor markets, and of course we should congratulate them on that considerable accomplishment.[64] Maybe, as the American Enterprise Institute has long claimed and as even Brookings economists now seem prepared to concede, virtually any "unskilled welfare recipient, if she is able-bodied and

---

[62] There is of course another, fiercer formulation of the conservative critic's objection in terms of the poor's wilfully exploiting taxpayers' largesse.

[63] For compelling back-of-the-envelope calculations, see Bane and Ellwood 1994, chap. 5. For more empirical evidence, see Holzer 1996, Wilson 1996b, and Kasarda 1990.

[64] Many more find even more lucrative employment in irregular ones, outside the law, judging from the evidence of Edin (1991; Edin and Jencks 1992). Curiously, advocates of self-reliance never seem to celebrate *their* enterprising spirit. Cf. Offe and Heinze 1992.

moderately resourceful, can almost certainly find an employer willing to offer her a job."[65] But it is a familiar fallacy to point to the successes of the few and conclude that, just because some have done it, then all could have done it.

If the structure of the situation is that one can succeed only on condition that not all do, then the freedom of the one is perfectly consistent with the "unfreedom" of the many.[66] For every one of the success stories recounted in Victorian best-sellers like Samuel Smiles's *Self-Help*, there were historically (and arguably had to be structurally) hundreds and thousands of untold stories of abject, blameless failures. Casual inspection of the limited job opportunities for single parents in the ghetto confirms that this is a pretty fair characterization of their plight. If there are a thousand people looking for work and only one job, one can get work only on condition that the remainder do not. That one person succeeds in getting a job, far from proving that all could, actually precludes others from doing so.[67]

The real labor market is of course more fluid than the simple static model of that example. For any given job, there will be many applicants and only one of them can get it; for any given job, therefore, one person's getting it really does preclude anyone else's getting it. But over time other jobs come up, and those who miss out on any one job have a chance at various others. So anyone's chances of getting some job, sometime or another, are far better than that person's chances of getting any particular job.

Alas, though, evidence from studies of labor markets in many places and many periods seems firmly to suggest that the longer you have been unemployed in the past, the longer you are likely

[65] Provided, of course, "she is willing to accept a low enough wage and an inexpensive package of fringe benefits" (Burtless 1995, 60); see similarly Novak et al. 1987, 94.

[66] Marxian economics provides reasons for believing that precisely that is true of the proletariat in any capitalist economy (Cohen 1983).

[67] At the very least, we may well doubt, with Burtless (1995, 61), that all "unskilled AFDC recipients could find [even] poorly paid jobs if hundreds of thousands of them were forced to find jobs within a one- or two-year period," as essentially is contemplated in the 1996 welfare reforms.

to remain unemployed in the future. The long-term unemployed in the inner-city ghettos really do seem to settle into some "unemployment sink" from which they have little chance of escaping.

2.2.3   Reliance, Planning, and Prudence

The conservative critic's objection to "welfare dependency," notice, is not to the poor receiving benefits. Rather, it is to their *depending* on them. If through some utterly unexpected eventuality people happen to come to need public assistance, then there is no objection (or anyway none that can properly be couched in terms of "welfare dependency") to their being given it.[68] The objection is instead to the intentional, forward-looking aspect – the perversion of prudent planning – that is associated with "the curse of relief *expected* and *relied upon.*"[69]

In this light, the demand for people to take "personal responsibility" for their own welfare can be separated into two interlocking demands. One is that they actually undertake a program of prudent planning for their own future. The other is that, in so doing, they plan to rely only on their own resources. I shall query exactly what should be treated as "their own" resources for these purposes: suffice it to say for now that the matter is less straightforward than it seems. What I want to query, first, is this notion of "prudent planning," which lies equally at the core of those demands.

Social reformers have long complained of the imprudence of the poor and of the ways in which poor relief contributes to that imprudence. Hear the words of the Reverend Malthus:

---

[68] Tocqueville (1835/1983, 118), for example, has no objection to emergency assistance that is "as spontaneous as unforeseen, as temporary as the evil itself." Similar distinctions between emergency and ongoing assistance were made by Bentham, Sidgwick, Pigou, and a host of their contemporaries, among both economists and charity workers; see Goodin 1988, chap. 12, for further references.

[69] In the words of the great Victorian social reformer, Charles Booth (1892, 182, emphasis added); see similarly Mill 1848, bk. 5, chap. 11. For further references, see Goodin 1988, chap. 12.

The labouring poor . . . seem always to live from hand to mouth. Their present wants employ their whole attention; and they seldom think of the future. Even when they have an opportunity of saving, they seldom exercise it; but all that they earn beyond their present necessities goes, generally speaking, to the alehouse. . . . [I]t is difficult to conceive that these men would not save a part of their . . . wages for the future support of their families, instead of spending it in drunkenness and dissipation, if they did not rely on parish assistance for support in case of accidents. . . . The poor laws may, therefore, be said to diminish . . . the will to save among the common people, and thus to weaken one of the strongest incentives to sobriety and industry, and consequently to happiness.[70]

It is not, however, merely moralizing clerics practicing the most dismal form of economic science who think that "the formation and steady pursuit of some particular plan of life" is "one of the most permanent sources of happiness."[71] Philosophers too make much of the moral importance attaching to people's "projects" and, indeed, whole "life plans."[72]

Notions of human beings as "project makers" and "life planners" can serve as valuable analytic devices, highly useful for making philosophical points of great importance. But taking that talk too literally can get us into trouble. The image of someone engaged in whole-life planning in the way that language suggests is utterly untrue to life as it actually is (and prudently ought to be) lived.

One reason, philosophically much discussed, is simply that people's preferences and, hence, plans change over time.[73] Though

---

[70] Malthus 1803/1992, bk. 3, chap. 6, pp. 101–2.

[71] Ibid., bk. 4, chap. 1, p. 211.

[72] Most notably, Bernard Williams (1973, 1981). David Schmidtz's (1995) earlier work is a judicious elaboration within this tradition. Perhaps the most ambitious attempt at applying such notions to the sorts of problems here in view is found in Daniels 1988: there, he develops a "prudential lifespan" model on the basis of such suggestions (chap. 3), and applies it to various issues concerning "justice between the young and old," particularly income support policy (chap. 7).

[73] Parfit 1984.

true and important, that is not what is most importantly wrong with the model of people as whole-life planners.[74] The larger problem is that, when people are deciding what to do at any point in time, reflecting on how the act in view fits with their "whole-life plans" is just not how they ordinarily behave or prudentially should behave.

Most of the things most of us do most of the time are more the product of local than of global maximization. We can see some reason for doing it, and no reason for not; and that, ordinarily, is the end of the matter. How the act fits with some larger whole-life plan we might have is ordinarily never mentally mooted. Indeed, most of us most of the time probably take a similarly opportunistic, locally maximizing attitude toward our "life plan" as such: we have in mind a variety of things we might like to do, should the opportunity arise; what we actually do depends upon the opportunities that arise.

Such opportunism, furthermore, seems perfectly prudent in the circumstances in which most of us ordinarily find ourselves. Planning is a good idea, in general and within limits, because in that way you are more likely to end up achieving more of what you want. But planning out every detail of one's life would only make sense for someone who enjoyed complete control over all the resources and other contingencies that would be required to realize the plan – which no one ever does. Other people and other forces, pure chance and complicated social happenstance, have crucial roles to play in determining how our lives turn out. That being so, prudence dictates a more open and pragmatic approach toward planning one's own future.[75] By all means plan what you reasonably can, in a loose sort of way and always subject to

---

[74] That would be consistent with their having a "whole-life plan" at each point in time, just one that changed at different points in time.

[75] There is much to be said for the sorts of rules of thumb Daniel Shapiro (personal correspondence 1996) recommends for keeping out of poverty: "1) Finish high school. 2) Get a job, any job; and stick with it. 3) Get married and stay married." I'm sure anyone who could would be well advised to follow those rules. By the same token, I'm equally sure that not everyone in the ghetto can.

revision: but do not overplan, setting in concrete intentions that are bound to need revising.

In loosely planning their lives in this way, people take all sorts of decisional shortcuts, which may well catch up with them, sooner or later.[76] When they do, we are tempted to say that they have only themselves to blame for having behaved "irresponsibly." That is a singularly ex post perspective on the situation, however. Ex ante, it may well have been a case of their acting on the basis of imperfect information, taking such shortcuts as were available to make the best decision they could within the time and resources that could reasonably be committed to the project.[77] Once the contingencies have played themselves out, people may well wish that they had done differently. But from the ex ante perspective of the situation they were in at the time they had to act, it is far from clear that they behaved other than perfectly responsibly – even if things eventually turned out badly.[78]

That looser image of forward planning probably better captures what lands most people on welfare rolls than does any starched-shirt Victorian model of "deliberate reliance." Except in fairly limited and contrived circumstances (such as deliberate "asset stripping" so as to qualify for meanly means-tested pensions), people rarely deliberately impoverish themselves with the conscious intention of relying on state support. More often, things go

---

[76] They employ arbitrary time horizons, lopping off consideration of further futures whatever the payoffs or probabilities associated with them; they are inept at processing probabilities, employing heuristics that systematically bias their decisions; and so on. See Slovic, Kahneman, and Tversky 1982 and Goodin 1982, chap. 8, and sources cited therein.

[77] That is to say, it is a matter of "bounded rationality," in the sense made famous by Simon (1954). Schmidtz (1992) makes precisely this point with respect to arbitrary time horizons.

[78] The alternative to acting partially in ignorance, taking computational and informational shortcuts like that, is never to do anything until all information is to hand – which usually amounts to saying not to do anything. Buridan's ass, I submit, is hardly a model of responsible social agency.

wrong in ways they did not anticipate: they lose their jobs; they lose their breadwinners; they fall unexpectedly pregnant, often despite their best efforts at contraception.[79]

Certainly in retrospect it can often be said that they should have anticipated those eventualities and should have hedged better against them. (Indeed, people themselves often say precisely that in self-recrimination, often quite unjustifiably.) But in prospect, they had certainly not been *planning* on receiving public assistance. They were not *relying* on it, in the relevant sense. Typically they were not thinking far enough ahead about the catastrophes that eventually befell them to be influenced by the prospect of public assistance as a fallback.

Furthermore, it is often right not to be thinking too far ahead, in these ways. The likelihood of something bad actually happening can sometimes increase with people's hedging against its happening. Marital breakdown is arguably rendered more likely, not less, the more you arrange your financial and other affairs within a marriage against that eventuality. Being laid off is rendered more likely, not less, by hedging your bets and giving your present employer less than "110 percent" of your loyalty. Of course, once one of those things actually has happened to you, then you regret not having hedged against it – in the same way, in Newcomb's paradox, you regret not having opted for the box with visibly more money in it once the accompanying opaque box turns out to be

---

[79] Even in the most dramatic cases, awful outcomes are more often the product of risks gone wrong. Antidrug rhetoric sometimes invites us to suppose that addicts "have only themselves to blame" for their addiction. But evidence submitted to the ACT Government's Heroin Task Force on which I recently sat suggests that even paradigmatic "drugs of dependence" such as heroin are not immediately addictive on first exposure, and many may take heroin (like alcohol) regularly for protracted periods without ever becoming addicted (see, e.g., McAllister, Moore, and Makkai 1991). If this is so, then for those unfortunates who eventually do become addicted their addiction cannot genuinely be said to be "the natural and inevitable consequence of their intentional acts": it is, rather, a matter of "a risk gone wrong" for those who had (no doubt recklessly) risked casual experimentation with the drug.

empty.[80] But ex ante, making the more trusting choice and hoping for the best were neither crazy nor necessarily irresponsible in any of those cases.

All that seems to be true of people in general. It seems particularly true of the specific groups most at the center of debates over "welfare dependency," impoverished young blacks in the American ghettos. Long-term, detailed planning makes most sense, as I have said, for those who have confident control over the resources required to carry out those plans. It makes virtually no sense for those eking out a marginal existence, buffeted by the random brutalization of the ghetto.

Welfare mothers may indeed be a partial exception to these more general strictures.[81] Some welfare mothers undoubtedly do deliberately get pregnant, with a view to securing AFDC and through it a household of their own.[82] And most teenaged girls in the ghetto know, at least in some more diffuse way, that if they have a baby they will receive welfare. It may well be that some

---

[80] The allusion is to a paradox in decision theory, owing to William Newcomb, which goes like this. There are two boxes in front of you. The first is opaque, but is said to contain either $1 million or nothing. The second is clear, and you can see it contains $1,000. You can choose to take the contents either of the first box alone or of both boxes. The "dominance" or "sure-thing" principle tells you to take both boxes: that way, you have $1,000 plus however much or little turns out to be in the opaque first box. But now suppose you are told a genie who with perfect insight into what sort of person you are manipulates the contents of the opaque first box, in such a way that if you are the greedy sort of person who opts for both boxes the opaque first box will in fact contain nothing, whereas if you are a trusting soul who opts for the opaque first box alone then that box will actually contain $1 million. Then the "dominance" and "expected utility" principles pull apart, the latter principle telling you to choose (or to be the sort of person who would choose) the first box alone (Nozick 1969, 1993, 41–50).

[81] Even if they constituted a *complete* exception, it is an open question how important an exception that would really be. After all (as shown in section 2.1.2), welfare mothers account for a small proportion of welfare expenditures overall.

[82] And, as I have said, that in itself is a step toward independence of a sort: in terms of minimizing dependency, it is unclear why dependency on the impersonal agency of the state should be so much more objectionable than personal dependency on parents.

welfare mothers plan in that stronger sense, and many in that weaker sense, to rely on welfare should they get pregnant. Still, in the ghetto as elsewhere, most young unattached women fall pregnant through an absence of planning rather than an excess of it.

Most of those who are most vulnerable and most likely to fall upon welfare rolls, more generally, simply do not – and are in no position to – plan their own futures with any degree of precision at all. They are no more in a position to "plan to 'rely' on welfare" than they are to plan much anything else about their lives.[83] To accuse them of a failure to take "personal responsibility" for their welfare is to ascribe to them a measure of control over their own lives that they can only wish that they actually enjoyed.[84]

2.2.4   Self-Reliance: But Who Is the "Self"?

Critics complain that generous social welfare provision encourages a "dependency culture," wherein people come to rely on state support rather than on their own efforts. The positive alternative that these critics offer is couched in terms of "self-reliance." As I have foreshadowed, however, the sense of "the self" involved in this notion of self-reliance is far from unproblematic.

On its face, "self-reliance" looks like a relatively straightforward notion. It implies relying upon oneself, and oneself alone. But however self-reliant, one inevitably relies on certain natural facts about the physical world (gravity, to return to our earlier example). However self-reliant, one inevitably relies on the persistence of certain social regularities (other drivers keeping in lane). However self-reliant, one inevitably relies to some greater or

---

[83] By the same token, it would be good if they could to avoid acquiring an arrest record: but in the ghetto these things are not always entirely within one's own power to control.

[84] The excusing condition here in view is logical, not merely psychological. The point is not just that social forces "overwhelm" these people, rendering them psychologically incapable of planning. The point is, instead, that, given the limited amount of control they can actually exert over their own lives with the limited resources available to them, it simply makes no sense to frame any very elaborate plans.

lesser extent on others honoring one's rightful claims and respecting one's rightful prerogatives (the bank cashing one's checks). No one would reasonably be said not to be self-reliant for having relied upon Newton's gravity, Greyhound's drivers, and Wells Fargo's cashiers in these ways. But no one relying on them could be said, strictly speaking, to be relying on oneself alone.

Maybe self-reliance is relative. Everyone *has* to rely on other people and forces to some extent – but those who rely on them no more than that should be deemed (relatively) self-reliant and, conversely, those who rely on them substantially more than that should be deemed to be (relatively) lacking in that attribute.

That is not the construction of "self-reliance" found in contemporary social welfare debates, however. On that construction, self-reliance would be a matter of not relying on other people or forces more than strictly necessary, physically or socially. In the social welfare debates here in view, people are indeed being urged to rely on some people and forces (state aid, most especially) no more than strictly necessary. But they are being urged to rely on other people and forces far more than anyone would care to claim is strictly necessary, on any credible construction of physical or social necessity. Thus, advocates of "self-reliance" urge grown "sons and daughters ... to live with their parents or relatives or friends" when they fall unemployed; "teen aged mothers ... to rely on support from their parents or the father of the child"; and "people laid off work ... to ... borrow from others to make do until the next job is found."[85] It is deemed consistent with "self-reliance" for stay-at-home mothers to depend on their husbands for financial support, and for the aged and infirm to be forced to depend similarly on subventions from children, siblings, grandparents, and even in-laws. And so on.

---

[85] Murray 1984, 228; see similarly his subsequent article (Murray 1985, 32). Others arguing broadly the same line include Margaret Thatcher and her ministers, Australian social security ministers, the secretary-general of the OECD, and a former archbishop of Canterbury; for references see Goodin 1988, chap. 12. Perhaps the most fully elaborated version of this argument is the American Enterprise Institute's report, *A community of self-reliance: The new consensus on family and welfare* (Novak et al. 1987).

In saying such things, perhaps it might be said that what advocates of "self-reliance" are taking for granted are just "natural forces" of some sort or another. It may well be that there is something genuinely "natural" about the affection that is ordinarily involved among family and friends, and maybe such affection characteristically manifests itself in mutual aid. Insofar as such assistance "flows automatically" from such sentiments, our reliance on it might be said to be akin to our reliance on natural forces (like gravity) or strong social conventions (like the rules of the road). Maybe our reliance on such assistance is not "*self-reliance*," strictly speaking, on any plausible standard.[86] But perhaps it is no more wanton or reckless or socially irresponsible than our relying on any of those other forces which we find relatively unproblematic.

Or again, perhaps there is something morally superior about relying on assistance from people who give it willingly and happily, and to whom you give something in return, rather than on assistance from people from whom it is coerced and to whom you give nothing in return. The former presumably characterizes ordinary relations within ordinary families. The latter arguably characterizes relations between welfare claimants and the taxpayers who constitute their reluctant benefactors.

All that is utterly beside the point of the policy debates here in view, though. No one wants to rule out the voluntary giving or receiving of assistance among family or friends; no one wants to denigrate either those who give or receive it. The policy question at issue is simply what to do when the mutual affection that we think natural among family and friends proves to be lacking, and when the mutual aid that we think ought flow automatically as a result of it proves not to be forthcoming.

One standard solution is legally compelling such assistance, nonetheless. Individualism is often said to lie at the heart of

---

[86] Even on the revised standard suggested a couple of paragraphs earlier, we do not *have* to rely on such assistance – however natural it may be – in the same ways we have to rely on gravity or even general social adherence to rules of the road.

contemporary Western philosophy, but actually it is more a form of "famialism."[87] And this ideology is powerfully reflected in the law. "Family responsibility" statutes require "every poor, old, blind, lame, and impotent or other poor person not able to work" to be maintained by parents, grandparents, or children, so far as they are able (and, often, reducing their entitlement to social assistance on the assumption, true or false, that they are). Such rules date from the Elizabethan Poor Law of 1601 and have figured in American poor laws from colonial times forward.[88] Although formally suspended in Britain in 1948, and in much of continental Europe over the next two or three decades, elsewhere (including in about half the American states) such rules remain officially in force, however rarely implemented.[89] In many places and under many guises, such rules are presently making a remarkable comeback, ironically enough under the banner of "personal responsibility."[90]

I do not necessarily want to argue here against those measures. In some cases they seem to me scandalous, in others less so; in a few, they seem to me to be positively desirable. The point I want to make in this connection has more to do with philosophical foundations than with policy prescriptions. The question I want to raise is whether (or in what peculiar sense) policies legally compelling reluctant people to rely on reluctant relatives for their support can count as contributions toward "self-reliance" and "personal responsibility."

A pair of particularly striking examples from recent American history might help sharpen this discussion. Consider, first, President Clinton's 1996 executive order mandating that young mothers receiving AFDC sign a "personal responsibility agreement" promising to remain living in the parental home. In all sorts of ways, perhaps that may well be the most responsible thing to do:

---

[87] A theme effectively developed by Kittay 1996.

[88] 43 Elizabeth I, C 2, § 7. Abbot 1940.

[89] Daniels 1988, 23. Another example is found in Articles 205 and 26 of the French *Code civil*.

[90] For further details, see Goodin 1988, chap. 12.

it may well facilitate their remaining in school, securing a job, and thus putting them in a better position in the longer term to take more responsibility for their own lives; it may constitute an "investment in their future" in a way premature independence would not; it may constitute "training in reciprocity" as they contribute (financially or otherwise) to the running of the shared household; and so on.[91]

Whatever those longer-term consequences of remaining in the parental home, however, there is surely another side to this story. A young adult's remaining in the parental home is ordinarily seen (and rightly so) as prolonging dependence on parents, as shunning the responsibility that comes with moving out and setting up house on one's own.

As I have said, in the circumstances of young unwed mothers that is just as well. It may well be irresponsible, in some larger sense, to take on more responsibilities than one is able to bear, or before one is ready to bear them. However we dress up the story, though, it is at best clearly one of trade-offs; it is a matter of abdicating responsibility now, so as to be better able to accept it later. It is a singularly one-eyed view of the situation that describes a young unwed mother's agreement to remain in the parental home as, unambiguously and unequivocally, a "personal responsibility" agreement.

Or, for a second example, consider persistent attempts, starting with the Social Security Amendments of 1974 and continuing through the Welfare Reform Act of 1996, to require delinquent fathers to pay child support.[92] Again, in itself that is an enormously desirable policy. It is eminently defensible, in terms of "personal responsibility" of fathers for the children they have sired; it is politically useful to shift the public focus away from

---

[91] It may also, not incidentally, discourage sexual promiscuity and further child-bearing.

[92] As has been tried many times before: the 1834 Poor Law, for example, contained identical provisions requiring unwed mothers to identify the child's father, and compelling the putative father to pay child support (4 & 5 Wm 4, C 76, §§ 69–70).

welfare mothers and onto "welfare fathers" as the true leaches on the commonweal.[93]

The question I want to raise about such policies is, again, a much narrower one. Whatever their many virtues, can such policies credibly claim to be reducing the mother's overall "dependency" on others? I submit that they cannot. What such policies do – and do most usefully – is merely to shift that dependency. The welfare mother's former dependency on the state is simply replaced, under such policies, by her dependency on child-support payments from the child's father.

Those advocating such policies do so in terms of "self-reliance," among many other important goals they hold out for us. But it is hard to see any increase in self-reliance, here. Welfare mothers who used to rely on the state for child support now rely on the children's fathers for child support (often still with the aid of the state in extracting those payments from delinquent fathers). Neither is a matter of relying on "oneself," in any ordinarily recognizable sense of the term.

The only way to make sense of this discourse, I submit, is to see that there is essentially a moral judgment at work here. "Self-reliance" is to be understood just as "appropriate" reliance. Judgments about appropriate and inappropriate reliance hinge, in turn, on moral judgments about rights and duties, obligations and responsibilities. Mothers *ought* be able to rely on a child's father to contribute to the child's support, in the same way we ought be able to rely on our bank to honor checks properly drawn against our accounts. That, rather than any funny definitional trick (stretching of the concept of "self" to embrace as part of the self all of one's extended family, and perhaps all one's friends to boot), is all that cultural conservatives mean when they say that

---

[93] Bane and Ellwood 1994, 150–6. As they say, it is unreasonable to expect one person to do the job of two: although perhaps inevitable in terms of care giving, in the case of abandoned mothers, at least we might hope to arrange social policy in such a way that they do not have to do double-duty financially as well. The eventual impact of such reforms is largely speculative, but there is some evidence to suggest that they might substantially reduce the numbers of AFDC claimants (Moffitt 1992, 51–5).

relying on the father's child support payments is consistent with values of "self-reliance."

2.2.5 The Costs of Moralized Definitions

There is no obvious and straightforward sense in which someone who is relying on persons other than oneself for needed assistance is being "*self*-reliant," taking full *personal* responsibility (taking full responsibility on one's *own* shoulders) for one's own welfare. Yet in some instances – such as instances of reliance on families or friends, commercial banks, or labor markets – that is said to be consistent with those values. In others, particularly in instances of reliance on state welfare, it is said not to be. On the face of it, at least, advocates of "personal responsibility" and "self-reliance" are being inconsistent, disingenuous, or worse in their arguments here.

My aim is not merely to trip up advocates of personal responsibility in embarrassing inconsistencies. Sloppy reasoning and suspect motives are the least of the problems plaguing their arguments. The larger problem arises from the way in which these inconsistencies are resolved – the way in which advocates of "self-reliance" and "personal responsibility for welfare" import *moral* premises to differentiate between dependencies that are and are not said to offend against those values.

Moralizing the definitions of these key terms prevents them from doing the work that those deploying them want them to do in their arguments. These advocates want to argue against certain social policies, on the grounds that they are bad "because" they promote welfare dependency and undermine self-reliance; they want to argue for other policies, on the grounds that they are good "because" they promote self-reliance and personal responsibility for welfare. That is to say, advocates of those arguments want the notions of self-reliance, dependency, and personal responsibility to do some *independent work* in their arguments. They want those notions to give us some *independent reasons* for doing one thing rather than another.

But what these advocates have done, in implicitly moralizing their definitions of those notions, is to prevent those notions from doing any independent work or providing any independent reasons. The way the moralized definitions function, schematically, is to say: "ϕ is to be considered an instance of dependency because it is morally bad." But if that moral judgment is built into the very definition of dependency in that way, then it is simply circular to go on to say: "ϕ is morally bad, because it is an instance of dependency." The argument is then an empty tautology. Similarly, if by definition "ϕ is to be considered an instance of self-reliance/personal responsibility because it is morally good," then it is simply tautological to say "ϕ is morally good, because it is an instance of self-reliance/personal responsibility."

Of course, there is nothing wrong or illogical in simultaneously asserting both halves of a tautology. Quite the contrary, classical logic commits you to doing precisely that. The point is just that it is not very informative to offer either half of a tautology as an answer to questions about the truth of the other. Each half of a tautology just restates the other, adding nothing in the process. It does not provide any independent reasons for the proposition in question. Asserting a tautology is just to repeat oneself, to stutter.

Now, of course, that is not what opponents of welfare dependency think they are doing when criticizing some welfare programs for engendering dependency or praising others for promoting self-reliance and personal responsibility. But that, I submit, is simply an error. They have simply failed to realize just how moralized their definitions of those key concepts are, and just how completely that moralization of their key concepts undercuts the power of those notions to provide any independent leverage on questions at hand.[94]

What opponents of welfare dependency need is some *further* analysis underwriting the moral judgments built into their moralized definitions of dependency, self-reliance, and personal

---

[94] The former is demonstrated in section 2.2.4, the latter earlier in the present section. Whether or not anyone explicitly commits the tautology here in view, everyone offering a moralized definition of "dependency" (as per section 2.4.4) is guilty of committing it implicitly.

responsibility. They need some analysis of why dependency on the market or on the family is morally acceptable, in a way that dependency on the state is not. Furthermore, that analysis needs to explain why depending on the state for some things (like security against assault or invasion) is permissible, whereas depending on the state for other things (like security against starvation) is not.[95]

It is no part of my brief here to argue that no such analysis can ever be found. But clearly some such analysis is needed. Intellectually, it will simply not suffice (even if rhetorically it might) merely to tar programs with the brush of "encouraging dependency," when dependency itself has been defined in such a highly moralized way. Neither will it suffice to praise other programs for "encouraging self-reliance and personal responsibility," when those terms have been defined in such highly moralized ways. To date, the further analysis that is needed at this point has not yet been provided. So far, this definitional pea-and-shell game of "hide the value premise" has, by and large, been the dominant feature of such arguments.

2.2.6 Family Values: An Aside

The reason the foregoing trick works, rhetorically, is that the dominant ideology of "famialism" leads us to supply, implicitly, the missing premise for ourselves. Both logically and rhetorically, what underlies more innocuous-sounding values like "self-reliance" and "personal responsibility" is what cultural conservatives have long been championing under the more ominous banner of "family values."[96]

Now, there is much that is agreeable – along with much that is not – about the traditional ideal encapsulated in the notion of

---

[95] Particularly when conditions giving rise to famines are themselves in part socially created, as often they are (Sen 1981; Dasgupta 1993).

[96] This link is drawn unashamedly in, e.g., the House Republicans' *Contract with America* (1994) and the American Enterprise Institute's *A community of self-reliance*, subtitled *The new consensus on family and welfare* (Novak et al. 1987).

the bourgeois family.[97] Happily, however, there is no need for us here to adjudicate just how "ideal" that ideal actually is, from a moral point of view. The policy question before us here, as in analyzing social welfare policy more generally, is simply what to do when families fail to live up to that traditional ideal stipulated by cultural conservatives.

Simply reasserting the ideal – simply saying it would have been better if these particular families had not gone wrong in these various ways – is of no practical consequence in such circumstances. The plain fact of the matter is that they have. The only real question before us is what we ought do about that fact.[98]

One option, much favored by self-styled defenders of "family values" as well as by advocates of "self-reliance" and "personal responsibility," is simply to ignore that fact. Often they seem to be saying we should just proceed as if that family breakdown had never occurred. Sometimes this stance would have us act as if we were simply *assuming* well-to-do parents will continue to support children whom they have disowned, well-to-do husbands and fathers will continue to support families they have abandoned, well-to-do husbands will share equitably with unemployed wives, and so on.[99] Other times, this stance would have us enact policies attempting to *make* them do so.

Once family values have broken down within any given family, however, there can hardly be any thought that enforcing (much less simply assuming) the effective discharge of ordinary family

---

[97] For a partisan defense nonetheless academic in presentation, see Berger and Berger 1983. For problems with it, from a moral point of view, see, e.g., Young 1995.

[98] Among other things, of course, to prevent any more from breaking down – perhaps even to the extent of writing off those who have broken down as a lesson that might help save those who have not yet but otherwise might. What policies are actually most effective in preventing family breakdown must necessarily be an open question of empirical sociology; but for my part I doubt, for reasons to be given, that punitive welfare policies will drive families in crisis away from breakdown rather than further into it.

[99] While such assumptions are rarely advocated as such, they are often enough employed – as, for example, when social assistance is means-tested on the basis of household income, on the (unexamined, and often unwarranted) assumption that each member of the household has equitable access to all the resources of the household as a whole.

responsibilities will actually restore ordinary family life, ordinary family affection, or ordinary family values to that wrecked family. In the words of Gilbert Steiner, "A broken family supported by a reluctant father is no stronger than a broken family supported by public assistance."[100] We can compel the outward performances, but we cannot compel the inner attitudes that are classically supposed to accompany them. It is those, in the end, to which all appeals to family values must ultimately appeal.[101]

Not only do the social welfare policies being urged in the name of "self-reliance" and "personal responsibility" not promote family values: they might even undermine them. One risk is this. If what really matters is the attitude and the motive, rather than the outward performance, then legally compelling the outward performance runs the risk of clouding motives and obscuring the real attitude underlying that performance. It is less a matter of "bad motives driving out good" than one of "multiple motives" doing so.[102]

Another danger, more worrying to my mind, is this. Family relationships are always enormously complex and invariably represent a delicately negotiated order. Compelling families to support "their own," in the name of "family values," will actually undermine those delicate balances. This has long been evident in relation to old-age pensioners. The earliest systematic surveys,

[100] Steiner 1981, 128. Even Reverend Malthus doubts the efficacy of the "exercise of civil power, however rigorous" in such affairs (1803/1992, bk. 4, chap. 8, p. 265).

[101] If they are going to have any *moral* appeal, anyway. It may well be that what really drives advocates of family values is a desire to reestablish patriarchical domination; and for that a social order built on notions of power and notions of duty enforced by it may quite suffice. There may be a few who still would try to sell that vision of social order as morally worthy or religiously mandated. Most advocating family values would surely eschew any such defense of them, however.

[102] I do not myself set great store by this argument: the existence of laws against starving our children does not undermine the social meaning of sharing a warm family meal. And I would be positively enthusiastic for "compelling performances, from whatever motives" if I thought that compulsion would secure more "good performances" than relying on "good motives" alone. Alas, in situations such as this I do not. For discussion of other cognate examples, see Goodin 1982, chap. 6, and, of converse cases, Goodin 1995, chap. 3.

conducted in Britain before the 1911 introduction of old-age pensions, consistently showed that even then parents did not want to live with their children or depend on them for support if they could possibly avoid it; throughout the century, those attitudes have simply hardened.[103] And if this is mainly a matter of pride, it is not altogether false pride.[104] Similarly, unemployed youth and the disabled are keen on "independent living" and autonomous households.[105] Insisting in the name of "family values" that they undo the achievements of adolescence by moving back under the parental roof and parental authority seems more a recipe for inducing family pathologies than for "strengthening families."

Whether or not family values are truly valuable, they cannot be wheeled in to provide the argument so sorely needed to bolster the peculiar construction of values of "self-reliance" and "personal responsibility" that is built into the moralized definitions of those terms that are adopted by their champions. Family values, if valuable, might justify a *positive* family policy promoting the traditional family. Those values, however valuable, lend no support whatever to punitive welfare policies that would impose those values on those whose family affairs have moved in other directions. Nor are those punitive policies the most plausible means of rebuilding family ties among families in the process of breaking down.

Where affection is waning or missing, it cannot simply be legally mandated or administratively presupposed. Some other strategy altogether is then required in order to cope with problems that, in happier circumstances, may well have been best handled by "families taking care of their own."[106]

---

[103] As Charles Booth found: "parents are unwilling to ask help from children and expect little"; they "prefer a pittance from the parish [in Poor Law relief], regarded as their due, to compulsory maintenance by their children" (Booth 1894, 169, 295). For results of more recent surveys, see Schorr 1980, chap. 2.

[104] Accepting the independence of one's growing children is only natural. Accepting one's own dependence on one's grown children, in contrast, seems to be more of an inversion of the natural order (Townsend 1957, 56; Schorr 1980, chap. 2; Shanas and Streib 1965).

[105] Morris 1993.

[106] An analogous point is developed in Waldron 1993b.

2.3   Collective Responsibility

Having completed my negative case against the current campaigns for "personal responsibility for welfare," I now turn to my more positive arguments for the alternative, "collective responsibility for welfare." In defining my own key terms, first I focus on the notion of "collective," carefully differentiating the sense of collectivism I shall be defending from other senses from which I want to distance myself. Next I discuss two notions of "responsibility," identifying clearly the one I think ought guide public policy and again differentiating it sharply from the one that is so often (mis)used in arguments for personal responsibility for welfare.

2.3.1   Alternative Kinds of Collectivism

A great many collectivist claims about human welfare seem to me to be simply untenable. Let me disassociate myself from the start from those more mystical, or more brutal, forms of collectivism.

Society, in my view, is made up of individual human beings and, significantly, interactions and interrelationships among them. "Welfare" is an attribute enjoyed by those natural individuals and, ultimately, by them alone. The welfare of society as a whole is nothing more than the aggregate of the well-being enjoyed by those individuals. They may, and typically do, derive much of their well-being from interactions with other individuals. (Adam Smith admits as much.) But in the final analysis well-being or welfare is just the well-being or welfare of those individuals, taken together. There is no entity called "society" that stands above those individuals and enjoys any welfare of its own. That is the first collectivist claim – call it "philosophical collectivism," for short – from which I would disassociate myself.

A second collectivist claim from which I would also disassociate myself – "economic collectivism" – is the sort that relates to central planning and command economies. This version asserts that collective social welfare can best be promoted through centrally orchestrated collective action. There is certainly some role for central authorities in facilitating and policing mutually beneficial interactions between private individuals. (Again, even Adam Smith concedes an important role for the state in building roads and enforcing contracts.) How big a role to assign collective authorities, relative to private individuals and free markets, in promoting social welfare is genuinely contested. But the contest in question is an empirical economic one. Virtually no one today believes that, as a matter of a priori social or economic truth, collective central planning and that alone can or will maximize social welfare.

There are other forms of collectivism to be similarly bracketed out of any serious discussion. Among them are "political collectivism," the tyranny of strong and especially central state authority over the rights and liberties of individuals and smaller-scale social units, and "social collectivism," the sociological analogue of that same phenomenon, putting central cultural arbiters of some sort or another in the place of central state authority. Again, there is something to be said for both political authority and cultural intermediation. But, again, giving central authorities absolute power in either dimension is something that virtually no one, nowadays, would care to defend. Certainly I would not.

Although I distance myself from all those forms of collectivism, there is one final form of collectivism I would want to defend – what I call "moral collectivism." By that I mean the collectivization of responsibility, morally, for one another's well-being. What exactly that means will be clarified over the coming pages. Still, I should say several things by way of clarification from the outset.

First, "collectivization of responsibility" here means, primarily, the *sharing* of responsibility. A collective responsibility in this sense is one that is distributed to each and every member of the group of individuals sharing it: the same responsibility falls to each and every one of them.

Since everybody's job is nobody's job, those individuals may well find that the best way for them actually to discharge that shared responsibility is to assign it to some one individual among their number. Or they may find that the best way for them to discharge it is to create some artificial person (a corporation, or a charitable trust, or a state), and assign their shared responsibility to that new collective entity.

The collectivization of moral responsibility might in this way lead to social or economic or political collectivization, as a second-order consequence of trying to meet our shared moral responsibility. But such further forms of collectivism are, on this account, justifiable merely as means to this primary moral end – and they are justifiable only insofar as they actually succeed in serving that end. In the final analysis, then, the collectivization here in view is firmly moral in character. Any implications that that might hold for collectivization of other sorts are purely instrumental in character.

Alternatively, the collectivization of moral responsibility I have in view might actually lead to individualization of moral responsibility, at least in the first instance. If (as is often claimed) each of us really is the best judge of our own interests and the best agent for promoting them, then the best way to meet our shared responsibilities for promoting one another's well-being collectively might be to assign each of us individually responsibility for his or her own welfare, at least in the first instance. Again, however, that individualization of responsibility would be purely instrumental, and purely provisional. We would be assigning responsibility to individuals themselves, not because doing so is good in itself, but merely as a means to discharging our shared collective responsibilities. And we would be assigning them that responsibility only provisionally, standing ready in the final analysis to step in with some other collective remedy whenever individuals themselves fail to discharge those responsibilities effectively for themselves. We must be ready to do so, in the final analysis, because the responsibilities themselves are, in the final analysis, shared collective responsibilities.

Second, the responsibility here in view is for *one another's* well-being. That is to say, responsibilities are shared, primarily (albeit only in the first instance), among groups of individuals who are already interacting with one another in some way or another.

There are several reasons for circumscribing shared responsibilities in this way, at least in the first instance. Sociologically and psychologically, norms of reciprocity ensure that members of an already interacting group will naturally feel a stronger sense of responsibility toward one another.[107] Purely pragmatically, the fact of already existing interactions makes it easier to specify the set of people among whom responsibility is to be shared.

Specifying what counts as "interaction" for these purposes is tricky, of course.[108] But it is unnecessary to get ourselves tied in knots over those issues, because the sheer fact of "interactions" as such ought not be privileged all that strongly from a moral point of view, anyway. Phenomenologically, the fact of interaction is undeniably helpful in making people *feel* the force of their moral responsibilities. Philosophically, however, the fact of interaction is of only passing and provisional importance, a convenience rather than a conclusive factor, in fixing ultimate moral responsibilities.

While we may well assign initial responsibility to those who are already interacting with one another, ultimate responsibility clearly ought not be limited to them and them alone. Ultimately, moral responsibilities are by their nature shared by all those who themselves count as moral agents. We divide up the social world in certain ways, assigning particular people special responsibility for particular others: the special responsibilities of family members to take care of one another are one example of that; the special responsibilities of fellow citizens toward one another are

---

[107] Barry 1989b.

[108] Possibilities range all the way from intimate social intercourse in a shared social space, through relatively impersonal exchanges of physical commodities, all the way to shared membership in largely anonymous and hence "imaginary" communities of class, race, or nation.

another; and the special responsibilities people have toward those with whom they are already interacting are yet another.[109] But inevitably there will be some people who are abused or are left out altogether in those interactions. If those with primary responsibility default, or if no one has been assigned primary responsibility in the first place, then the only way to meet our ultimately shared responsibilities toward these people is for someone else to be assigned responsibilities of a secondary or backup sort for discharging them.[110]

Third, the collectivization I here have in view is merely for one another's *well-being* or welfare. I shall further narrow my focus, for the narrow purposes of this book, to people's material well-being. There are, of course, other aspects of one's well-being for which we might want to ascribe responsibility. We might think, here, of people's spiritual well-being. But allocating responsibility for the salvation of one's soul is, again, beyond the remit of my discussion here.

2.3.2 Two Senses of Responsibility

Before launching into my more specific arguments about the collectivization of moral responsibility and how that plays itself out in the social welfare setting, I must say something more about the notion of moral responsibility as such.

Many distinctions might be drawn, and correspondingly many kinds of responsibility might be distinguished. (In earlier portions of this book, Schmidtz obviously draws the distinctions differently than I do.)[111] Without belaboring how my distinctions fit with others', let me simply set out what my distinctions are.

---

[109] Goodin 1985b; 1995, chap. 16; Goodin and Pettit 1986.

[110] Goodin 1995, chap. 5; see also Goodin 1985b, chap. 5.

[111] Both the models I shall introduce below are "dynamic," at least in the colloquial sense that both the backward-looking and forward-looking models involve at least two points in time (the former sometime past and now; the former now and sometime later). In section 1.1.1, Schmidtz seems to build deterrent intentions into the very definition of "dynamic"; and it is by virtue of that idiosyncratic feature of his terminology that only blame responsibility comes out as dynamic and task responsibility would come out as "static."

I want to distinguish basically two kinds of responsibility. One is the forward-looking, task-oriented sort of responsibility I shall be championing. The other is the backward-looking, blame-allocating sort of responsibility, which I think should be shunned for policy purposes but which nonetheless seems to dominate discussions of social welfare.

The dominant sense of responsibility in discussions of social welfare policy is that essentially backward-looking notion, which aims primarily at allocating praise and blame. Of course, we might have some larger forward-looking purpose in invoking backward-looking notions of responsibility in this way. We may well want to assign people credit or blame for consequences of their past actions and choices, with a view to shaping their future actions and choices. Knowing you will be held to account in this way for what you have done, in the past, may well make you do better, in future.

Such incentive effects associated with backward-looking notions of responsibility sometimes figure largely in arguments for holding people personally responsible for actions and choices impacting on their own welfare, in ways I shall discuss in due course. The point to notice for now is simply that, at root, such invocations of responsibility are essentially backward looking. Fundamentally, they praise or blame people for what they have done in the past – even if the aim in doing so is to shape future behavior.

My preferred kind of responsibility, in contrast, is in itself essentially forward looking. The aim here is, fundamentally, to tell us what we should do in the future. This forward-looking notion is best conceptualized as a model of "task responsibility." It works by specifying whose job it is to see to it that certain tasks are performed and that certain things are accomplished.

There will, of course, inevitably be a certain retrospective accounting involved in deciding whether this task responsibility has been discharged well or badly. Thus there is a "shadow of the past" associated even with the essentially forward-looking notion of task responsibility – just as there is, thanks to incentive effects, a "shadow of the future" associated with the essentially backward-looking notion of blame responsibility. Both kinds of shadow clearly matter. Each has important consequences for the practical operation of each kind of responsibility. Nonetheless, each clearly is a shadow, a further consequence rather than the principal substance of each respective form of responsibility.

Philosophers often stand accused of pointless distinction mongering, making fine distinctions apparently just for the sake of it, never showing what, if any, material difference the distinctions might make. Against that standing charge, I offer this as an example of a distinction with a real difference. All too often, public policy conflates the two sorts of responsibility I have been distinguishing, with consequences that are catastrophically nonsensical and utterly indefensible.

Task responsibility is often thought to flow, automatically (indeed, analytically), from blame responsibility. To determine whose responsibility it should be to correct some unfortunate state of affairs, we should on such logic simply determine who was responsible for having caused that state of affairs in the first place. Those who are responsible for causing an unfortunate situation are responsible for fixing it. "Responsibility is responsibility," or so the thought goes. Nothing, it seems, could be simpler, more analytically straightforward.[112]

Applied to the realm of social welfare policy, such logic can, however, have some very dire consequences. Suppose people are poor, in part, through some fault of their own. They had babies they could not afford, they dropped out of school, they got in trouble with the law, or they simply failed to look for work when there was work on offer. In each of those cases they would then be partly responsible, in the backward-looking, causal sense, for their own plight. And on the logic here in view, those who are responsible should be held responsible. Insofar as they got themselves into this situation, it should be their responsibility to get themselves out of it.

---

[112] Indeed, a whole body of the law – the law of torts – is for better or worse built on precisely this foundation.

But that amounts to "policy by pun." The two senses of responsibility are importantly different, in ways that that eliding of them perversely collapses. History is not always easily reversible. People cannot always get themselves out of the jam as easily as they got themselves into it. Sometimes no one can. But sometimes others are better situated to get them out of a jam that they and they alone got themselves into. In such circumstances, who "caused" the problem (whom to assign backward-looking "blame responsibility" for it) is one thing. Who can best remedy it (whom to assign forward-looking "task responsibility" for it) is another thing altogether.[113]

I shall be elaborating this argument with reference to social welfare claimants throughout the rest of my discussion. That application will obviously be contested and clearly depends on a variety of further empirical facts, which are themselves in dispute. But the validity of my general point about the importance of distinguishing these two senses of responsibility for policy purposes is, I think, beyond dispute.

Just to fix that general point, consider a pair of other examples.[114] The first is a stylized example of the sort beloved among philosophers. Suppose a man has just jumped out of a six-story building. The owner of the ground-floor shop just below happens to be standing where she can see him jump; and she happens to have her finger on the button which, virtually instantaneously, drops her awning to protect against the afternoon sun.

---

[113] Even in tort law, liabilities are sometimes apportioned among joint tortfeasors by assigning the greater share of the costs to those with "deep pockets" and who can therefore best afford to pay – which represents an element of my "task responsibility" model, even in the bastion of "blame responsibility" (Calabresi 1970, chap. 4).

   Sometimes it will of course be the case – as oftentimes, presumably, it will be with rich corporations, for example – that the same people who caused the problem will also be the best placed to alleviate it, in which case I am of course perfectly happy for them to be assigned *both* blame responsibility *and* task responsibility.

[114] For fuller statements of the moral theory that these examples evoke, see Goodin 1985b linking responsibilities to dependencies and Kittay 1997 linking dependencies to justice.

Now, the jumper has only himself to blame for jumping and, hence, for anything that happens to him in consequence of his jump. In terms of blame responsibility, the responsibility is all his. But once he is falling through the air, there is nothing further he can do to save himself from death or serious injury. The shopkeeper, in contrast, has no blame responsibility: she has done nothing to cause the jump. Nor, let us suppose, does she have any antecedent moral relationship with the man: she is neither family nor friend nor lover; she has never promised to save him or people in general if they jumped. Still, the shopkeeper and she alone can do something to help mitigate the consequences of his fall; and because of that fact, the task responsibility falls to her to put out her awning to help break his fall. In the final reckoning of accounts, once the jumper has been released from hospital, we may well think that blame responsibility ought determine allocation of costs (so the jumper ought buy the shopkeeper a new awning to replace the one wrecked saving him). But in terms of task responsibility, at the time the jumper is in midair, there can be no question of that credibly being ascribed to the jumper (despite his clear blame responsibility) or of its being credibly denied the shopkeeper (despite the clear absence of any blame responsibility on her part).

Or, for another more policy-relevant example, consider the question of what we should do about the treatment of smoking-related cancers. Smokers, let us assume, have only themselves to blame for their cancers. They could have prevented the disease by never smoking, in the first place. But once they have contracted the disease there is, let us suppose, nothing further that they could do to cure themselves of it. (Even surgeons with cancer cannot operate on themselves.) Task responsibility, once again, necessarily falls upon others to cure cancers for which they are in no way to blame.[115] And, once again, backward-looking

---

[115] The task of wielding the knife, at least: we can, of course, move later to recover the costs of the surgery from rich and reckless smokers, just as the Swiss mountain rescue service sends reckless trekkers bills for the costs of their rescues.

considerations of blame responsibility are a woefully inadequate guide to forward-looking questions of the proper allocation of the tasks at hand.[116]

---

[116] Some, of course, argue against treating (anyway, as a matter of high priority in a time of competing claims) those who have through their own irresponsible behavior brought illness on themselves. The more civilized version of this argument works through a sort of triage logic, noting that smokers have worse prognoses (in part because of the risk that, being addicted, they will continue or resume smoking); the more brutal versions of the argument talk more bluntly in terms of letting smokers bear the natural consequences of their actions. For discussion of these and related issues, see Goodin 1989, 15–30; cf. Littlechild and Wiseman 1984 and Schelling 1986.

2.4 The Classic Case for Collectivization Restated

As I have said, my argument here aims first and foremost at defending "moral collectivism" and, most especially, the collectivization of ultimate responsibility for many aspects of people's material well-being. Any connection between that form of "moral collectivism" and "political collectivism" – policies pursued through some central state apparatus – is, as I have said earlier, a purely contingent one. Having said all that, I want now to show that that contingent connection is nonetheless a strong one.

There are good reasons, of a once familiar and still fairly standard sort, for pursuing certain sorts of goals through some sort of coordinated, collective apparatus like the state. My brief rehearsal of the early history of expanding state responsibility for social welfare is meant merely to remind us of those good reasons and to show that those reasons remain strong ones to this day.

Responsibilities get collectivized in the first instance and politicized in the second simply because that is the only realistic way (or, anyway, much the most effective way) of discharging them. If we take the responsibilities seriously in the first instance – in the first instance, even just as individual personal responsibilities – reflections on those contingent facts about the world as we know it should lead us to accept them ultimately as collective responsibilities to be collectively discharged through our political agencies.

2.4.1   Fault and the Folly of Disentangling Causes

In the bad old days of the New Poor Law – of workhouses and poorhouses – character tests served to differentiate the "deserving" from the "undeserving" poor. The former were those who came to their plight through no fault of their own, the latter those who had only themselves to blame.[117] The most crucial step away from a Poor Law approach to the relief of poverty and social distress came with the abandonment, for all practical purposes, of fault-based distinctions between the deserving and the undeserving.[118]

Abandonment of inquiries into fault came first, and most significantly, in connection with "workers compensation" policies around the beginning of the twentieth century. Workers injured on the job had long been entitled, under tort law, to sue their employer or their co-workers for injuries suffered at their hands. But central to tort actions is the apportioning of fault and hence blame. Insofar as the injured worker was partly to blame, any tort award would be reduced proportionately. And insofar as the injury occurred through some complicated set of causal interactions, blame would be somehow apportioned among all those whose negligence contributed to the outcome.

Those features of the law had several consequences for tort remedies for industrial accidents and injuries. One was to make injured workers usually bear at least part of the costs of their own injuries at precisely a time when, being incapacitated, their ordinary income flows were interrupted and they were least able to bear the burden. Another was to make compensation claims almost always complicated and expensive to litigate, sometimes stymieing them altogether (particularly where causal contributions were particularly complex or inextricably intertwined). For all too many injured workers, seeking compensation for industrial

---

[117] Accordingly, the 1834 Poor Law provided that "Relief shall be given to any adult Person who shall from Old Age or Infirmity of Body be wholly unable to work, without requiring that such Persons shall reside in any Workhouse" (4 & 5 Wm 4, C 76, § 27).

[118] Finger-wagging moralism may remain, but it no longer carried any material consequences.

injuries quite simply cost more than it was (or was likely to be) worth.

The problem was rightly seen as lying in the inquiry into fault, which is at the core of any assessment of tort liability. The obvious solution was a system of "no-fault" compensation for industrial injuries. Workers compensation was therefore instituted on an insurance-based footing. All employers were obliged to carry insurance against the costs of industrial injuries. Any injured employees could lodge a claim against their employer's insurance simply by establishing the fact of a work-related injury, without any inquiry into fault or blame.[119]

Under such arrangements, of course, careless workers get more compensation than they might be said to "deserve" in fault-based terms. But so too, under the old tort system, victims of work-related injuries always received less compensation than they really deserved, net of the costs of litigation (and given those costs, a great many other deserving victims never lodged any claims at all). So, on balance, the no-fault scheme was hailed as a great success, and the workers compensation model was extended to many other areas ranging from no-fault automobile insurance to no-fault divorce.[120] There, too, the benefits from reduced costs of litigation were generally seen as more than counterbalancing any undue reward to those who were really at fault for the car crash or marital breakdown.[121]

This brief history of workers compensation and cognate no-fault insurance schemes holds clear lessons for the larger issues

---

[119] The best short account of these developments is found in Atiyah (1980, chaps. 14, 15). (Later editions truncate philosophical discussions in favor of fuller discussions of recent legal developments.) On connections to social insurance schemes more broadly, see de Swaan 1988, 177–217; on the fault system more generally, see Calabresi 1970.

[120] Though the way the rule has been implemented is far from satisfactory, particularly regarding the economic consequences for women upon divorce (Weitzman 1985; Folbre 1994).

[121] Abandoning inquiries into fault does not bar inquiries into issues of sheer fraud, of course. It is perfectly consistent with no-fault schemes to prosecute those who fake injuries and so on.

of "personal responsibility." Where causes are complex and inter-twined, it typically costs more than it is worth to try disentangling them so as to allocate "personal responsibility" among particu-lar individuals (not to mention other more impersonal causal factors).[122] In such circumstances we have, for all sorts of pur-poses, abandoned distinctions based upon ascriptions of personal responsibility, liability, and blame. We have, for all sorts of good reasons, shifted instead to no-fault schemes of compensation. Re-calling those reasons ought make us wary of reverting to models of "personal responsibility" in other social welfare contexts where causal factors are similarly complex and intertwined.

2.4.2   The Collectivization of Risks

The workers compensation model holds a second lesson for us, as well. In moving away from fault-based remedies for industrial accidents and injuries, we have moved toward insurance-based schemes. Those have many charms. One, related to my previous discussion, is that they avoid inquiry into fault or blame.[123] So long as the policy is in force (premiums have been duly paid, and so on), the underwriters must pay out whenever the insured-against contingency has arisen. It is simply irrelevant, for the practical purposes of determining who should pay what, *how*

---

[122]   Indeed, as I shall go on to argue in section 2.4.3, it often is logically incoherent even to try. Often there are many equally good ways to disaggregate causal responsibility, the choice among them being dictated not by the structure of causation but by the more forward-looking purposes we have in trying to allocate responsibility. Often it makes more sense to allocate a larger share of the responsibility to those who can best afford to pay (the "deep pockets" principle, already discussed) or, as I have urged, to those who are best able to do something to remedy the problem now or to prevent recurrence of similar ones in the future.

[123]   For any practical purposes, anyway: moral recrimination will inevitably re-main, although one cannot help thinking that the sooner people who have been injured in an industrial accident or car crash or bruising divorce get past the stage of recriminations and on with the task of reconstructing their lives, the better off they will be.

the insured-against contingency has come about or whose "fault"
it was.[124]

Another charm, particularly relevant in the present context,
is that insurance schemes constitute collective "risk-pooling"
strategies.[125] All those party to an insurance scheme pool their
risks with everyone else party to that scheme. Some "win" the
gambles of life, and the insured-against contingencies do not happen to them. Others, facing the same ex ante risks, "lose." If we
assume the premiums charged corresponded to the real risks that
each person was running, the premiums from the winners in such
a mutual-insurance risk pool should just suffice to pay the claims
of the losers.

The problem with individualized tort-based claims for compensation, recall, lay in the nature of complex and confused causation. It was unclear how to apportion fault, and hence financial
liabilities, among all those sharing responsibility for the accident
(co-workers, supervisors, owners, and so on). A collectivized
insurance-based solution does not try to individualize liabilities
in that way. Instead it imposes a collective obligation to pay on
roughly the same group of people who have among themselves
collectively contributed to causing the accident in the first place.

---

[124] Except in cases – limited enough even in private insurance, and virtually
nonexistent in social insurance schemes – where the policy contains explicit
"exclusions" touching on such issues.

[125] They are also, in consequence, collective "cost-pooling" strategies. One of the
things that rightly frightens people when they are thinking of dependency
in personal, individual terms is the prospect that caring for the dependent
will soak up literally all their resources. In a world devoid of decent public
provision, we worry about that on a personal basis when it comes to caring
for aged parents or handicapped children; we worry about it, in a more
intellectual way, when moral theories like utilitarianism seem to generate
duties that might end up being virtual "blank checks" against our resources.
Looking at it from an individual point of view, such worries are real. But
looking at it from a collective point of view, the burdens are potentially
much more manageable: it is a matter of everyone, collectively, who has
spare resources taking care of everyone, collectively, who is in need. Seen in
that light, the costs of welfare mothers are not exorbitant (as shown by the
statistics given in section 2.1.2).

The great virtue of workers compensation in that connection is that it compulsorily pools risks, for insurance purposes, in a way that roughly corresponds to the pool of causes that have conspired to produce the accident in the first place.[126] The collectivization of the policy response effectively maps (and, indeed, is dictated by) the collectivity of the causes contributing to the problem in view.

The whole point of state provision for "social security" is precisely to collectivize risks in just that way. Historically, that is how such programs have been set up, as "social insurance" of one form or another: as Old Age, Survivors, and Disability Insurance in the United States or National Insurance in Britain; as unemployment insurance; as medical insurance, publicly or privately provided; and so on.[127] Economically, risk pooling is one among the many ways such programs have been justified: collecting "insurance premiums" (typically, in the form of earmarked "social security taxes") from everyone at risk and using the payments from the lucky ones to pay the costs of the unlucky.[128]

The argument so far has merely served to justify the collectivization of risks by means of risk pooling. Nothing said so far

---

[126] That is to say, such schemes go far toward providing the "internalization" Schmidtz calls for in section 1.2.

[127] See de Swaan 1988, 177–217. In the very first years of their operation, of course, old-age pension schemes paid pensioners who retired without making any (or many) contributions; after that initial period as a sheer transfer program, insurance aspects of the scheme then came to the fore.

[128] Or taking from them *when* they are rich and giving to them *when* they are poor. That is to say, "social insurance" is often more a matter of what underwriters technically term "assurance." A "life assurance policy" is insurance-like in the first instance (if you die before your policy is paid up, your survivors will receive its full, paid-up value), but in the long run and for most people it will function simply as a savings scheme (with people withdrawing in the end just what they have paid in, plus interest). That is a good model for the welfare state's role in smoothing people's income over the life course, taxing away some of their high earnings in their middle years and paying them subsidies in low-earning periods of youth and old age. On social insurance, economically understood, see Atkinson 1995c and Barr 1987, 1989.

speaks to the question of whether that risk pooling should be voluntary or compulsory. Compulsory "social insurance" operating through the state is importantly different from privately organized "mutual insurance" schemes. Scornful though they may be of compulsory state schemes, advocates of "self-reliance" and "personal responsibility" often speak powerfully in favor of voluntary private ones.[129]

Such private risk-pooling arrangements for social security have a long history. Precursors range from the guilds of the early Middle Ages through Victorian "friendly societies," which remained major social forces well into the early years of the twentieth century.[130] Such risk-pooling practices remain the standard form of social protection in less developed countries.[131] Even in the most developed countries they persist to this day in the form of private retirement plans, private medical and disability insurance, and so on.

Many on the New Right advocate extending such private provision for welfare in the name of promoting "voluntarism" and "intermediary institutions."[132] They aim to resurrect the friendly society tradition, with "mutual aid" among members of voluntary (often fraternal or religious) organizations literally taking the place of many or most state welfare services.[133] The example of General Pinochet's privatization of Chile's old-age pension system is repeatedly offered as emblematic of their preferred policy reforms – and rightly so, given the mounting evidence on the

---

[129]   As does Schmidtz in section 1.4.1. We may well wonder at the sense in which private insurance – pooling your risks with many others, and counting on assistance from the fund thus created should you need it – might credibly be said to constitute "*self*-reliance." Indeed, calling those plans "private" at all is something of a misnomer, masking as it does the essential mutuality that lies at the core of all such risk-pooling, insurance-based arrangements. But, again, let us simply note the inconsistency and let it pass.

[130]   Berman 1983, 390–2; Thompson 1980, chap. 12, pt. 2, esp. pp. 457–62; de Swaan 1988, chap. 5.

[131]   Ahmad et al. 1991; United Nations 1995, 268.

[132]   Novak et al. 1987, esp. chap. 7; Berger and Neuhaus 1977.

[133]   Cornuelle 1965; Green and Cromwell 1984.

fiscally regressive impact of shifting from tax-funded to private insurance schemes in various sectors.[134]

To justify social welfare provision in its present form, therefore, we must not only defend the collectivization that is entailed by risk pooling in mutual insurance (which can, after all, be done on a purely private, voluntary basis). We must also provide a defense of the further collectivization that comes with compulsory membership and state provision.

As it happens, that defense perfectly parallels the other. Here as before, the compulsory state-based collectivization of the risk pool is justified (indeed, dictated) by nature of the collective risks in view. Here, I shall be talking in terms of risks that are "collective" in a sense that is rather different and even more compelling than before. So far I have been talking about risks that are collective, just in the sense that everyone in the group at risk runs the same ex ante risk (has the same ex ante odds) of bad things happening to them. Next, I shall be talking about risks which are "collective" in the stronger sense that people experience not only the same ex ante odds but also the same ex post outcome.[135]

For an example of a collective risk in that stronger sense, think of a general economic depression. If depression hits and I lose

---

[134] Here, the agenda of right-wing think-tanks like the Cato Institute (1996, 3) is coming to be discussed, albeit cautiously and critically, even by mainstream international institutions (United Nations 1995, 278–9; Diamond and Váldes-Prieto 1994). On the spread of the model across Latin America, see Privatization 1994. Burchardt and Hills (1997, 28, 36, 45) examine three schemes for private insurance to replace public cover in the United Kingdom: unemployment insurance for home mortgagers; insurance against long-trem incapacity for work; and long-term care insurance. They find that across all those programs, the poor would pay more privately than publicly for the same cover; that they would pay dramatically more (16 percent more, for those in the lowest income decile) for long-term care insurance; and that everyone, rich or poor, would pay between 3 and 9 percent more for insurance against long-term incapacity for work.

[135] This "linking of individual risks" (Burchardt and Hills 1997, 6, 57–8) in insurance is akin to what economists call "public goods" (Samuelson 1954).

my job, the depression does not touch me alone. It also touches everyone else in my community, a great many of whom will lose their jobs at the same time and for the same reason as I do.[136] (Of course, not everyone loses his job, so risks are never *completely* collective, in this stronger sense: but they can be more or less collective, in this sense.) Or, for another example, think of an epidemic: when cholera or a killer flu strikes a neighborhood, many (if not quite everyone) of those exposed fall ill around the same time and for the same reason.[137]

The more collective risks are in that sense, the more trouble they pose for the logic of privately organized mutual insurance. The risk-pooling logic underlying mutual insurance is predicated upon the risks in question being statistically independent events – some winning, while others are losing – so that premiums collected from the one will cover payouts to the other. Collective risks of the strong sort I have just been discussing are the very opposite of that. Those risks are interdependent. If the insured-against contingency occurs for one member of the pool, it occurs for virtually every member of the pool. But then, of course, the logic of mutual insurance breaks down. Where everyone wins or everyone loses, rather than some winning while others are losing, premiums from the winners will not cover the payouts to the losers.[138] If the losing card comes

---

[136] The United Nations (1995, 280) points out that "unemployment is not an insurable risk" in private markets for precisely that reason.

[137] This "homogeneity of membership and consequent accumulation of risks" historically had precisely the predicted effect, bankrupting many friendly societies' mutual insurance schemes for sickness benefits or unemployment insurance (de Swaan 1988, 146).

[138] It is acknowledged even by advocates of privatizing unemployment insurance that, in the case of the catastrophe of another Great Depression, the only solution within a mutual insurance scheme would be "retrospective rating," reducing benefits paid to the unemployed (and/or increasing insurance premiums to the still working) to balance the books. The only alternative to that is to rely on savings, either within the insurance fund or among the individuals insured (Rappaport 1992, 101–2).

up, it comes up for everyone and the mutual insurance fund is bankrupted.[139]

In this connection, the great virtue of *social* insurance – insurance underwritten by the state – is that it does not necessarily depend on the premiums it has collected to pay off claims against the scheme. If social insurance premiums and trust funds fed by them do not suffice to meet claims in any given year, the state always has recourse to "general fund revenue" generated by general taxes to pay them. The state and the state alone has the power to levy and to collect coercively such taxes; it and it alone has access to the general tax revenues thus collected.[140] That is the sense in which we need a coercively collectivized solution – a solution underwritten by a state with coercive taxing powers – to the problems posed by collective risks of the stronger sort. The weaker collectivization represented by mere risk pooling of a private "mutual insurance" sort will simply not suffice.

This is only to say that a state system has a mechanism of protecting against collective risks of this stronger sort, which private mutual insurance systems lack. Whether the state finds the will actually to employ that mechanism – levying taxes sufficient to meet the shortfalls in social insurance trust funds – is another matter altogether. But it is important to recognize that that is just a matter of political will. We tend to talk loosely of the looming "bankruptcy" of Medicare and Social Security in the United

---

[139] Unless the fund has managed to collect premiums over the course of previous "all-win" years sufficient to tide it over these "all-lose" years. But if it has, that will have been purely fortuitous. It would be akin to someone declining to take out medical insurance, putting what would have been paid in premiums instead into a bank account, hoping that by the time serious illness hits the balance in that account has grown large enough to pay the bills. It may, if the illness is not too costly and comes sufficiently late; but there is obviously no guarantee that the converse will not be the case.

[140] Private insurance markets have to rely on "reinsurers" at this point. While initially these function as "metainsurance," pooling risks of other risk pools, such reinsurance markets must ultimately rest on something other than the logic of insurance if there is any real risk of massive and interdependent risks. That is where the deep pockets of Lloyds' "names" come in, staking their personal fortunes in the company to underwrite the risks they reinsure. The precariousness of the scheme is well represented by the recent disasters that have befallen many Lloyds syndicates and the near collapse of Lloyds as a whole.

States. All that means, however, is that the funds will be exhausted *unless* we change the laws that set them up (increasing individual contributions, delaying the age at which one can start drawing Social Security, or whatever). And, of course, any law enacted can be, and in such circumstances should be, simply altered by subsequent enactments.[141]

Politicians may be reluctant to do so for all sorts of reasons, some good, some bad. They may perfectly properly prefer to treat legislatively mandated expenditures as if they are literally "uncontrollable," and legislatively established trust funds as inviolate, in order to take certain issues "out of politics."[142] At the end of the day, however, those are just self-denying ordinances adopted by legislators themselves. If the only way to safeguard the very existence of a trust fund is to restructure it, then it is entirely within the power of legislators to do so. If the fund "goes bankrupt" – and many have over the years[143] – that is not through some inexorable workings of external forces beyond politicians' powers to control. It is merely because politicians have chosen to let it. Unlike private mutual insurance schemes, the agents of the state have within their power an instrument – coercive taxation – that can always be used to prevent the collapse of any social insurance scheme, if only they have the political will to use it.

Among the many other features of compulsory state insurance which arouse controversy, another worth mentioning briefly concerns risk rating. In an ideal world of perfect competition, private insurance underwriters would charge people an "actuarially fair" premium strictly proportional to the risks they are running. Social insurance organized through the coercive agency of the state not only need not (being immune to competitive pressures that force down private insurance rates) but also will not, since after all social insurance serves a social (which is to say, redistributive) function as well as a strictly insurance one. The premiums it charges thus typically diverge from standards of "actuarial fairness": the rich are typically charged more and paid less (and the

---

[141]   Dauster 1996.
[142]   Derthick 1975; Patashnik 1995.
[143]   Rose and Peters 1979.

poor conversely) by compulsory public schemes than they would have been in perfectly competitive private markets.[144]

Before we get too exercised by such actuarial unfairness, though, we should pause to reflect on the fantasy of a "perfectly competitive market" in these realms. Not only is perfect competition probably an impossible ideal, here as elsewhere. More to the point, no one would really *want* a perfectly competitive market here. Competitive pressures work their efficiency-producing magic, remember, by noncompetitive traders being driven out of the market; and no one would willingly run the risk of his or her retirement plan or life insurer going bankrupt, any more than anyone would happily run the risk of themselves becoming uninsurable. Both of those are risks that, by their nature, private insurance markets cannot insure against.[145] Both are things that social insurance, underwritten by the state, can and does insure us against.[146]

It is an open question – and, given familiar problems in demand revelation for public goods, a fundamentally unanswerable one – how much state-provided insurance against those catastrophic outcomes is "really worth" to any of us. But just note how relatively low the savings are which "good risks" could have made by opting out of such schemes, taking out actuarially fair private insurance instead. The value to all of us (and, indeed, to each of them) of the "insurance against becoming uninsured

---

[144] The extreme case perhaps is Australian legislation governing private medical insurance, which explicitly prohibits risk rating and dictates uniform premiums for all regardless of the likelihood of their claiming. The young thus cross-subsidize the old, the healthy cross-subsidize the unhealthy, small families cross-subsidize large ones (Australia, Senate Select Committee on Health Legislation and Health Insurance 1990, 6–7).

[145] The inability of private reinsurers to insure against bankruptcies in retirement plans or private insurance funds has again to do with the notion of "collective risks in the stronger sense," wherein lots of underwriters fail all at the same time in consequence of the same larger social and economic forces. To underwrite reinsurance of that sort, we need some equivalent of the Federal Deposit Insurance Corporation (which protects U.S. bank deposits in similar fashion), with rights to draw on general fund revenue in the last resort.

[146] Notably, under the "privatized" Chilean old-age pension, the state reinsures against the former risk through the guarantee of a minimum pension for anyone who has contributed to a private scheme for twenty years or more, the state supplementing the private pension's payments as necessary to bring people up to that minimum level (United Nations 1995, 278; Privatization 1994).

or uninsurable" that a compulsory state scheme provides must surely exceed that, on almost any credible assessment.

I shall not attempt to survey the many other controversies surrounding social insurance.[147] Let us merely recall our purpose in revisiting those old debates. The issue before us is one of "personal" versus "collective" responsibility for welfare. The lesson old debates over social insurance hold for us, in that context, is that, in very many respects, personal responsibility is best exercised through some collective agency. The best way for individuals prudently to provide for their own future welfare is by collectively pooling risks, through some sort of mutual insurance, rather than "self-insuring" and bearing the full weight of those risks on their own shoulders. And where those risks are themselves collective in the stronger sense – where everyone's fate really does, to any significant extent, rise and fall together – then the same prudential calculations recommend compulsory state insurance to protect against the risk of bankrupting private mutual insurance schemes.[148]

---

[147] Another arises from the fact that social insurance is typically organized on a "pay-as-you-go" basis: contributions from today's workers are used to pay the pensions of today's pensioners, rather than going into an "individually vested account" against which those workers will be able to draw when they reach pensionable age – as would happen with a private retirement fund, for example. While the present generation of economists seems keen on individually vested accounts, an earlier generation of economists advising the founders of the scheme warned of the dire macroeconomic consequences that would result from a large vested fund building up over time, which could not (or anyway probably would not) be put to good productive uses for one reason or another (Ball 1988, 23–4).

[148] How exactly we set up this social insurance is infinitely variable. It is perfectly possible for compulsory insurance to be provided through private underwriters subject to state regulation and with the state as reinsurer of last resort, as is done with workers compensation schemes in most states of the United States. In setting up a scheme, we would want to make it legally compulsory for everyone to carry insurance, and for insurance companies to insure everyone seeking insurance through a pool of "assigned" (i.e., bad) risks which underwriters would have to share out among themselves; we would want the state to police (and perhaps even set) rates and in any case tightly regulate the insurers; but we would also want the state to act as "underwriter of last resort," reinsuring (as through the U.S. Federal Deposit Insurance Corporation) against the risks that claims will vastly exceed the insurers' reserves. A system of "compulsory private old-age insurance" is canvassed by Shapiro (1997).

2.4.3   The Efficiencies of Collective Provision

A final plank in the classic case for collectivization points to the greater efficiencies of collective provision of certain things in certain circumstances. Consider here the case for sanitary sewers. It is not impossible for each household to dig its own hole in the ground, or for there to be some private service collecting waste pans from each household's outhouse; indeed, such arrangements have prevailed in even moderately large cities in the developed world in living memory. The case for sanitary sewers is simply that it is so much more efficient (and, in sanitation terms, so much more effective as well) for those services to be centrally organized. In that sense, waste pooling is akin to risk pooling in the previous discussion. We can all simply cope better with the problems posed by wastes, as by risks, if we develop schemes for dealing with all of them together rather than one by one.

The example of sanitary sewers is deliberately quaint.[149] But there are all sorts of other areas in which we have genuine options of public or private, collectivized or individualized solutions to shared problems. In the words of Brian Barry's inaugural:

> Does the public health service have long waiting lists and inadequate facilities? Buy private insurance. Has public transport broken down? Buy a car for each member of the family above driving age. Has the countryside been built over or the footpaths eradicated? Buy some elaborate exercise machinery and work out at home. Is air pollution intolerable? Buy an air-filtering unit and stay indoors. Is what comes out of the tap foul to the taste and chock-full of carcinogens? Buy bottled water.... We know it can all happen because it has: I have been doing little more than describing Southern California.[150]

There are many things to be said against such a vision of the future. Many of us would bemoan the lack of sociability that is conjured up by visions of privatized, individual consumers barricaded

---

[149] But not so quaint as to be *altogether* without contemporary relevance, in a world where British water authorities are being reprivatized.

[150] Barry 1989a, 541.

within their own homes, riding their exercise bikes nowhere, and gulping water from their own flasks. There is much to be said, in those terms, for the sort of "café society socialism" – a socialism that had more to do with sociability than with redistribution – as was championed by Anthony Crosland in his *Future of Socialism*.[151] But anyone not independently attracted to that way of life is unlikely to be persuaded by anything I can say in describing or defending it. Some people apparently really do (or anyway clearly want to) believe that they are an island, genuinely preferring to bowl alone.[152]

Rather than launching a headlong assault on their settled values and preferences in that respect, I shall here launch a more oblique if less high-minded challenge to the purely privatized existence that they say they prefer. I shall focus simply on one particular aspect of the comparative efficiencies of collective provision in so many of these areas. Again, there are of course many aspects to efficiency;[153] again, there is no space to canvass all of that large and often largely inconclusive literature here.

There is however one thing that can usually be said, fairly conclusively, in favor of collectivized responses to social problems in this regard. The general point I want to develop here has to do with what sort of notions of "causation" are most appropriate for purposes of making public policy. There are, of course, a great many subtle philosophical discussions of the notion of causation and correspondingly many ways of construing the basic concept.[154] I do not intend to survey them all here, however briefly. Instead I shall merely pick out one in particular that, although perhaps not particularly appealing as a general

---

[151] 1954, esp. chap. 21.

[152] Though it must be said even of Barry's Southern Californians that they tend to join health clubs, working out alongside one another (if not literally "together") and, at least in one notable Pasadena spa, on Nautilus machines in the front windows of the establishment for all the passing world to see. Even private exhibitionists need a public for an audience.

[153] These are surveyed and critiqued, as they relate to welfare state debates, in Goodin 1988, chap. 8.

[154] See, e.g., the essays collected in Sosa 1975.

philosophical account, is particularly apt for forward-looking purposes of public policy.

The notion of causation that I commend for those purposes is Collingwood's notion of "contributory factors with handles on them."[155] The basic idea here is just this. In answering the question, What is the cause of x? we must inquire first as to our purpose in asking. If the purpose is allocating post hoc blame for having caused something to happen, then the answer will focus on one set of variables. But if the purpose is exercising control over future events, then what we are looking for are those variables which are within our present power, ones over which we can manipulate to desired effects. This seems to be a notion of particular relevance to public policy makers – and more generally to any agents, be they public or private, trying to work their will on the world.

Applying this standard to questions like pollution control, for example, policy makers should be looking across the many things that contribute to pollution for those variables which have the best "handles" on them, and which are most subject to manipulation and control. They could try to change the behavior of each individual, one by one: but getting effective control over the behavior of lots of independent actors is difficult; far better to focus on manufacturers, restricting the range of polluting products on the market available for those consumers to buy. In trying to control the dumping of oil at sea, it is far more effective to exercise control over the manufacture of oil tankers (which is done at only a few shipyards) than to try to exercise control over the behavior of a vast fleet on the high seas.[156] We should be looking, in this way, for "pressure points" where policy might be most effective.

In the funnel of causation, lots of little erratic factors often funnel through the narrow neck of one particular crucial factor before producing the effects they do. In trying to control the effects, policy makers ought be looking for the necks of the funnels. And

---

[155] Resurrected by Feinberg (1970, 144).
[156] Mitchell 1994a, 1994b.

those, almost invariably, are collectivizing. The various erratic factors that feed into the wide mouth of the funnel are individual and idiosyncratic in character. The funnel's narrowing neck, by its nature, pools those individual contributions and melds them together.

Examples of this phenomenon abound in social policy. If you are trying to reduce road fatalities, it makes more sense to compel a handful of automobile manufacturers to fit airbags and other "passive restraints" than to try to compel a multitude of drivers to buckle their seatbelts each time they drive. If you are trying to reduce the health effects of tobacco, "stop smoking" advertising campaigns aimed at altering the behavior of multitudes of addicted smokers make less sense than restrictions on where tobacco can be bought and where it can be consumed, limiting sales to registered outlets and prohibiting smoking in public places.[157] If you are trying to reduce deaths from firearms, campaigns to persuade individuals to hand in weapons make less sense than restrictions on the manufacture and sale of ammunition to be used in those weapons.

Ideals of "personal responsibility" would presumably dictate a behavior-modification approach in each of those cases. If we can get people to modify their behavior in those ways, we would have better, more responsible people in consequence. But in each of those cases, the attempt to encourage more "responsible" behavior on an individual basis is almost certainly the less effective way of achieving desirable outcomes overall. We merely have to decide what we want, better people or fewer dead bodies. My own preferences are clear from the prejudicial way I unapologetically cast that choice.

---

[157] Goodin 1989, 41–56, 80–8.

2.5 The Morality of Incentives and Deterrence

I T IS standardly said that public policy ought to provide positive incentives to encourage good behavior and negative disincentives to deter bad. It is commonly alleged that, instead, public policy in general and social welfare policy in particular provide "perverse incentives," making vice pay more than virtue.

Such complaints have long been familiar. Reverend Malthus and his followers criticized the old poor law's lax assistance regime for discouraging taxpayers from saving, industrialists from investing, and welfare administrators from vigorously enforcing the law. They demoralized recipients, undermining their character and their morals, encouraging them to lie, cheat, and steal, to cut corners, and to live as leeches on the commonweal rather than as upright, self-reliant citizens.[158]

Of course, the "impotent poor" – those too old or infirm to earn their own living – were always supposed to be bracketed out and treated more generously.[159] But as for the "able-bodied poor," the guiding rule of the 1834 reforms to the English Poor Law (which in turn guided Anglo-American social welfare policy throughout the next century) was the infamous "principle of lesser eligibility." According to that principle, every incentive should be given

---

[158] Checkland and Checkland 1974, 130ff.; Malthus 1803/1992, bk. 4, chap. 10.

[159] But not all that generous. The commissioners, notice, were at pains to emphasize that the business of poor relief was merely to relieve "indigence": literally, just to prevent people from starving (Checkland and Checkland 1974, 65ff.).

to the able-bodied poor to find paid labor if they possibly can. Relying on public support should be made the "least eligible" option. "As regards [any] able-bodied labourers who apply for relief," the authors of the *Poor Law Report of 1834* bluntly recommend giving them "hard work at low wages by the piece, and extracting more work at a lower price than is paid for any other labour in the parish. In short,... let the labourer find that the parish is the hardest taskmaster and the worst paymaster he can find, and thus induce him to make his application to the parish his last and not his first resort."[160] Such logic is powerfully reflected in our own time in the simple and oft-expressed thought that "no one ought be better off on welfare than in work."[161] Without dissenting from that proposition itself, necessarily, I shall here be offering some arguments against setting welfare benefits deliberately low in hopes of driving prospective claimants to work.

2.5.1   Deterrence: Punishing the Blameless

Disincentives and deterrents generally pose a host of familiar moral problems, mostly to do with issues of blaming the victim and punishing the innocent in one way or another. In the realm of nuclear deterrence, for example, many moralists question the ethics of threatening (and, in extremis, of actually killing) masses of innocent civilians.[162] Within the philosophy of punishment, many moralists similarly query the utilitarian readiness to punish people who are themselves innocent of any wrongdoing, simply in order to deter others from committing future crimes.[163]

Within social welfare policy, the "principle of lesser eligibility" arrays its deterrents and disincentives with the aim of promoting personal responsibility and reducing social dependency. It has long been acknowledged that that might cause unintended

---

[160]   Checkland and Checkland 1974, 337.
[161]   The most humane version of which thought is found in Bane and Ellwood 1994, chap. 4.
[162]   Hardin et al. 1985.
[163]   Mabbott 1939.

harm to innocents. Thomas Malthus proposed literally starving children in order to shame their fathers into feeding them, confessing that this smacked of "visiting the sins of the father upon the child" but saying that he simply could not think of any other way of inducing personal responsibility and deterring prospective fathers from reckless procreation.[164] Two centuries later, we hear analogous proposals for making the life of welfare mothers more intolerable. The official aim, once again, is to induce more responsible behavior and deter reckless breeding. Once again, however, it is conceded even by staunch advocates of those schemes that innocent children will inevitably suffer "collateral damage" in the process.[165]

Calling it "collateral damage" suggests that the harm is accidental and incidental and that it ought be judged more leniently for that reason. Most of us would indeed be inclined to excuse complete accidents, outcomes that were entirely outside people's control. Most of us would similarly excuse people from blame for outcomes that, although perhaps within their control in some sense, were nonetheless genuinely unforseen and unforeseeable.[166] But fewer of us would be prepared to excuse people from blame for outcomes which they could and should have foreseen (even if they did not actually do so).[167] Fewer still would be prepared to excuse people from blame for consequences of their actions which they clearly foresaw at the time of acting.[168]

In my own frankly consequentialistic view, how much of a moral discount ought be applied even to sheer accidents depends on just how foreseeable they were in advance. If we knew (or

---

[164] Malthus 1803/1992, bk. 4, chap. 8, p. 266.

[165] Novak et al. 1987, 114–5. Commentators as diverse as Senator Moynihan and columnist George Will speak powerfully against such proposals for that very reason (Moynihan 1996, 34).

[166] Cf. Bernard Williams 1981, chap. 2, where he seems to advocate a standard of "strict liability" in such matters.

[167] That is in the law of tort the defining feature of "negligence," to which blame (albeit of a reduced form) legally attaches.

[168] Jesuitical defenders of the doctrine of "double effect" apart: cf. Anscombe 1965 and Dworkin 1985, 37–52.

could and should have known) fully well that innocents will suffer as a result of what we do, then we ought in my view to be held fully to account for that foreseeable suffering. It is of no consequence to say that we did not "mean" for them to suffer, that we did not do what we did "for the sake" or "with the express purpose" of causing their suffering. Neither is it much of an excuse to say that we tried to set things up in such a way as to avoid innocents' suffering, if we knew (or could and should have known) fully well that our scheme will not work as planned and that innocents will indeed end up suffering in consequence.

Note, in this connection, a striking oddity about the disincentives that Malthus and his heirs want to build into social welfare policy. The more those disincentives succeed as deterrents – the more they succeed in persuading anyone to avoid them who possibly can, by getting paid work or a rich benefactor, for example, rather than relying on poor relief – the greater the extent to which the remaining pool of welfare recipients will consist of people who literally cannot do anything to help themselves. In other words, the more this deterrent policy works precisely as intended, the lower will be the proportion of "undeserving poor" (and the greater will be the proportion of "deserving poor") among those left receiving the deliberately and punitively inadequate assistance.[169]

Here, then, harming innocents is in no sense an accident. It is not the unintended consequence of a deterrent policy misfiring. Rather it is a direct and utterly foreseeable consequence of the policy's working precisely according to plan. In that sense, Malthusian deterrents and disincentives built into punitive Poor Laws are morally more obnoxious than anything Herman Kahn or Jeremy Bentham ever envisaged.

Of course, whereas the latter would nuke innocents or hang them, a punitive social welfare policy would merely starve them instead. The fact remains that, in order for the punitive aspects of social welfare policies to serve as disincentives to would-be

---

[169] I offer a structurally similar argument in Goodin 1985a.

recipients, the treatment meted out must be *punishingly* bad (the sums paid out punishingly low,[170] the time limits painfully truncated, the stigma attached severely humiliating) by some generally accepted social benchmark. The more socially unacceptable the plight of welfare recipients, the more the undeserving poor will be driven to avoid it. But the inevitable consequence, as I have said, is that that socially unacceptable fate will disproportionately be visited upon those who are least able to avoid (and hence who least deserve) that fate.

The "two-tier welfare policy" discussed at the outset of this section is one attempt to address that problem. The aim there is to separate out all of the "deserving poor" and subject them to a different and less harsh welfare regime, reserving the punitive regime of deterrents and disincentives purely for the "able-bodied" and hence "undeserving" poor. If we assume all of them could find gainful employment on ordinary labor markets if they really tried (an assumption I query in section 2.5.4), any of them who nonetheless fall back on public assistance deserve whatever harsh treatment they received there. Or so it is hoped.

That is not how "two-tier welfare policies" actually operate in practice, though. Historically, the less-favored tier has traditionally been reserved not for the morally less deserving but rather for the economically more superfluous (the top tier being the prerogative of workers, the lower being reserved for women and children).[171] Operationally, sorting claimants into "deserving" and "undeserving" entails an individualized "character test" requiring welfare administrators to make discretionary judgments of an often arbitrary and objectionable sort.[172] In an attempt to minimize such arbitrary discretion, we try to work through blunt instruments of a more broadly categorical sort.[173] But such bluntly categorical mechanisms inevitably sort some people into

---

[170] As indeed welfare benefits already are, on the evidence of Edin (1991; Edin and Jencks 1992).

[171] Nelson 1990; Gordon 1994.

[172] See further section 2.2.2.

[173] See further Goodin 1995, chaps. 1, 4, 14.

the wrong class; and the more who are genuinely deserving among the population at large, the more people who will be misclassified as undeserving and wrongly subjected to the deterrent sanctions of the "principle of lesser eligibility" in consequence.[174]

Thus the sorts of deterrents and disincentives that advocates of a "principle of lesser eligibility" would build into a welfare regime seem inevitably destined to end up penalizing the deserving as well as the undeserving poor. And, ironically, the harsher those deterrents – the more they succeed in deterring those who have it within their power to avoid them – the more those who are left suffering their penalties are those who do not in any way deserve them.[175]

2.5.2 Opportunities versus Incentives

In trying to manipulate people's behavior through sanctions and incentives, we can work on either side (or both) of the motivational ledger. The "principle of lesser eligibility" works on the negative side of the ledger, giving prospective welfare claimants every reason to avoid falling back on state assistance if they possibly can. Rather than (or in addition to) making public assistance less attractive in that way, we might take a more positive approach, making it more attractive for people to take personal initiatives in finding paid employment.

There are many aspects to such a policy.[176] Much can be done to increase take-home pay: increasing the minimum wage,

---

[174] Goodin 1985a.

[175] Other ironies arise in the process of implementing such strategies, as welfare administrators inadvertently create disincentives to people getting off the welfare rolls. "Poverty traps" can be created by earnings thresholds (or even steep tapers) in benefit structures, such that taking paid employment would cost welfare recipients more in lost welfare benefits than a job would actually pay. No one defends poverty traps, of course. But although inadvertent, they are a natural and not always easily avoidable consequence of punitive welfare policies aimed at "weaning" recipients off welfare at the earliest opportunity and making them "personally responsible" for their own welfare.

[176] See, e.g., Bane and Ellwood 1994, chaps. 4, 5.

introducing earned income tax credits for low-paid workers, subsidizing the costs of working (such as transportation and child care), and so on. All this would make it more financially worthwhile for poor people to work. But most of today's welfare recipients are not in paid work, not primarily because work does not pay enough (though that may be true too), but rather because they lack genuine opportunities to work. There are no jobs where they live, and no affordable housing available to them where there are jobs; they have too few of the sorts of skills that employers want; they have too little information about what is wanted and what is available; and so on.[177]

It is thus widely agreed on all sides of the welfare debate that moving people from welfare to paid employment requires active labor market policies and energetic programs of education and training. People cannot get jobs if there are no jobs: so job creation is crucial. People cannot get jobs if they are unfit for jobs: so increasing the skills of the unemployed is also crucial. There are of course many particular ways to tailor job creation and education and training programs; and some clearly work better than others. But which precise schemes are to be preferred in any particular circumstances is an empirical question, and beyond the philosophical remit of this discussion.[178]

Here let us focus instead on a generic feature of all such schemes. However exactly they are organized, job creation, education, and training schemes all aim essentially at increasing the *opportunities* (rather than the rewards and, hence, incentives) for people to work. Such schemes take for granted that the will to work already exists, independently of the policies themselves.[179] What those policies do is simply make paid employment – taking

---

[177] This is the theme of Wilson (1991, 1996a, 1996b). For variations on these themes, see Jencks 1992, chaps. 4 and 5, and the contributors to Jencks and Peterson 1991.

[178] I shall comment in section 2.5.3 upon the distinctively moral defects of some ways of setting up such schemes.

[179] That formulation intentionally straddles two possibilities: one is that people are predisposed that way, naturally; the other is that other distinct policies serve to provide the requisite incentives.

"personal responsibility for one's own welfare," in that sense – a viable option for those for whom it presently is not.

This way of constructing social reality is importantly different from the one implied by talk of "incentives," even of the more positive sort. The language of incentives suggests that the poor do not work because they have coldly, calculatedly determined that it is not worth their while working. Manipulating incentives so as to make work relatively more attractive, and welfare relatively less so, presupposes that people decide (*choose*, in some meaningful sense) to go and to remain on welfare.[180] Then and only then can we say that people have truly "abdicated" personal responsibility for their own welfare.

That implication does not follow, however, on the "opportunity" construction of the problem. Insofar as people do not work because they have no realistic chances of finding paid employment, we cannot to that extent say that they have genuinely "decided" or "chosen" to rely on state welfare rather than their own efforts to support themselves. To the extent that labor market and education and training policies constitute solutions to these problems at all (and it is agreed on all sides of the debate that they do, at least in part), then to that extent we cannot honestly say that people have "abdicated" personal responsibility for their own welfare.

Thus, whereas the "incentive" construction of the problem of welfare dependency necessarily denigrates the motives and character of welfare recipients, the "providing opportunities" construction does not. On the latter account, it is an open question (in a way that on the former it is not) whether or not poor people would be predisposed to take "personal responsibility" for their own welfare, if only they had the chance.[181] Since even advocates of the "incentive" perspective concede an important role for policies "enhancing opportunities," even they must admit that the

---

[180] Or could have chosen otherwise, insofar as they remain on welfare through sheer inertia.

[181] They may or may not be: insofar as they have never had (or known they had) the chance, we cannot know for sure what they will do if given it.

question is rather more open than their initial cut at the problem would seem to suggest.

2.5.3   Offers You Can't Refuse

Few would object to "workfare" if it merely offered to increase the opportunities available to the poor. But that is not how workfare works. Workfare is a paradigm case of what philosophers call a "throffer": the conjunction of a threat and an offer.[182]

Ordinary threats threaten to make you worse off, whereas ordinary offers offer to make you better off. A "throffer" does both at once. It presents a pair of options: one would make you worse off than you would otherwise be, absent any intervention; and the other would make you better off than you would otherwise be, again absent any intervention. Remaining as you would otherwise be, absent any intervention, is simply not an option.

Shifting public policy from "welfare" to "workfare" presents recipients of state assistance with an analogous proposition. Continuing to receive state assistance on the present basis ceases to be an option. Instead, welfare recipients are offered the work–welfare package as an all-or-nothing proposition. Either they accept education and training to make them work-ready, along with their welfare check (which would, hopefully, make them better off than they are under the present regime);[183] or, alternatively, they can reject the package as a whole, in which case they will

---

[182]   Owing to Steiner (1974–5; 1994, chap. 2).

[183]   Though probably not by much: on the basis of his survey of the empirical evidence on the performance of such schemes, Moffitt (1992, 50) regards it as a "relatively optimistic view that the programs can consistently increase earnings by $1,000 per year for AFDC female heads"; given that, and given how far below the poverty line most of them are at present, "a large change in the poverty rate of female heads is not likely to result from implementing the program." In their extended analysis of workfare programs in four locales, Friedlander and Burtless (1995, 11) are even more pessimistic: they find that the *cumulative* increase in earnings over five years range from $1,079 in Arkansas to $2,119 in Baltimore for the average participant in those programs.

get neither welfare nor work training (which would clearly leave them worse off than they are under the present regime).

We ordinarily seem inclined to take a relatively sanguine view of throffers. The threatening half of the throffer – the fork that would make the person worse off – is in itself ordinarily morally odious.[184] But in a throffer a threat is conjoined with another option that would make the person better off than he or she would otherwise be. And we seem ordinarily inclined to think that the attractiveness of that other half of the throffer powerfully mitigates the unattractiveness (morally and otherwise) of the other.[185]

This relatively sanguine view of throffers, however, is implicitly contingent on the choice between the options being a genuinely viable choice. No doubt taking the "threat" fork of the decision tree is always going to be a relatively undesirable option, but it must be at least a *viable* option.[186] The gunman's "Your money or your life" is not merely a threat masquerading as an offer; insofar as death is the only option, handing over your money is

---

[184] In general, anyway. It may well be that advocates of workfare have no moral hesitancy in compelling the poor and morally corrupted in this way (and would justify such coercion in frankly paternalistic terms, as discussed later).

[185] It is not erased completely. People are still being "forced," in some sense or another, to take the offer (on pain of suffering the threatened outcome that constitutes its alternative). But they are being forced to no greater extent than they are "forced" to remain with the status quo in the standard case of an offer (which, after all, presents them with the single choice of "be better off in this particular way, or remain in the status quo"). So in terms of freedom, victims of a throffer are no worse off than in the standard case of an offer; and in terms of welfare, they are considerably better off than in the standard case of a threat.

[186] How we cash out "viable" here is of course crucial. Minimally, as the gunman analogy suggests, to be viable an option must be consistent with sustaining life itself. But for purposes of moral assessment of a throffer, surely we would similarly treat as "morally unviable" an option that would force you to commit a morally heinous crime. By extension, we might morally condemn the workfare throffer if the welfare mother who rejects the offer would have no option but to sell her body to support her baby: we may say that is an unviable option morally, even if it is in the circumstances of ghetto life an all-too-viable one practically.

not in any important sense a choice at all.[187] So too, sometimes, with throffers. The "threat" fork must leave people in at least a viable position, in order for the "offer" fork to count as a choice (and hence an offer) at all. You may be made better off than you presently are by taking the "offer" fork. But that does nothing to diminish the involuntariness of the act, if you effectively had no choice but to act thusly.[188]

That may well be true of the workfare throffer. Some of those who are presently receiving welfare benefits may well be able to sustain themselves without those payments: refusing to enter education and training schemes, even at the cost of losing all public assistance, would for them be a perfectly viable (albeit perhaps undesirable) option; and workfare would therefore be a genuine throffer. Most welfare recipients, however, genuinely do not see how they could possibly sustain themselves without state support.[189] They see no choice but to accept the throffer of workfare: but then their accepting the throffer cannot be seen as representing their own "free choice" in any meaningful sense at all. For them, workfare constitutes an "offer they can't refuse."

Of course advocates of workfare are confident that education and training *will* make people better off, and we can always invoke purely paternalistic principles to justify making people better

---

[187]   A samurai might see things differently. So might an ancient Greek. No matter. The welfare policies under discussion in this book are those of the Anglo-American democracies, wherein the truth of this proposition could not be doubted.

[188]   Hume (1760, pt. 2, chap. 12) remarks similarly upon the "voluntariness" of consenting to government. Note that the same could be said of even simple "offers" made to people who are in an unviable status quo: they, too, would have no choice but to accept the "offer."

[189]   That may represent a failure of imagination, of course, rather than any genuine assessment of their options. But unless people perceive options they obviously cannot act upon them; so the options they see themselves as having, rather than those that they "actually" have, are what matter here. (Ironically, criticisms of beneficiaries as being "unimaginative" in their search for alternatives to state support here backfire on opponents of state welfare.) But, in any case, the evidence offered by Edin (1991; Edin and Jencks 1992) as to the budgets AFDC recipients have to manage on clearly suggests that the failure here is hardly just one of imagination.

off without giving them any free choice in the matter. But note that it is an insistently external, paternalistic notion of other people's welfare that must be at work here.

Just as it would be wrong to infer anything about such people's "free choice" from their reactions to the throffer of workfare, however, so too would it be wrong in these circumstances to infer anything about their self-perceived "welfare" from those responses, either. Ordinarily we assume people are good judges of their own interests. Accordingly, when we see that they choose to accept workfare rather than doing without welfare altogether, we ordinarily infer that workfare makes them better off (subjectively, at least). And so it does in one sense: they clearly are better off than they would be with any other option on the table. But that way of framing the issue suppresses any inquiry into options *not* on the table, which must also be considered in coming to an overall assessment of the impact of the policy upon those subject to it.

Consider, by analogy, Daniel Ellsberg's famous discussion of "the reluctant duelist."[190] True, if I am forced to fight a duel, I would much rather shoot first than be shot. But fixing our focus too tightly upon *that* choice obscures a much larger and more important fact. Instead of either of those two options, I would much rather not fight the duel at all.

So too, perhaps, with workfare. Many of those who are told that their welfare benefits will be withdrawn unless they sign up for workfare agree to do so as reluctantly as Ellsberg's duelist. As between workfare or nothing, they choose workfare. But all that proves is that workfare is, for them, better than nothing. It does not prove that workfare is, in their view, better than welfare as presently constituted.[191] Like Ellsberg's reluctant duelist, our reluctant workfare client might vastly have preferred welfare as presently constituted to the choice of workfare or nothing, of shooting or being shot.

---

[190] Ellsberg 1956.

[191] Any more than their acceptance of welfare checks, as presently drawn, means that they would not prefer some yet more generous scheme.

Of course, many recipients might actually welcome the opportunities workfare provides, particularly if workfare is structured in genuinely enabling rather than more purely punitive ways. Many others involuntarily subjected to that regime might retrospectively come to be glad of it. And, in any case, the views of welfare and workfare clients are not the only preferences to be considered here. Even if they are made worse off by being forced to work for a living, the rest of us might derive sufficient satisfaction from that to outweigh their own preferences in the matter. Hence, none of this constitutes a conclusive case against workfare. Still, all of these moral points, familiarly weighty in other contexts, surely should count for *something* in those contexts. They ought not simply be ignored, as they typically are, in coming to an overall assessment of workfare-style policies.

2.5.4   Welfare as Compensation for Structural Unemployment

All too many welfare recipients simply have "no choice" but to rely on state assistance, on whatever terms the state chooses to offer it. They cannot simply "opt" to help themselves in the ordinary way through ordinary labor markets. In part that is because they are "unemployable," having no skills for which there exists any market demand (which is the part of the problem to which workfare is addressed). In part, too, they are unemployed because of the way work is structured (where it is located, how well it is remunerated, what child-care arrangements are, and so on: problems that various other reforms hope to address).

Another important part of the problem, however, has to do with "structural unemployment." New technologies have radically transformed both the manufacturing and service sectors. More is now being done with fewer people, and there is simply no realistic place in the modern economy for many of the workers thus displaced.[192] This is not the place for detailed inquiries into those new economic realities, their causes and longer-term

---

[192]   Head 1996; Thurow 1996; Reich 1991; Porter 1990.

consequences.[193] For present purposes suffice it to say that, at least for the foreseeable future, we will inevitably be experiencing a surplus of labor rather than a shortage. The gap between the number of workers looking for jobs and the number of available jobs for them to fill constitutes the extent of "structural unemployment." That represents the number of people who are inevitably and unavoidably unemployed in our economy – people who are unemployed, simply because there is no job to be found for them in our economy as it is presently constituted.[194]

In various respects, the welfare state has always been predicated on the assumption of "full employment."[195] Administratively, we base social insurance on workplace contributions, thus presupposing that everyone is either in paid employment or in some stable relationship with someone who is.[196] Fiscally, we operate social insurance on a "pay as you go" basis, paying claimants out of premiums collected from current employees, which

---

[193] Some say that these new technologies cause more unemployment only in the short term. But according to the famous Keynesian aphorism, "In the long run, we're all dead" – and none more so than those displaced from the labor market for even as "little" as five or ten years, absent a social safety net to take care of their needs.

[194] That sense of "structural unemployment" points to the structure of the economy. There might be another, more sociological sense of "structural unemployment," which points to the structure of society and the distribution of "caring work" within it, which "structures" certain people (typically women) out of the labor market (Land 1978; Ungerson 1987; Kittay 1996).

[195] There were three legs to William Beveridge's vision of how the postwar British welfare state was supposed to work – one represented by his more famous report, *Social insurance and allied services* (1942), the other two by his *Full employment in a free society* (1945) and *Voluntary action* (1948).

[196] That is to say that social insurance schemes essentially enshrine a "breadwinner's welfare state," and traditionally a "male" one at that. Some feminists urge a nongendered version of same, while others urge a different model altogether; see, e.g., Fraser 1994 and Sainsbury 1996.

Ironically, when the U.S. Social Security Act was initially passed in 1935, its provisions for "Aid to Dependent Children" (as AFDC was then called) were regarded as almost purely transitional arrangements. Those provisions were envisaged primarily as aid to widows and their dependent children and, as "survivor's insurance" would increasingly absorb those into the mainstream social security arrangements, that class of claimants would gradually fade away (Gilbert 1995, 30).

presupposes a relatively high ratio of workers to claimants. High levels of structural unemployment are awkward in both respects: administratively, increasing numbers are thereby thrown into the residual pool claiming "social assistance" rather than "social insurance"; fiscally, increasingly large contributions must be extracted from a decreasingly small work force to pay the welfare bill. But neither of these more familiar problems is what I want to discuss here.[197]

Structural unemployment raises distinctively moral implications for the ideal of taking "personal responsibility" for the welfare of yourself and your family. For anyone who is not independently wealthy or the beneficiary of a large charitable largesse, that necessarily means finding work that pays enough to meet the needs of oneself and one's family. But in situations of structural unemployment, it is simply not possible for everyone who needs work in order to discharge that responsibility to find it. There is just not enough work to go around.

What then follows from the fact of structural unemployment for the ideal of personal responsibility? Clearly, we ought excuse those for whom no work can be found from any moral obligation to earn their own living. But implementing this principle on an individualized basis will inevitably prove devilishly difficult. There will always be more people who are actually unemployed than who are structurally unemployed; and it is sheer folly to try to determine, on a case-by-case basis, which among the actually unemployed are structurally so.[198] Structural unemployment is

---

[197] Nor shall I, except here in passing, note that the most obvious remedy for structural unemployment is a program of public works. There is much that a resurrected Civilian Conservation Corps could usefully do in repairing national infrastructure; but politically that is simply not in the cards.

[198] Familiar "availability for work" tests, administered by local employment offices as part of unemployment insurance schemes, aim somewhat more modestly to distinguish "voluntary" from "involuntary" unemployment. There, people's unemployment is defined as "voluntary" if they persistently refuse to accept jobs for which they are qualified. Those classed as "involuntarily unemployed" in those terms include both those for whom there are no jobs (the structurally unemployed) and those for whom the labor exchange has simply failed to find a job.

by definition a structural feature of the economy, a systemic artifact that cannot credibly be attributed to any individual worker
in particular.

Here, as before, an individualized response makes little sense
precisely because the phenomenon is by its nature a collective,
structural one. If structural unemployment is a feature of the
overall pattern of the economy which we all share, then it makes
more sense to try to pool our risks of being structurally unemployed, sharing the benefits of employment and the costs of structural unemployment among all those party to the pool.

There are various ways to do that. Here is one deliberately
fanciful proposal. Issue everyone with "labor permits" (conceived
as a "license to hunt for a job"), those permits being issued to
everyone equally but strictly in proportion to the number of jobs
actually available. Thus, for example, in a world of 10 percent
structural unemployment each person would get nine-tenths of
a labor permit. Since anyone in full-time paid employment will
need a full permit licensing them to hold such a post, anyone
wanting full-time paid employment would then have to buy his
or her last one-tenth of a permit from someone else. Those people,
in turn, will have to live off the proceeds of selling their fractional
labor permits in this way.[199]

Now, nobody seriously proposes organizing any actual labor
market in exactly that way.[200] But that way of thinking about
how to share out the benefits and burdens of structural unemployment does help us think differently – and, I think, more ap-
propriately – about the nature of public assistance to those who
are, or can credibly claim to be, its victims.[201] Instead of regarding welfare payments as "transfers" of a gratuitously redistributive
sort, thinking in terms of a market in labor permits helps us see
them as "compensation" to people who have done something for

---

[199]   Haminga 1995.

[200]   Though we do require various people to have "licenses" of some sort before
going into business, and "market socialists" propose redistributing basic social
capital in just such ways (see, e.g., Roemer 1994).

[201]   Broadly similar thoughts drive Meade (1995), for example, to endorse a
"basic income" policy.

us.[202] Thinking in terms of a market in labor permits leads us to think of welfare beneficiaries not as "leaches" living off the rest of us but, rather, as petty bourgeois capitalists (of a degenerate *rentier* sort) living off the sale or rent of their assets.[203] Of course, there is no actual market in labor permits. No actual welfare recipients have actually agreed to sell their partial rights to work to us in exchange for the welfare benefits that they receive. Real people typically become unemployed through no (particular) choice of their own.[204] But surely that fact makes them more, rather than less, deserving of public sympathy and support.

My larger point is just this. Telling people to "get a job" – and in that most standard of ways to "take personal responsibility" for the welfare of themselves and their families – may be well and good, so long as there are jobs enough to go around. The American economy (like most other OECD economies) is not like that, however, and it is likely to remain unlike that for some time to come. Where there are simply not enough jobs to go around, we cannot reasonably blame welfare recipients across the board for not earning their own keep on the ordinary labor market.[205] On the contrary, in situations of structural unemployment we ought not just regard welfare recipients as blameless victims, akin to the

---

[202] What they are "doing for us" is occupying slots among the unemployed that someone has to occupy, in an economy with any appreciable level of structural unemployment; and unemployment benefits can be conceived as "payments" to them for that service. Alternatively, we can conceive of them as, literally, insurance benefits paid to those who have been unlucky in a lottery to which we too were parties (and will be once again, in future rounds of the game).

[203] Thinking in terms of all the unpaid "caring" work that is done outside the market, and which needs to be done to keep markets operating, leads us to think of them in different ways yet again. See, e.g., Atkinson 1996 and Kittay 1996.

[204] As argued in section 2.2.3, it more often is a matter of their taking risks – doing things that increase the chances of their being unemployed, without strictly determining that outcome.

[205] Whether we would object to coercing people to take jobs, even if there were one for everyone, is a separate issue that simply does not arise in the economy as it is presently structured.

"impotent poor" of old. Welfare is then not so much a matter of charitable succoring of the poor as it is "just compensation" paid to victims of our economic system. Insofar as unemployment is structural, and insofar as the rest of us benefit from the economic structures that render those people unemployed, we are rich because they are poor – and vice versa. In that light, any welfare payments we make to them are better conceived as discharge of a debt rather than as a charitable benefaction.[206]

[206] Waldron (1993a) tries to derive a similar conclusion from what seems to me a less plausible chain of reasoning (the destitute would otherwise be morally entitled to steal from us; by paying them off with welfare, we cancel the moral permissibility of that act).

2.6   The Point of Politics

M ANY of those who advocate privatized, personal solutions in
preference to collectivized, public ones do so out of a frank
abhorrence of politics as such. They view politics as essentially
a distributional struggle, and they suppose that all those efforts
devoted to redistributing things from one to another could better be devoted to producing more things for everyone. "All float
higher on a rising tide," as the saying goes among all those world-
wide who admire the "Asian tiger" combination of high-growth
economies and a minimum of democratic encumbrances.

Politics, on this view, constitutes a deadweight loss on a par
with legal fees in divorce courts. It is joint madness, which could
only afflict couples no longer capable of joint decision making,
to squander a quarter of their joint assets squabbling over the
distribution of those assets between them. It would be far better for both parties to forswear costly legal arguments and agree
(by just flipping a metaphorical coin) on any settlement falling
within the broad region bracketed by those prospective legal
fees.

Similarly, those who view politics as a mere distributive squab-
ble say that it is far better for all of us if we avoid mutually can-
celing efforts at snatching things from one another – efforts that,
taken together gain nothing for anyone – and to devote those efforts instead to productive endeavors, which would make more
for everyone. Just as the divorcing couple ought be broadly indifferent among distributions within the region bracketed by prospective legal fees, so too on this model ought citizens content

themselves with any allocation of riches that brings them more than they would have secured through the full play of the democratic process, net of the very substantial snatching-and-snatching-back costs of that process.

That, however, is a peculiarly jaundiced way of looking at politics.[207] What it ignores is the perspective of what we want collectively to be, to do, and to represent. The market is one world, one aspect of life, one side to our selves. The ethical and social side is another, which can (if it is done right) be evoked by politics. Certainly it can be pursued in private, in part; in part it can even be pursued through the market (people can, and occasionally do, donate part of their market earnings to nonprofits and charities). But it can be pursued most fully only in public, political interactions.

Those who urge "personal responsibility" do not really dispute any of that. Maybe they sometimes slip into the baldly anti-political language of the Asian tigers. But clearly they do not really mean it. Their vision of sturdy self-reliance is just as much a vision of who we are and what we stand for as a people as is any other. What they urge in pursuit of that vision is clearly political action, as collective and coercive as any other. Supposing they are sincere in their arguments on this score, theirs is just as much a collective political project as the one I have here been advocating. The question is simply which of those rival political projects has the better claim to our moral and political allegiance – which sort of people we really are and really want to be, as a people.

---

[207] It may also be actually incoherent, as stated. It appeals to a sense of what is "good for all of us," to the notion that everyone would be better off if everyone desisted from political wrangling. But its analysis of the pathology of politics works through the notion of a maximizing individual or group, smashing and grabbing to get as much as he can for himself and his group. Why should a maximizing individual or faction care about what is "good for all"? On the logic of collective action at work here, each is better off fighting his or her own corner, whatever others do; the fact that each fighting his or her own corner leaves them all worse off than they would be if no one were to do so is strictly irrelevant, from the point of view of the individual simply maximizing his or her own holdings.

2.6.1   Rising Tides, Wasted Lives: Money Is Not Like Water

Those are themes to which I shall return in closing. First, however, I want to offer a few responses, more empirical than philosophical in character, to Asian tiger–style suggestions that policies promoting "personal responsibility for welfare" will stimulate economic growth, which will, in turn, increase the well-being of even the worst-off members of the society.

In a way, that just amounts to a restatement of the old creed of "supply-side economics" and the correlative theory of "trickle down." Last heard in the heady days of high profligacy during the Reagan administration, few can now be found who would advocate that creed explicitly. Its fallacies are just too familiar.[208]

Wealth just does not trickle down to the worst off. That is unsurprising, given that economic rewards attach to slots in the economy ("capitalist" or "laborer," in standard Cobb-Douglas production functions) that the unemployed poor simply do not occupy.[209] It is unsurprising, given what we know about "transaction costs" and other economic imperfections that prevent markets from clearing – blockages likely to be most concentrated around those who are most peripheral to the ordinary operation of economic markets (the estranged poor, the unemployed, and so on).[210] It is unsurprising, given what we know about competition for "positional goods" and the "social limits to growth."[211]

Neither is real national wealth and genuine economic growth likely to be particularly well promoted by more personalized approaches to social welfare policy.[212] Conservative critics have long argued that pay-as-you-go public pensions reduce personal

---

[208] I survey some of them in Goodin 1988, chap. 9.

[209] National income is distributed among factors of production. In a market equilibrium, those who play no part in the productive process get no income.

[210] Coase 1937, 1960; Williamson 1985.

[211] Hirsch 1976; Sen 1981.

[212] This popular old theme has recently been reinvigorated by, e.g., Lindbeck et al. 1994 and Drèze and Malinvaud 1994. But the econometric evidence in support of such propositions is unclear, cross-nationally, and economic theory suggests far more attention to institutional and program details (Atkinson 1995a, 1997).

savings and investment.[213] The empirical evidence on that is terribly mixed.[214] But in any case, it is far from clear that shifting everyone over to a genuinely personalized, properly "vested" private pension plan would be particularly productive of venture capital of the sort that is required for robust economic growth: most people will not (or, anyway, ought not rationally) be taking many risks with capital that they need to save to see them through their final years.[215] Similarly, however much or little welfare recipients might reduce their labor supply in response to social benefits, marginal reductions of low-paid (and hence, presumably, low-value) labor inputs will hardly make much difference to the overall performance of the national economy.

The long and the short of it seems to be that supply-side fantasies fail on both fronts. There is little reason to think that any "economic miracles" overall will be produced by reducing the public role in welfare provision and shifting responsibility back on individuals themselves. Neither is there any reason to think that the benefits of any economic growth that does occur will trickle down to the neediest members of society.[216]

2.6.2   Who We Are and What We Stand For

Self-styled communitarians make much of the collective and social nature of the "sources of the self" that stand behind the

---

[213] Most recently, Feldstein 1996.

[214] Estimates of the reduction in private savings attributable to the current U.S. Social Security system range from 0 to 50 percent (Danziger, Haveman, and Plotnick 1981, 1003–6).

[215] Rationally, people ought be seeking supersafe investments (or, rather, a diversified portfolio of holdings that is in aggregate supersafe) for their old age – and that will ordinarily be inconsistent, once again, with investing as much as socially desirable in high-risk entrepreneurial ventures. Pension fund and IRA investment practices are more adventuresome, no doubt in part because they are competing with one another for members. But insofar as those organizations are competitively driven to risky investments in this way, their members ought to worry that they will go bankrupt just when they are most needed: when there is an economic downturn that forces many of their members into early retirement.

[216] The experience of the past dozen years or so in the United States belies that myth (Danziger and Gottschalk 1993).

machinations of the atomistic, autonomous freebooter of liberal fantasy.[217] Biologically, any given individual is the product of a prior union between two others. Biologically, human young are physically dependent on others for a protracted period. Sociologically and psychologically, no one can learn to maneuver around the social world without considerable tutelage from others. Psychologically, the "conception of self" we harbor is inherently defined in relation to others and their conceptions of us in turn. In all these ways, individuals are inherently social products.

How telling a criticism that might be of liberalism as such is an open question. I think not very.[218] But this is not the place to enter into that other discussion. My purpose in raising these issues in the present context is rather different. Where self-styled communitarians say that individuals *have* to be social in nature, what I shall be claiming here is merely that they *can* and most typically *want* to be. In terms of sloganeering, whereas self-styled communitarians focus on each individual's "sense of self" and its ultimately social sources, I focus on our collective "sense of ourselves."

We have a sense, which we share (however imperfectly) with others, of what sorts of groups we belong to and want to belong to. We have a sense, however imperfectly shared, of what those groups are like, what they stand for, and what we want them to stand for. We have a sense, however imperfectly shared, of what is good for the group collectively, quite apart from our judgments of what is good for each of us individually.

How exactly that collective sense of who we are and what we stand for is actually evoked is an interesting empirical issue. Sometimes it seems to be essentially a matter of what is the question. Some ways of asking the question (What is it worth to you?)

---

[217] Or their fantasies about liberal fantasies: I leave open the question of whether any historical liberal ever said most of the things contained in these caricatures.

[218] Wherever individuals come from (however "social" the sources of the self, and so on), once they have been fully formed, liberalism provides a pretty good account of what they do and of how we should treat them. See further Goodin 1998.

naturally evoke a more privatized, individualistic response of an essentially market-oriented sort; other ways of asking the question (What is for the best?) seem more naturally to evoke more reflective responses of a more communally oriented sort.[219]

That may be no more than a simple matter of "role responsibilities." People have various roles in their lives, switching among them endlessly throughout their ordinary working day. Different ways of framing the question might be just ways of priming people to think in terms of different ones among their many roles. No one of those roles can be utterly preeminent, taking complete priority over all others all the time; and how individuals trade off their various role responsibilities for one another is, inevitably, largely something for them to decide for themselves.

Be all that as it may, there does seem to be in ordinary people's ordinary preference functions a clear sense of the "public interest," separate from mere "private interests."[220] People internalize that notion, and perfectly properly make demands of one another in the name of it. There are some goals that we can best pursue, and others that we can only pursue, through concerted collective action. Promoting the common good and the collective welfare is, in many respects, among them. Personal responsibility for welfare is a good thing, in its place. Our task must be to keep it firmly in its place.

---

[219] This is a theme of Sagoff 1988. Evidence of "sociotropic" voting seems to bear out those speculations (Kiewiet 1983; Rohrschneider 1988).

[220] Goodin 1996.

References

Abbot, Edith. 1940. *Public Assistance*. Chicago: University of Chicago Press.

Ackerman, Bruce. 1983. On getting what we don't deserve. *Social Philosophy and Policy* 1: 60–70.

Aesop. n.d./1960. The drover and Heracles. In Valerius Babrius, ed., *Aesop's fables*, 20. Trans. D. B. Hull. Chicago: University of Chicago Press.

Ahmad, Ehtisham, Jean Drèze, John Hills, and Amartya Sen, eds. 1991. *Social security in developing countries*. Oxford: Clarendon Press.

Akerlof, George A., Janet L. Yellen, and Michael L. Katz. 1996. An analysis of out-of-wedlock childrearing in the United States. *Quarterly Journal of Economics* 111: 277–317.

Anscombe, G. E. M. 1965. War and murder. In Walter Stein, ed., *Nuclear weapons: A Catholic response*, 45–62. London: Merlin Press.

Arneson, Richard J. 1997. Egalitarianism and the undeserving poor. *Journal of Political Philosophy* 5: 327–50.

Arnold, N. Scott. 1994. *The philosophy and economics of market socialism*. New York: Oxford University Press.

Atiyah, P. S. 1980. *Accidents, compensation and the law*. 3rd ed. London: Weidenfeld & Nicolson.

Atkinson, A. B. 1995a. Is the welfare state necessarily a barrier to economic growth? In Atkinson, *Incomes and the welfare state*, 121–31. Cambridge: Cambridge University Press.

1995b. *Public economics in action: The basic income/flat tax proposal*. Oxford: Oxford University Press.

1995c. Social insurance. In Atkinson, *Incomes and the welfare state*, 205–19. Cambridge: Cambridge University Press.

1996. The case for a participation income. *Political Quarterly* 67: 67–70.

1997. *The economic consequences of rolling back the welfare state*. Cambridge, Mass.: MIT Press.

Australia, Senate Select Committee on Health Legislation and Health Insurance. 1990. What price care? Hospital costs and health insurance. *Parliamentary Papers* 33, no. 446: 6–7.

Badhwar, Neera Kapur. 1993. The circumstances of justice: Pluralism, community and friendship. *Journal of Political Philosophy* 1: 250–76.

Baker, Edwin. 1974. Utility and rights: Two justifications for state action increasing equality. *Yale Law Journal* 84: 39–59.

Baldwin, Peter. 1995. *Beyond the safety net.* Canberra: Australian Government Publishing Service.

Ball, Robert M. 1988. The original understanding on social security: Implications for later development. In Theodore R. Marmor and Jerry L. Mashaw, eds., *Social security: Beyond the rhetoric of crisis,* 17–39. Princeton: Princeton University Press.

Bane, Mary Jo, and David T. Ellwood. 1994. *Welfare realities: From rhetoric to reform.* Cambridge, Mass.: Harvard University Press.

Barr, Nick. 1987. *Economics of the welfare state.* London: Weidenfeld & Nicolson.

——— 1989. Social insurance as an efficiency device. *Journal of Public Policy* 9: 59–82.

Barry, Brian. 1989a. The continuing relevance of socialism. In Barry, *Democracy, power and justice,* 526–42. Oxford: Clarendon Press.

——— 1989b. Humanity and justice in global perspective. In Barry, *Democracy, power and justice,* 434–62. Oxford: Clarendon Press.

Bartlett, Bruce. 1995. *How poor are the poor?* National Center for Policy Analysis, Brief Analysis no. 185.

Baugher, Eleanor, and Leatha Lamison-White. 1996. *Poverty in the United States: 1995.* U.S. Bureau of the Census, Current Population Reports, P60-194. Washington, D.C.: Government Printing Office.

Becker, Gary S. 1996. Unemployment in Europe and the United States. *Journal des Economistes et des Etudes Humaines* 7: 99–101.

Beito, David T. 1990. Mutual aid for social welfare. *Critical Review* 4: 711–36.

——— 1996. Fraternal societies and social services: From mutual aid to the welfare state. Mimeographed.

——— 1997a. The "lodge practice evil" reconsidered: Medical care through fraternal societies, 1900–1930. *Journal of Urban History* 23: 569–600.

——— 1997b. "This enormous army": The mutual aid tradition of American fraternal societies before the twentieth century. *Social Philosophy and Policy* 14, no. 2: 20–38.

Berger, Brigette, and Peter L. Berger. 1983. *The war over the family.* New York: Doubleday.

Berger, Peter L., and Richard John Neuhaus. 1977. *To empower people: The role of mediating structures in public policy.* Washington, D.C.: American Enterprise Institute.

Berman, Harold. 1983. *Law and revolution: The formation of the Western legal tradition.* Cambridge, Mass.: Harvard University Press.

Beveridge, William H. 1942. *Social insurance and allied services.* Cmnd. 6404. London: HMSO.

1945. *Full employment in a free society.* New York: Norton.

1948. *Voluntary action.* London: Allen & Unwin.

Blaug, Marc. 1963. The myth of the old Poor Law and the making of the new. *Journal of Economic History* 23: 151–84.

Block, Fred, Richard A. Cloward, Barbara Ehrenreich, and Frances Fox Piven. 1987. *The mean season: The attack on the welfare state.* New York: Pantheon.

Blomfield, L., et al. 1834. *Report from His Majesty's Commission for Enquiring into the Administration and Practical Operation of the Poor Law.* London: HMSO. Reprinted in part in Checkland and Checkland 1974.

Blum, Lawrence A. 1980. *Friendship, altruism and morality.* London: Routledge & Kegan Paul.

Boettke, Peter J. 1993. *Why perestroika failed: The politics and economics of socialist transformation.* New York: Routledge.

Bogart, J. H. 1985. Lockean provisos and state of nature theories. *Ethics* 95: 828–36.

Booth, Charles. 1892. *Pauperism and the endowment of old age.* London: Macmillan.

1894. *The aged poor in England and Wales.* London: Macmillan.

Branden, Nathaniel. 1996. *Taking responsibility.* New York: Simon and Schuster.

Burchardt, Tania, and John Hills. 1997. *Private welfare insurance and social security: Pushing the boundaries.* York: York Publishing Services, for the Joseph Rowntree Foundation.

Burtless, Gary. 1995. How much work should be expected of AFDC mothers? What supportive services are needed to increase their labor force participation? In R. Kent Weaver and William T. Dickens, eds., *Looking before we leap: Social science and welfare reform,* 58–62. Brookings Occasional Paper. Washington, D.C.: Governmental Studies Program, Brookings Institution.

Calabresi, Guido. 1970. *The costs of accidents.* New Haven: Yale University Press.

Cato Institute. 1996. Social Security privatization's Chilean model. *Cato Policy Report* 18, no. 1 (Jan.–Feb.): 3.

Checkland, S. G., and E. O. A. Checkland, eds. 1974. *The Poor Law report of 1834.* Harmondsworth: Penguin.

Chesher, R. 1985. Practical problems in coral reef utilization and management: A Tongan case study. *Proceedings of the Fifth International Coral Reef Congress* 4: 213–24.

Church, George J., and Richard Lacayo. 1995. Social insecurity. *Time,* March 20, pp. 24–32.

Clinton, William J. 1996a. Presidential news conference: Clinton says welfare bill is a "real step forward." *Congressional Quarterly Weekly Report* 54, no. 31 (August 3): 2216–8.

1996b. Statement upon signing H.R. 3734 [Welfare Reform Act of 1996]. *United States Code, Congressional and Administrative News, 104th Congress – Second Session*, 5: 2891–3.

Coase, R. H. 1937. The nature of the firm. *Economica* 4: 386–405.

1960. The problem of social cost. *Journal of Law & Economics* 3: 1–44.

Cohen, G. A. 1983. The structure of proletarian unfreedom. *Philosophy & Public Affairs* 12: 3–33.

Commission on Social Justice, U.K. Labour Party. 1994. *Social justice: Strategies for national renewal*. London: Vintage.

Cornuelle, Richard C. 1965. *Reclaiming the American dream*. New York: Random House.

Cowen, Tyler. 1998. *In praise of commercial culture*. Cambridge, Mass.: Harvard University Press.

Cox, W. Michael, and Richard Alm. 1995. By your own bootstraps. *Federal Reserve Bank of Dallas Annual Report*, 2–24.

Crosland, Anthony. 1954. *Future of socialism*. London: Jonathan Cape.

Daniels, Norman. 1988. *Am I my parents' keeper*? New York: Oxford University Press.

Danziger, Sheldon, and Peter Gottschalk, eds. 1993. *Uneven tides: Rising inequality in America*. New York: Russell Sage Foundation.

Danziger, Sheldon, Robert Haveman, and Robert Plotnick. 1981. How income transfer programs affect work, savings and income distribution. *Journal of Economic Literature* 19: 975–1028.

Dasgupta, Partha. 1993. *An inquiry into well-being and destitution*. Oxford: Clarendon Press.

Dauster, William G. 1996. Protecting social security and medicare. *Harvard Journal on Legislation* 33, no. 2 (Summer): 461–509.

de Swaan, Abram. 1988. *In the care of the state*. Oxford: Polity.

Demsetz, Harold. 1967. Toward a theory of property rights. *American Economic Review (Papers & Proceedings)* 57: 347–59.

Derthick, Martha. 1975. *Uncontrollable spending for social services grants*. Washington, D.C.: Brookings Institution.

Diamond, Peter, and Salvador Valdés-Prieto. 1994. Social security reform. In Barry Bosworth, Rudiger Dornbusch, and R. Labán, eds., *The Chilean economy*, 257–320. Washington, D.C.: Brookings Institution.

Drèze, Jacques H., and Edmond Malinvaud. 1994. Growth and employment: The scope for a European initiative. *European Economy (Reports & Studies)*, no. 1: 77–106.

Dukeminier, Jesse, and James E. Krier. 1993. *Property*, 3rd ed. Boston: Little, Brown.

Duncan, Greg J. 1984. *Years of poverty, years of plenty*. Ann Arbor: Institute for Social Research, University of Michigan.

Duncan, Greg J., and Jeanne Brooks-Gunn, eds. 1997. *Consequences of growing up poor*. New York: Russell Sage Foundation.

Dworkin, Gerald. 1985. Nuclear intentions. In Russell Hardin, John Mearsheimer, Gerald Dworkin, and Robert E. Goodin, eds., *Nuclear deterrence: Ethics and strategy*, 37–52. Chicago: University of Chicago Press.

Ecenbarger, William. 1996. What welfare did for Thomas Dutton. *Reader's Digest* 149 (December): 169–76.

Edin, Kathryn. 1991. Surviving the welfare system: How AFDC recipients make ends meet in Chicago. *Social Problems* 38: 462–74.

Edin, Kathryn, and Christopher Jencks. 1992. Reforming welfare. In Jencks, *Rethinking social policy: Race, poverty and the underclass*, 204–36. Cambridge, Mass.: Harvard University Press.

Ellickson, Robert C. 1993. Property in land. *Yale Law Journal* 102: 1315–1400.

Ellsberg, Daniel. 1956. Theory of the reluctant duelist. *American Economic Review* 46: 909–23.

Elman, Richard M. 1966. *The poorhouse state*. New York: Pantheon Books.

Emerson, Ralph Waldo. 1841. Self-reliance. In Emerson, *Collected Works*, ed. J. Slater, A. R. Ferguson, and J. F. Carr, 2: 25–51. Cambridge, Mass.: Harvard University Press, 1971.

Feinberg, Joel. 1970. *Doing and deserving*. Princeton: Princeton University Press.

Feldstein, Martin. 1996. The missing piece in policy analysis: Social security reform. *American Economic Review (Papers & Proceedings)* 86: 1–14.

Ferrara, Peter J. 1997. Privatization of social security: The transition issue. *Social Philosophy and Policy* 14, no. 2: 145–64.

Filmer, Robert. 1652/1991. *Patriarcha and other writings*. Ed. J. P. Sommerville. Cambridge: Cambridge University Press.

Folbre, Nancy. 1994. *Who pays for the kids? Gender and the structures of constraint*. London: Routledge.

Fosdick, Peggy, and Sam Fosdick. 1994. *Last chance lost?* York, Pa.: Irvin S. Naylor Publishing.

Frankfurt, Harry G. 1988. *The importance of what we care about*. Cambridge: Cambridge University Press.

Fraser, Nancy. 1994. After the family wage: Gender equity and the welfare state. *Political Theory* 22: 591–618.

Fraser, Nancy, and Linda Gordon. 1994. "Dependency" demystified: Inscriptions of power in a keyword of the welfare state. *Social Politics* 1 (Spring): 4–31. Originally published in *Signs* 19 (1994): 1–29.

Fried, Barbara. 1995. Wilt Chamberlain revisited: Nozick's "justice in transfer" and the problem of market-based distribution. *Philosophy and Public Affairs* 24: 226–45.

Friedlander, Daniel, and Gary Burtless. 1995. *Five years after: The long-term effects of welfare-to-work programs*. New York: Russell Sage Foundation.

Fukuyama, Francis. 1995. *Trust: The social virtues and the creation of prosperity*. New York: Free Press.

Galston, William A. 1991. *Liberal purposes*. Cambridge: Cambridge University Press.

Gans, Herbert J. 1995. *The war against the poor: The underclass and antipoverty policy*. New York: Basic Books.

Gauthier, David. 1997. Political contractarianism. *Journal of Political Philosophy* 5: 132–48.

Geddes, R. Richard, and Dean Lueck. 1997. Self-ownership and the rights of women. Fordham University economics working paper.

Gibson, D. M. 1985. The dormouse syndrome. *Australian and New Zealand Journal of Sociology* 21: 87–103.

Gilbert, Neil. 1995. *Welfare justice: Restoring social equity*. New Haven: Yale University Press.

Gilder, George. 1987. Welfare's "new consensus": The collapse of the American family. *Public Interest*, no. 89: 20–5.

Gilligan, Carol, and Mary Field Belenky. 1980. A naturalistic study of abortion decisions. In Robert L. Selman and Regina Yando, eds., *Clinical-developmental psychology: New directions for child development* no. 7, 69–90. San Francisco: Jossey-Bass.

Gomez, E., A. Alcala, and A. San Diego. 1981. Status of Philippine coral reefs – 1981. *Proceedings of the Fourth International Coral Reef Symposium* 1: 275–85.

Goodin, Robert E. 1982. *Political theory and public policy*. Chicago: University of Chicago Press.

1985a. Erring on the side of kindness in social welfare policy. *Policy Sciences* 18: 141–56.

1985b. *Protecting the vulnerable: Toward a reanalysis of our social responsibilities*. Chicago: University of Chicago Press.

1988. *Reasons for welfare*. Princeton: Princeton University Press.

1989. *No smoking: The ethical issues*. Chicago: University of Chicago Press.

1995. *Utilitarianism as a public philosophy*. Cambridge: Cambridge University Press.

1996. Institutionalizing the public interest. *American Political Science Review* 90: 331–43.

1998. Communities of enlightenment. *British Journal of Political Science*.

Goodin, Robert E., and Philip Pettit. 1986. The possibility of special duties. *Canadian Journal of Philosophy* 16: 651–76.

Gordon, Linda. 1994. *Pitied but not entitled: Single mothers and the history of welfare, 1890–1935*. Cambridge, Mass.: Harvard University Press.

Green, David G. 1985. *Working class patients and the medical establishment: Self-help in Britain from the mid-nineteenth century to 1948*. Aldershot: Gower.

1993. *Reinventing civil society: The rediscovery of welfare without politics*. London: IEA Health and Welfare Unit.

Green, David G., and Lawrence Cromwell. 1984. *Mutual aid or welfare state: Australia's friendly societies.* Sydney: Allen & Unwin.

Grose, Thomas K. 1996. Labor, social costs taking toll on governments. *USA Today,* September 19, B1–2.

Haminga, Bert. 1995. Demoralizing the labor market. *Journal of Political Philosophy* 3: 23–35.

Handler, Joel F. 1979. *Protecting the social service client.* New York: Academic Press.

Handler, Joel F., and Yeheskel Hasenfeld. 1991. *The moral construction of poverty: Welfare reform in America.* Newbury Park, Calif.: Sage.

Hardie, Ann. 1995. Why we're living longer. *Atlanta Journal Constitution,* August 28, A3.

Hardin, Garrett. 1968. A tragedy of the commons. *Science.* 162: 1243–8.

  1977. The ethical implications of carrying capacity. In G. Hardin and J. Baden, eds., *Managing the commons,* 112–26. San Francisco: W. H. Freeman.

Hardin, Russell, John Mearsheimer, Gerald Dworkin, and Robert E. Goodin, eds. 1985. *Nuclear deterrence: Ethics and strategy.* Chicago: University of Chicago Press.

Hart, H. L. A., and Tony Honoré. 1985. *Causation in the law.* 2nd ed. Oxford: Clarendon Press.

Head, Simon. 1996. The new, ruthless economy. *New York Review of Books* 43, no. 4 (February 29): 47–52.

Hechter, Michael. 1983. A theory of group solidarity. In Hechter, ed., *Microfoundations of macrosociology,* 16–57. Philadelphia: Temple University Press.

  1987. *Principles of group solidarity.* Berkeley: University of California Press.

Held, Virginia. 1980. Introduction. In Held, ed., *Property, profits, and economic justice.* Belmont, Calif.: Wadsworth.

Himmelfarb, Gertrude. 1984. *The idea of poverty.* London: Faber & Faber.

  1994a. *The de-moralization of society: From Victorian values to modern values.* New York: Knopf.

  1994b. A demoralized society. *Public Interest,* no. 117: 57–80.

Hinderaker, John H., and Scott W. Johnson. 1996. Wage wars. *National Review,* April 22, pp. 34–8.

Hirsch, Fred. 1976. *Social limits to growth.* Cambridge, Mass.: Harvard University Press.

Hochschild, Jennifer L. 1991. The politics of the estranged poor. *Ethics* 101: 560–78.

  1995. *Facing up to the American dream.* Princeton: Princeton University Press.

Hohfeld, Wesley Newcomb. 1919. *Fundamental legal conceptions.* New Haven: Yale University Press.

Holzer, Harry J. 1996. *What employers want: Job prospects for less-educated workers*. New York: Russell Sage Foundation.

House Republicans. 1994. *Contract with America*. New York: Times Books, Random House.

Hume, David. 1760. Of the original contract. In Hume, *Essays, literary, moral and political*, pt. 2, chap. 12. London: A. Millar.

Husock, Howard. 1997. Standards versus struggle: The failure of public housing and the welfare state impulse. *Social Philosophy and Policy* 14: 69–94.

Ikeda, Sanford. 1997. *Dynamics of the mixed economy: Toward a theory of interventionism*. New York: Routledge.

Jencks, Christopher. 1992. *Rethinking social policy: Race, poverty and the underclass*. Cambridge, Mass.: Harvard University Press.

Jencks, Christopher, and Susan Mayer. 1996. Do official poverty rates provide useful information about trends in children's economic welfare? Working paper.

Jencks, Christopher, and Paul E. Peterson, eds. 1991. *The urban underclass*. Washington, D.C.: Brookings Institution.

Kasarda, J. D. 1990. Structural factors affecting the location and timing of urban underclass growth. *Urban Geography* 11: 234–64.

Katz, Jeffrey L. 1996a. Provisions of the welfare bill. *Congressional Quarterly Weekly Report* 54, no. 31 (August 3): 2192–6.

    1996b. Welfare showdown looms as GOP readies plan. *Congressional Quarterly Weekly Report* 54, no. 30 (July 27): 2115–9.

Kiewiet, D. Roderick. 1983. *Micropolitics and macroeconomics*. Chicago: University of Chicago Press.

King, Desmond S. 1995. *Actively seeking work?* Chicago: University of Chicago Press.

Kittay, Eva Feder. 1995. Taking dependency seriously: The Family and Medical Leave Act considered in light of the social organization of dependency work and gender equality. *Hypatia* 10: 8–29.

    1996. Equality, feminism and dependency work. Paper presented to the Annual Meetings of the American Political Science Association, San Francisco.

    1997. Human dependency and Rawlsian equality. In Diana T. Meyers, ed., *Rethinking the self*. Boulder: Westview Press.

Kreps, David M. 1990. Corporate culture and economic theory. In James Alt and Kenneth Shepsle, eds., *Perspectives on positive political economy*, 90–143. Cambridge: Cambridge University Press.

Land, Hilary. 1978. Who cares for the family? *Journal of Social Policy* 7: 257–84.

Levitan, Sar A. 1990. *Programs in aid of the poor*. Baltimore: Johns Hopkins University Press.

Lewis, Jane. 1995. The problem of lone mother families in twentieth century Britain. Discussion Paper WSP/114, Welfare State Program, STICERD, London School of Economics.

Lindbeck, Assar, Per Molander, Torsten Persson, Olof Petersson, Agnar Sandmo, Birgitta Swedenborg, and Niels Thygesen. 1994. *Turning Sweden around*. Cambridge, Mass.: MIT Press.

Littlechild, S. C., and J. Wiseman. 1984. Principles of public policy relevant to smoking. *Policy Studies* 4, no. 3: 54–67.

Locke, John. 1690/1960. *Second treatise of government*. Ed. P. Laslett. Cambridge: Cambridge University Press.

Luker, Kristin. 1996. *Dubious conceptions: The politics of teenage pregnancy*. Cambridge, Mass.: Harvard University Press.

Lundberg, Shelly, and Robert D. Plotnick. 1995. Adolescent premarital childbearing: Do economic incentives matter? *Journal of Labor Economics* 13: 177–200.

Mabbott, J. D. 1939. Punishment. *Mind* 48: 152–67.

Malthus, T. R. 1803/1992. *Essay on the principle of population*. 5th ed. Ed. Donald Winch. Cambridge: Cambridge University Press.

Mautner, Thomas. 1982. Locke on original appropriation. *American Philosophical Quarterly* 19: 259–70.

Mayer, Susan E. 1997. *What money can't buy*. Cambridge, Mass.: Harvard University Press.

McAllister, Ian, Rhonda Moore, and Toni Makkai. 1991. *Drugs in Australian society: Patterns, attitudes and policies*. Sydney: Longman Cheshire.

Mead, Lawrence M. 1986. *Beyond entitlement*. New York: Basic Books.

    1992. *The new politics of poverty: The nonworking poor in America*. New York: Basic Books.

Meade, James. 1995. *Full employment regained?* Cambridge: Cambridge University Press.

Mill, John Stuart. 1848. *Principles of political economy*. London: Parker & Son.

Miller, Fred D., Jr. 1995. *Nature, justice, and rights in Aristotle's* Politics. New York: Oxford University Press.

Mitchell, Ronald B. 1994a. *International oil pollution at sea: Environmental policy and treaty compliance*. Cambridge, Mass.: MIT Press.

    1994b. Regime design matters: International oil pollution and treaty compliance. *International Organization* 48: 425–58.

Moffitt, Robert. 1992. Incentive effects of the U.S. welfare system: A review. *Journal of Economic Literature* 30: 1–61.

Morris, Jenny. 1993. *Independent lives: Community care and disabled people*. London: Macmillan.

Moynihan, Daniel Patrick. 1996. Congress builds a coffin. *New York Review of Books* 43, no. 1 (January 11): 33–6.

Murray, Charles. 1984. *Losing ground: American social policy, 1950–80*. New York: Basic Books.

1985. Helping the poor: A few modest proposals. *Commentary* 79, no. 5: 27–34.

1994. Does welfare bring more babies? *Public Interest*, no. 115: 17–30.

1995. The next British revolution. *Public Interest*, no. 118: 3–29.

Myrdal, Gunnar. 1940. *Population: A problem for democracy.* Cambridge, Mass.: Harvard University Press.

Nagel, Thomas. 1991. *Equality and partiality.* New York: Oxford University Press.

Nash, J. Madeleine. 1996. Wrecking the reefs. *Time*, September 30, pp. 60–2.

Nechyba, Thomas J. 1997. Social approval, values, and AFDC. Stanford University economics working paper.

Nelson, Barbara J. 1990. The origins of the two-channel welfare state: Workmen's compensation and mothers' aid. In Linda Gordon, ed., *Women, the state and welfare*, 123–51. Madison: University of Wisconsin Press.

Novak, Michael, et al. 1987. *A community of self-reliance: The new consensus on family and welfare.* Report of the Working Seminar on the Family and American Welfare Policy. Washington, D.C.: American Enterprise Institute.

Nozick, Robert. 1969. Newcomb's problem and two principles of choice. In Nicholas Rescher, ed., *Essays in Honor of C. G. Hempel*, 114–46. Dordrecht: Reidel.

1993. *The nature of rationality.* Princeton: Princeton University Press.

Offe, Claus, and Rolf G. Heinze. 1992. *Beyond employment: Time, work, and the informal economy*, trans. Alan Braley. Oxford: Polity.

Orloff, Ann Shola. 1993. Gender and the social rights of citizenship: The comparative analysis of gender relations and welfare states. *American Sociological Review* 58: 303–28.

Ostrom, Elinor, Roy Gardner, and James Walker. 1994. *Rules, games, and common pool resources.* Ann Arbor: University of Michigan Press.

Palmer, Tom G. 1990. Are patents and copyrights morally justified? The philosophy of property rights and ideal objects. *Harvard Journal of Law and Public Policy* 13: 817–65.

Parfit, Derek. 1984. *Reasons and persons.* Oxford: Clarendon Press.

Patashnik, Eric. 1995. Credible commitments? The politics of federal trust funds. Paper presented to the Annual Meetings of the American Political Science Association, Chicago.

Pateman, Carole. 1988. The patriarchal welfare state. In Amy Gutmann, ed., *Democracy and the welfare state*, 231–60. Princeton: Princeton University Press.

Petchesky, Rosalind Pollack. 1981. Antiabortion, antifeminism and the rise of the new right. *Feminist Studies* 7: 206–46.

Pitsch, Peter K. 1995. Creative destruction and the innovation age. Hudson Briefing Paper no. 179. Indianapolis.

Piven, Frances Fox, and Richard A. Cloward. 1971. *Regulating the poor*. New York: Pantheon.

Porter, Michael E. 1990. *The competitive advantage of nations*. New York: Free Press.

Privatization of pensions in Latin America. 1994. *International Review of Labour* 133, no. 1: 134–41.

Rappaport, Michael B. 1992. The private provision of unemployment insurance. *Wisconsin Law Review* 61: 61–129.

Rawls, John. 1958. Justice as fairness. *Philosophical Review* 67: 164–94.

1971. *Theory of justice*. Cambridge, Mass.: Harvard University Press.

Reich, Charles A. 1963. Midnight welfare searches and the Social Security Act. *Yale Law Journal* 72: 1347–60.

Reich, Robert B. 1991. *The work of nations: Preparing ourselves for twenty-first century capitalism*. New York: Knopf.

Roemer, John E. 1994. *A future for socialism*. Cambridge, Mass.: Harvard University Press.

Rohrschneider, Richard. 1988. Citizens' attitudes toward environmental issues: Selfish or selfless? *Comparative Political Studies* 21: 347–67.

Rose, Carol. 1985. Possession as the origin of property. *University of Chicago Law Review* 52: 73–88.

1986. The comedy of the commons: Custom, commerce, and inherently public property. *University of Chicago Law Review* 53: 711–87.

Rose, Richard, and B. Guy Peters. 1979. *Can government go bankrupt?* London: Macmillan.

Rothschild, Emma. 1996. The debate on economic and social security in the late eighteenth century: Lessons of a road not taken. *Development and Change* 27: 331–51.

Sagoff, Mark. 1988. *The economy of the earth*. Cambridge: Cambridge University Press.

Sainsbury, Diane. 1996. *Gender, equality and welfare states*. Cambridge: Cambridge University Press.

Samuelson, Paul A. 1954. The pure theory of public expenditure. *Review of Economics & Statistics* 36: 387–89.

Samuelson, Robert J. 1996. Great expectations. *Newsweek*, January 8, pp. 24–33.

Sanders, John T. 1987. Justice and the initial acquisition of private property. *Harvard Journal of Law and Public Policy* 10: 367–99.

Sapiro, Virginia. 1990. The gender basis of American social policy. In Linda Gordon, ed., *Women, the state and welfare*, 36–54. Madison: University of Wisconsin Press.

Sartorius, Rolf. 1984. Persons and property. In Ray Frey, ed., *Utility and rights*, 196–214. Minneapolis: University of Minnesota Press.

Scanlon, T. M., Jr. 1988. The significance of choice. *Tanner Lectures* 8: 149–216.

Scarlett, Lynn. 1994. Clear thinking about the earth. In John Baden, ed., *Environmental Gore*, 249–56. San Francisco: Pacific Research Institute.

Schansberg, D. Eric. 1996. *Poor policy*. Boulder, Colo.: Westview Press.

Schelling, Thomas C. 1986. Whose business is good behavior? In W. Knowlton and R. Zeckhauser, eds., *American society: Public and private responsibilities*, 153–80. Cambridge, Mass.: Ballinger.

Schmidtz, David. 1990. Justifying the state. *Ethics* 101: 89–102.

   1991. *Limits of government*. Boulder, Colo.: Westview Press.

   1992. Rationality within reason. *Journal of Philosophy* 89: 445–66.

   1994. Choosing ends. *Ethics* 104: 226–51.

   1995. *Rational choice and moral agency*. Princeton: Princeton University Press.

Schoeman, Ferdinand, ed. 1987. *Responsibility, character and the emotions*. Cambridge: Cambridge University Press.

Schorr, Alvin. 1980. "*. . . Thy father and thy mother. . .*": A second look at filial responsibility and family policy. Washington, D.C.: Government Printing Office.

Sen, Amartya. 1981. *Poverty and famines*. Oxford: Clarendon Press.

   1996. Fertility and coercion. *University of Chicago Law Review* 63: 1035–61.

Shanas, E., and G. F. Streib, eds. 1965. *Social structure and the family: Generational relations*. Englewood Cliffs, N.J.: Prentice-Hall.

Shapiro, Daniel. 1997. Can old-age social insurance be justified? *Social Philosophy and Policy* 14, no. 2: 116–44.

Short, Eugenie D. 1985. FDIC settlement practices and the size of failed banks. *Economic Review* (March): 12–20.

Short, Eugenie D., Jeffrey W. Gunther, and Kelly Klemme. 1991. A perspective on banking reform. *Financial Industry Issues* (Third Quarter): 1–4.

Short, Eugenie D., and Kenneth J. Robinson. 1991. Deposit insurance reform in the post-FIRREA environment: Lessons from the Texas deposit market. *Quarterly Report* 45: 128–34.

Siegel, Fred. 1996. Planned disaster. *New Democrat* (November–December): 14–18.

Simmons, John. 1992. *The Lockean theory of rights*. Princeton: Princeton University Press.

Simon, Herbert A. 1954. A behavioral theory of rational choice. *Quarterly Journal of Economics* 69: 99–118.

Skocpol, Theda. 1992. *Protecting soldiers and mothers: The political origins of social policy in the United States*. Cambridge, Mass.: Harvard University Press.

Slovic, Paul, Daniel Kahneman, and Amos Tversky, eds. 1982. *Judgment under uncertainty*. Cambridge: Cambridge University Press.

Smiles, Samuel. 1859/1996. *Self-help*. London: J. Murray. Reprinted with a foreword by Lord Harris of High Cross, London: IEA Health and Welfare Unit.

Sosa, Ernest, ed. 1975. *Causation and conditionals*. Oxford: Oxford University Press.

Steiner, Gilbert Y. 1981. *The futility of family policy*. Washington, D.C.: Brookings Institution.

Steiner, Hillel. 1974–5. Individual liberty. *Proceedings of the Aristotelian Society* 75: 33–50.

Steiner, Hillel. 1994. *Essay on rights*. Oxford: Blackwell.

Tanner, Michael. 1996. *The end of welfare*. Washington, D.C.: Cato Institute.

Tanner, Michael, Stephen Moore, and David Hartman. 1995. The work vs. welfare trade-off. *Policy Analysis* 240: 1–53.

Taylor, Charles. 1976. Responsibility for self. In Amelie Rorty, ed., *The identities of persons*, 281–99. Berkeley: University of California Press.

   1985. *Human agency and language: Philosophical papers 1*. Cambridge: Cambridge University Press.

Thompson, E. P. 1980. *The making of the English working class*. Harmondsworth: Penguin.

Thomson, Judith Jarvis. 1990. *The realm of rights*. Cambridge, Mass.: Harvard University Press.

Thurow, Lester C. 1996. *The future of capitalism: How today's economic forces will shape tomorrow's world*. New York: Morrow.

Tilton, Timothy A. 1990. *The political theory of Swedish social democracy*. Oxford: Clarendon Press.

Titmuss, Richard M. 1958. The social division of welfare: Some reflections on the search for equity. In Titmuss, *Essays on "the welfare state,"* 34–55. London: Allen & Unwin.

Tocqueville, Alexis de. 1835/1983. Address to the Royal Academy of Cherbourg. Reprinted as "Memoir on pauperism," trans. Seymour Drescher, *Public Interest*, no. 70 (Winter): 102–20.

Tollison, Robert D., and Richard E. Wagner. 1988. *Smoking and the state: Social costs, rent seeking and public policy*. Lexington, Mass.: D.C. Heath/Lexington Books.

Townsend, Peter. 1957. *The family life of old people*. London: Routledge & Kegan Paul.

Tully, James. 1994. Aboriginal property and Western theory: Recovering a middle ground. *Social Philosophy and Policy* 11: 42–62.

Ungerson, Clare. 1987. *Policy is personal: Sex, gender and informal care*. London: Tavistock.

United Nations. 1995. Current issues in social security policy. In UN Department for Economic and Social Information and Policy Analysis, *World economic and social survey 1995: Current trends and policies in the world economy*, 263–82. E/1995/50, ST/ESA, 243. New York: United Nations.

U.S. Census Bureau. 1995. *Statistical abstract of the United States: 1995*. 115th ed. Washington, D.C.: Government Printing Office.

1996a. *Income, poverty, and valuation of noncash benefits: 1994*. Series P60-189. Washington, D.C.: Government Printing Office.

1996b. *Money income in the United States: 1995*. Current Population Reports. Series P60-193. Washington, D.C.: Government Printing Office.

1996c. *65+ in the United States*. Current Population Reports. Series P23-190. Washington, D.C.: Government Printing Office.

U.S. Congress. 1996. Personal Responsibility and Work Opportunity Reconciliation Act of 1996 [Welfare Reform Act of 1996]. PL 104-193 [HR 3734], August 22, 1996, 100 Stat 2105.

U.S. Department of Labor. 1995. *Consumer expenditure survey, 1992–93*. Bureau of Labor Statistics. Bulletin no. 2462. Washington, D.C.: Government Printing Office.

1996. *Consumer expenditures in 1994*. Bureau of Labor Statistics. Washington, D.C.: Government Printing Office.

U.S. House of Representatives. 1996. House Report on Personal Responsibility and Work Opportunity Reconciliation Act of 1996. House Report No. 104-651. *United States Code, Congressional and Administrative News, 104th Congress – Second Session*, 5: 2183–648.

Van Parijs, Philippe. 1991. Why surfers should be fed: The liberal case for an unconditional basic income. *Philosophy and Public Affairs* 20: 101–31.

Vobejda, Barbara. 1996. Clinton sets teen welfare standards. *Washington Post*. Reprinted in *Guardian Weekly* 154, no. 19 (May 12): 16.

Waldron, Jeremy. 1993a. Welfare and the images of charity. In Waldron, *Liberal rights*, 225–49. Cambridge: Cambridge University Press.

1993b. When justice replaces affection: The need for rights. In Waldron, *Liberal rights*, 370–91. Cambridge: Cambridge University Press.

Weaver, R. Kent, and William T. Dickens, ed. 1995. *Looking before we leap: Social science and welfare reform*. Brookings Occasional Paper. Washington, D.C.: Governmental Studies Program, Brookings Institution.

Weitzman, Lenore J. 1985. *The divorce revolution: The unexpected social and economic consequences for women and children in America*. New York: Free Press.

Welfare Reform Act. *See* U.S. Congress 1996.

Wikler, Daniel. 1978. Persuasion and coercion for health: Ethical issues in government efforts to change life-styles. *Health & Society* (now *Milbank*

Quarterly) 56: 383–438.

1987. Personal responsibility for illness. In D. van de Veer and T. Regan, eds., *Health care ethics*, 326–58. Philadelphia: Temple University Press.

Williams, Bernard. 1973. Critique of utilitarianism. In J. J. C. Smart and B. Williams, *Utilitarianism, for and against*, 75–150. Cambridge: Cambridge University Press.

1981. *Moral luck*. Cambridge: Cambridge University Press.

Williamson, Oliver E. 1985. *The economic institutions of capitalism: Firms, markets, relational contracting*. New York: Free Press.

Williamson, Oliver E., and Sidney G. Winter, eds. 1991. *The nature of the firm: Origins, evolution, and development*. New York: Oxford University Press.

Wilson, J. R. S. 1978. In one another's power. *Ethics* 88: 299–315.

Wilson, William Julius. 1987. *The truly disadvantaged: The inner city, the underclass, and public policy*. Chicago: University of Chicago Press.

1991. *The truly disadvantaged* revisited. *Ethics* 101: 593–609.

1996a. The poorest of the urban poor: Race, class and social isolation in America's inner-city ghettos. In Martin Blumer and Anthony M. Rees, eds., *Citizenship today*, 223–48. London: UCL Press.

1996b. *When work disappears: The world of the new urban poor*. New York: Knopf.

Wolf, Richard. 1997a. In Florida, welfare reform standing test of time. *USA Today*, May 12, p. 6.

1997b. Six-month welfare drop sets record. *USA Today*, June 9, p. 3.

Worsham, James. 1996. Taking the taxes out of health care. *Nation's Business* 84 (December): 29–30.

Young, Iris Marion. 1995. Mothers, citizenship and independence: A critique of pure family values. *Ethics* 105: 535–56.

Index

Abbot, Edith, 136n88
able-bodied poor, 100–3, 119, 172–3, 176
Aborigines, 16–17, 91
abortion, 105, 110n35, 112
accidents, 174–5
Ackerman, Bruce, 82–3
ACT Government's Heroin Task Force, 131n79
addiction, 131n79
advantage, 80n151; overall/mutual, 87n161
Aesop, 103
African Americans, 15, 65
Ahmad, Ehtisham, 161n131
Aid to Dependent Children, 185n196
Aid to Families with Dependent Children (AFDC), 18, 20, 104, 109, 124, 132, 136, 180n183, 182n119, 185n196; effects of, 78; spending for, 106–7; time limits on, 19n27, 110
Akerlof, George A., 112n40
Alcala, A., 31n49
alienation, 76
Alm, Richard, 39n61, 40n64
altruism, 76
Amana colonies, 54
American Enterprise Institute, 101n4, 111n36, 125, 134n85, 141n96
Anscombe, G. E. M., 174n168
appropriation: the commons before, 31–3; justification of, 33–6; not zero-sum game, 29–31; *see also* original appropriation
Arneson, Richard J., 99n1, 113n44
Arnold, N. Scott, 60n105
arts (the), 4n1
"Asian tiger," 190, 191, 192
assistance to others: legally compelled, 135–8, 142–4

Atiyah, P. S., 157n119
Atkinson, A. B., 123n58, 160n128, 188n203, 192n212
Atlantic green turtle, 31–2
Australia, 109n32, 166n144
"availability for work" tests, 186n198

babies: born destitute, 77–9
Badhwar, Neera Kapur, 119n50
Baker, Edwin, 9
Baldwin, Peter, 109n32
Ball, Robert M., 167n147
Bane, Mary Jo, 103n13, 105n18, 108n29, 109nn31,32, 110n34, 125n63, 138n93, 173n161, 177n176
Barr, Nick, 160n128
Barro, Robert J., 61n107
Barry, Brian, 148n107, 168, 169n152
Bartlett, Bruce, 42n75
basic income: policy, 187n201; guaranteed, 91–2; unconditional, 123n58, and right to, 85n158, 89, 91
Baugher, Eleanor, 40n66, 41n70
Becker, Gary, 15n16
behavior modification, 170, 171
Beito, David T., 65, 67, 68, 70n134
Belenky, Mary Field, 110n35
Bentham, Jeremy, 127n68, 175
Berger, Brigette, 142n97
Berger, Peter L., 142n97, 161n132
Berman, Harold, 161n130
Beveridge, William, 185n195
birth control, ban on: Hutterites, 55–6
blacks, 114, 132; *see also* African Americans
blame, 5, 150, 156, 158; in accidents, 174–5; allocating, 170; assigning, 10–12; for health problems, 106; in planning failures, 130; for poverty, 101–2; structural unemployment

blame (*cont.*)
   and, 188–9; for unplanned
   pregnancy, 111, 112–13
blame responsibility, 7n5, 150–4
blameless (the): punishing, 173–7
blaming the victim, 173
Blaug, Marc, 100n2
Block, Fred, 103n11
Blomfield, L., 100n2
Blum, Lawrence A., 119n50
Boettke, Peter J., 60n105
Booth, Charles, 144n103
Boskin, Michael, 38
bounded rationality, 130n77
Branden, Nathaniel, 22n34
Brooks-Gunn, Jeanne, 74
Buchanan, James, 76n148
Burchardt, Tania, 162nn134,135
Buridan's ass, 130n78
Burtless, Gary, 126nn65,67, 180n183

Calabresi, Guido, 152n113, 157n119
Canada: Great Depression, 14
"caring" work, 185n194, 188n203
carrying capacity of land, 46–8
categorical benefits, nondiscretionary,
   123n58
Cato Institute, 162n134
causal responsibility: disaggregating,
   158n122
causation, 159; joint, 11; and public
   policy, 169–71
causes: collectivity of, 160; folly of
   disentangling, 156–8
Cayman Farm, 32–3
Cayman Islands, 32–3
central state; *see* state
"character test," 176
charity, 20, 63, 79, 123n57
Checkland, E. O. A., 100n2, 101n3,
   172nn158,159, 173n160
Checkland, S. G., 100n2, 101n3,
   172nn158,159, 173n160
Chesher, R., 31n49
Chicago: African Americans in, 65
child care, 101n4
child poverty rates, 40–1
child rearing, 45; commodification of,
   45n78
child support, 111, 137–9
children, 5, 22, 36, 93, 94, 95, 106;
   "collateral damage" to, 174; in/and
   market society, 16; parents'
   investment in educating, 62n112;
   preserving resources for, 31–2, 35;
   punishing, 90; unequal opportunities
   of, 74; of unwed mothers, 78, 124; of

welfare mothers, 111, 112, 113,
   122n55; and welfare programs, 19,
   20; *see also* babies
"children having children," 102
Chile, 161, 166n146
choice(s): in dependency, 119; lack of,
   in dependent's perspective, 123, 124,
   125; taking responsibility for, 11; in
   throffers, 181–2, 183; of values and
   preferences, 99n1; of welfare
   mothers, 110–12
Church, George J., 61n109, 89n163
Civilian Conservation Corps, 186n197
Clinton, Hillary, 60
Clinton, William J., 15, 63, 102n7, 104,
   105n20, 136
Cloward, Richard A., 124n60
Coase, R. H., 192n210
Cobb-Douglas production functions,
   192
coercion: in workfare, 181n184
cohabitation rules, 124
Cohen, G. A., 126n66
collateral damage, 174
collective action, 191n207, 195
collective provision: efficiencies of,
   168–71
collective responsibility, 56, 72, 78–9,
   145–54; versus individual
   responsibility, 7–9; institutions of,
   63–4; for medical care, 67; in
   public/communal property, 48
collective sense of ourselves, 194–5
collectivism: alternative kinds of, 145–9
collectivization of responsibility, 80,
   146–8, 149; classic case for, 168–71;
   classic case for, restated, 155–71;
   compulsory state-based, 162–7; in
   friendly societies, 72; for risks, 158–67
Collingwood, R. G., 170
command economies, 146
Commission on Social Justice, 105n19
commodification of child rearing, 45n78
common good, 4n3, 195
common law, 33–4
common property: management of, 57
commons (the): before appropriation,
   31–3; parceling, 30n48; preserving,
   33; regulation of, 56–7; unregulated,
   34, 35, 36, 46–8, 49, 52
commons problems, 76; *see also* tragedy
   of the commons
communal dining and worship:
   Hutterites, 55
communal ownership, 76, 95
communal property, 22–3, 46, 48–9, 50,
   51

communal responsibility, 58
communes, 48–9, 53–6, 58, 59; monitoring costs in, 50; right of exclusion, 25; two-member, 76n150
communitarians, 77, 193–4
community: responsibility and, 44–59; sense of, 76, 77
Community of self-reliance, A (Novak et al.), 101n4, 134n85, 141n96
competence, 72n141; assumption of, 75; of poor people, 74
Congressional Budget Office, 37
consequences, 86–8
conservation, 34, 46
conservatives, 64, 124–5, 127, 138–9, 141, 192–3
Consumer Expenditure Survey, 41n73
Consumer Price Index, 38
contract law, 52
Contract with America, 101n4, 103–4, 105n19, 141n96
"contributing factors with handles on them," 170
contributions: rewards according to, 91
control: exclusive, 58; local, 59; over one's life, 105, 133
Convention on International Trade in Endangered Species, 32
conventions, 52, 53; *see also* social conventions
cooperative ventures, 21; alternative to departure from status quo view, 91–3; capacity to contribute to, 93; friendly societies as, 80; individual contributions to, 44–6; *see also* society as cooperative venture for mutual advantage
coral reefs, 31–2
Cornuelle, Richard C., 161n133
"cost-pooling" strategies, 159n125
courts, 10–11
Cowen, Tyler, 4n1
Cox, W. Michael, 39n61, 40n64
credit, 10, 150
Cromwell, Lawrence, 65, 161n133
Crosland, Anthony, 169
culture, 6, 23; of poverty, 102
custom(s), 52; governance by, 56–8

Dale, Thomas, 53–4, 55, 59
Daniels, Norman, 128n72, 136n89
Danziger, Sheldon, 14, 19, 20, 60, 61, 193nn214,216
Dasgupta, Partha, 114n45, 141n91
Dauster, William G., 165n141
decision theory, 132n80
decisional shortcuts, 130

"deep pockets" principle, 152n113, 158n122, 164n140
democracy, direct, 69
Demsetz, Harold, 46, 47, 50, 51n88
dependability, 120–1
dependency, 18, 59, 62n113, 78, 107; defined, 116–17; from dependent's perspective, 123–7; on grown children, 144; as key word, 116–22; moralized definition of, 107, 118, 123, 139–40; objectionable/ unobjectionable, 118–22, 132n82; on parents, 137; reducing through deterrence, 173–4; and resource depletion, 159n125; of welfare mothers, 138; *see also* public dependency; welfare dependency
dependency culture, 133
Derthick, Martha, 165n142
"deserving poor," 101n4
destitution, 77–9, 86, 87
de Swaan, Abram, 100n2, 157n119, 160n127, 161n130, 163n137
determinism: free will versus, 99n1
deterrence: morality of, 172–89; as punishing the blameless, 173–7
Diamond, Peter, 162n134
Dickens, William T., 101n4, 108n29
discretionary power: over welfare resources, 123, 124
disincentives, 173, 175–6, 177
distributional struggle: politics as, 190–1
doctors: friendly societies, 65, 66, 69
"double effect" doctrine, 174n168
Drèze, Jacques H., 192n212
Dukeminier, Jesse, 47nn80,81
Duncan, Greg J., 74, 108n28
Dutton, Thomas, 16–17
Dworkin, Gerald, 174n168
dynamic perspective, 6–7, 43, 61

Ecenbarger, William, 16–17
economic collectivism, 146, 147
economic depression, 162–3
economic growth, 192–3
economic relations, 121
Economist, 38n57, 41n68
Edin, Kathryn, 125n64, 176n170, 182n189
Edison, Thomas, 45, 85
efficacy, 94
efficiencies: of collective provision, 168–71
egoism: assumption of, 5
Elizabethan Poor Law of 1601, 136
Ellickson, Robert, 46, 48, 49–50, 51, 53, 54n93, 56, 57

Ellsberg, Daniel, 183
Ellwood, David T., 103n13, 105n18,
    108n29, 109nn31,32, 110n34,
    125n63, 138n93, 173n161, 177n176
Elman, Richard, 18
Emerson, Ralph Waldo, 103n12
employer-provided benefit packages, 67
employment, 125–6, 178–9; *see also* job
    market
Endangered Species Act, 32–3
England: health care, 66, 68
equal opportunity, 84–6, 95
equal respect: and equalization, 82–6
equal shares, 82–4, 89, 91, 92, 95
equalization: equal respect and, 82–6
Escambia County, Florida, 19n27
exclusion, right of, 25, 26, 35, 48, 56
expropriation, 27–8
external forces, reliance on, 117–18,
    122, 133–4
externalities: cost of, 49, 50, 55;
    internalizing, 24; local versus
    remote, 49–53; negative/positive, 8,
    24, 34, 45, 52
externality problems: in property
    ownership, 48–9
externalized responsibility, 8–9, 11, 18,
    21–2, 47, 59, 64, 79, 80; entitlement
    to, 59; federal deposit insurance as,
    12–14; through welfare programs,
    73; in welfare state, 77

failure of will, 125
fairness, 113n44
false negatives/positives, 109n33
familialism, 136, 141
family: compelling assistance from,
    142–4; ideal of, 142; reliance on,
    117, 118–19, 122, 134, 135, 136–8,
    139, 141
family breakdown, 142–3
family household, 56
family members, responsibilities of, 148
"family responsibility" statutes, 136
family values, 141–4
fathers: child support, 137–9
fault, 5, 11, 156–8, 159; apportioning,
    159
federal deposit insurance, 12–14
Federal Deposit Insurance Corporation
    (FDIC), 12–14, 166n145, 167n148
Feinberg, Joel, 170n155
Feldstein, Martin, 61, 193n213
feminists, 124, 185n196
feminization of poverty, 115
Ferrara, Peter J., 90n165
Filmer, Robert, 26n37

first possession principle, 83–4, 95
Folbre, Nancy, 157n120
Fosdick, Peggy, 31n49
France, 113n43; unemployment rate, 15
Frankfurt, 99n1
Fraser, Nancy, 101n4, 124n61, 185n196
fraternal feeling, 76–7
free-riding, 59, 88, 113
free will: versus determinism, 99n1
freedom: throffers and, 181n185
French *Code civil*, 136n89
Friedlander, Daniel, 180n183
friendly societies, 63–9, 74–5, 79, 80,
    161, 163n137; participation in, 65–6;
    possibility of, in twenty-first century,
    69–72; reasons for decline of, 67–9
friends: reliance on, 117, 118–19, 122,
    134, 135, 139
Fukuyama, Francis, 63
full employment, 185–6
Full employment in a free society
    (Beveridge), 185n195
future generations, 27, 46; costs of
    current consumption to, 89;
    preserving opportunities for, 58; and
    resource appropriation, 36
Future of Socialism (Crosland), 169

Galston, William, 84
game(s): appropriation as, 33–6
Gans, Herbert J., 101n4, 102n8
Gardner, Roy, 58n102
Gauthier, David, 12n8, 106n23, 113n44
Geddes, R. Richard, 42n76
gender: in welfare dependence debates,
    114–15
Germany: unemployment rate in, 15
ghettos, 132
Gibson, D. M., 123n57
Gilbert, Neil, 101n4, 185n196
Gilder, George, 111n36
Gilligan, Carol, 110n35
Ginsberg, Mitchell, 18–19
Gomez, E., 31n49
good (the), theory of, 86–7
Goodin, Robert E., 5, 7n5, 12n8, 16, 19,
    61, 62, 70–1, 74, 87, 103nn10,13,
    109n33, 117nn47,49, 121n53,
    123nn57,58, 127nn68,69, 130n76,
    134n85, 136n90, 143n102,
    149nn109,110, 152n114, 154n116,
    169n153, 171n157, 175n169,
    176n173, 177n174, 192n208,
    194n218, 195n220
Gordon, Linda, 101n4, 115n46, 176n171
Gottschalk, Peter, 193n216
governance by custom, 56–8

government: and commodification of
child rearing, 45n78; in health care,
68, 70; in/and insurance programs,
71–2; and public property, 46;
redistribution by, 16, 60–1; role of,
57, 77; and welfare, 21, 78; welfare
responsibility of, 64
Grand Lodge of Maryland, 67
Great Depression, 14, 163n138
Green, David G., 64, 65, 66, 68n131,
161n133
Grose, Thomas K., 15n16
gross domestic product (GDP), 61–2, 73
group(s), 194; interaction of individuals
in, 148–9; internalized responsibility,
8; taking responsibility as, 23
group solidarity, 59
guarantee(s): to equal share regardless
of contribution, 59; of welfare, 78–9
guaranteed basic income; *see* basic
income
guaranteed provision, 9
guilds, 161
Gunther, Jeffrey W., 13n10

Haminga, Bert, 187n199
handicaps, 93
Handler, Joel F., 101n4, 105n18, 124n59
Hardie, Ann, 42n77
Hardin, Garrett, 22n35, 46n79
Hardin, Russell, 173n162
Harris, Lord, of High Cross, 103n12
Hart, H. L. A., 112n41
Hartman, David, 20n32
Hasenfeld, Yeheskel, 101n4, 105n18
Haveman, Robert, 14, 193n214
"having to" rely on public assistance:
moralized analysis of, 122n55,
135n86
Head, Simon, 184n192
health care, 63, 64–70, 74–5; adequacy
of, in friendly societies, 66
health care costs, 65
health maintenance organizations, 69
Hechter, Michael, 59, 67n130
Heinze, Rolf G., 125n64
helping others, 17, 20–1; helping people
who cannot help themselves, 5, 6, 7
Hills, John, 162nn134,135
Himmelfarb, Gertrude, 100n2, 102nn7,9
Hinderaker, John H., 37n55
Hirsch, Fred, 192n211
Hochschild, Jennifer L., 102n8
Hohfeld, Wesley Newcomb, 25n36
Holzer, Harry J., 125n63
Honoré, Tony, 112n41
hospitals, fraternal, 69–70

House Republicans, 101n4, 103–4,
105n19, 141n96
human commerce: as zero-sum game, 3,
85
Hume, David, 182n188
hunter-gatherers, 34–5
Husock, Howard, 6n4
Hutterites, 55–6, 58–9

Ikeda, Sanford, 13n13
illegitimacy rates, 111nn37,38
"impotent poor" (the), 119, 122n55,
172, 189
incentives, 5, 6, 178, 179; morality of,
172–89; opportunities versus,
177–80; perverse, 18
income, 37–40, 41; contingent on
production, 78; unearned, 92
income inequality, 73–4
income smoothing, 160n128
income support policy, 128n72
income transfers, 74, 92
individual responsibility, 22–3; versus
collective responsibility, 7–9; and
general welfare, 4–5, 95; in health
care/retirement, 72; and
internalizing responsibility, 58–9;
one's own welfare as, 5, 7; in private
property, 48; welfare state and, 64
individuals: providing for future
welfare, 167; are social products,
194; and social welfare, 145–6, 147
individualism, 135–6
individuation of moral responsibility,
147
inflation, 38
institutions, 5–6, 7; affect behavior,
87–8; of collective responsibility,
63–4; intermediary, 161; just, 86,
87; and self-esteem, 93; and taking
responsibility, 10, 11–12, 14–15, 21,
22, 94–6; that regulate appropriation,
33–4, 36; *see also* property institutions
insurance-based schemes, 157, 158–67
insurance programs, 70–1
intellectual property, 28n41
interactions, 148–9
International Order of Foresters, 66n125
internalized responsibility, 8–9, 10–11,
14, 24, 36, 46, 59, 160n126; in
agricultural practices, 57; in
collective sense, 72, 79, 80; in
friendly societies, 79; in health
care/retirement, 72; individual
responsibility and, 58–9; institutions
and, 94–5; justice of, 80; in market
society, 96; and material progress, 21;

internalized responsibility (*cont.*)
  privatization and, 52–3; property
  institutions in, 25, 27
inventions, 45–6
investments, 193n215
Israel: kibbutzim, 56n96
Italy, 15

James, Marquis, 72n139
Jamestown colony, 29, 53–6, 59, 78, 79,
  87, 88
Japan, 17
Jencks, Christopher, 41n68, 125n64,
  176n170, 178n177, 182n189
job creation, 15
job education and training programs,
  178–9, 180–1, 182
job market: as zero-sum game, 85–6
job opportunities, 125, 126
Johnson, Scott W., 37n55
justice, 80–96; as cluster concept, 82,
  83, 84, 85; conceptions of, 80–2, 86,
  95, 96; of status quo, 89

Kahn, Herman, 175
Kahneman, Daniel, 130n76
Kasarda, J. D., 125n63
Katz, Jeffrey L., 104n17
Katz, Michael L., 112n40
key words (social policy debates),
  116–44
Kittay, Eva Feder, 101n4, 112n39,
  136n87, 152n114, 185n194,
  188n203
kibbutzim, 56
Kiewiet, D. Roderick, 195n219
King, Desmond S., 105n18
Klemme, Kelly, 13n10
Knights and Daughters of Tabor, 70
Kreps, David M., 121n54
Krier, James E., 47nn80,81

labor inputs, 193; and product value,
  30n48
labor market, 126–7, 187–8
"labor permits," 187–8
Lacayo, Richard, 61n109, 89n163
Ladies Friends of Faith, 67
Lamison-White, Leatha, 40n66, 41n70
Land, Hilary, 185n194
large events, 49, 51–3, 55; communal
  regimes and, 53–6
"last clear chance" principle of
  responsibility, 112n41
latecomers: and original appropriation,
  29, 30
laws, 52
Levitan, Sar A., 40n65

Lewis, Jane, 101n4
liberalism, 194
liberties: rights differ from, 25–6
life insurance, 69, 71
life plans, 12n8, 128–9
Lindbeck, Assar, 192n12
Lindsay, John, 18
Littlechild, S. C., 154n116
Lloyds (co.), 164n140
Lockean proviso, 26–7, 28, 29, 35–6,
  47–8
Locke, John, 26–7, 30
Lueck, Dean, 42n76
Luker, Kristin, 111n37
Lundberg, Shelly, 18n22

Mabbott, J. D., 173n163
McAllister, Ian, 131n79
Makkai, Toni, 131n79
Malinvaud, Edmond, 192n212
Malthus, T. R., 100n2, 101n4, 111n38,
  113, 123nn57,58, 127–8, 143n100,
  172, 174, 175
market economy, 85
market society(ies), 3, 16, 17, 20, 24,
  45, 96; and human capital, 93; life
  in, 42; success in helping people
  prosper, 94–6
material progress, 3, 4; internalized
  responsibility in, 21
material well-being, 149, 155
Mautner, Thomas, 28n40
maximization, 129
maximizing individual/group, 191n207
Mayer, Susan, 41n68, 73–4
Mead, Lawrence M., 19n28, 72n141,
  102n8
Meade, James, 187n201
means testing, 66, 107, 142n99
medical care; *see* health care
medical insurance, 160; Australia,
  166n144
medical profession: and friendly
  societies, 65, 68
medical savings accounts, 72
Medicare, 106, 107, 164–5
medium events, 49, 50–1, 55
Metropolitan Life of New York, 71–2
Mexicans, 62
Microsoft software programs, 28
Mill, John Stuart, 127n69
Miller, Fred D., 87n161
mistakes, paying for, 14, 24
Mitchell, Ronald B., 170n156
Moffitt, Robert, 108n29, 111n38,
  138n93, 180n183
monitoring, 49, 59

monitoring costs, 50
Moore, Rhonda, 131n79
Moore, Stephen, 20n32
moral appropriateness/inappropriate-
    ness of relying on others, 122, 135
moral collectivism, 146, 147, 155
moral judgment, 138–9, 140; *see also*
    moralized definitions
moral recrimination, 158n123
moral responsibility, 149–54
moralism, 156n118; punitive, 101n4
morality: of incentives and
    disincentives, 172–89
moralized definitions, 144; cost of,
    138–41; of dependency, 107, 118,
    123, 139–40
Mormons, 54
Morris, Jenny, 144n105
mothers, abandoned, 138n93
Moynihan, Daniel Patrick, 73, 174n165
Murray, Charles, 111n37, 134n85
mutual aid, 10, 60–79, 135, 161
mutual aid societies, 58–9, 71, 75, 78
mutual insurance, 71, 161, 162, 163–4,
    167
mutual support: self-reliance and, 95
Myrdal, Gunnar, 113n43

Nagel, Thomas, 39, 91–2, 94
Nash, J. Madeleine, 31n50
National Health Service, 117n48
national income: distribution of,
    192n209
National Insurance (England), 66, 160
National Insurance Act (England), 65,
    68, 75
National Park Service, 25
Native American culture, 47n81
natural conditions, 54–5, 59
natural forces, reliance on, 119, 122,
    135
natural/unnatural dependencies,
    118–19
Nature Conservancy, 33n51
Nechyba, Thomas J., 17n20, 18n23
need-based redistribution, 60
needs: and need satisfaction, 9, 16
negative externalities, 8, 52; created by
    original appropriation, 34
negative-sum game, 25, 31, 35, 36
neighbors, 50, 51, 52, 53, 95
negligence, 174n167
Nelson, Barbara J., 115n46, 176n171
Neuhaus, Richard John, 161n132
New Age Democrats, 100, 103–4
New Deal, 63
New Labour Party (U.K.), 105n19

New Poor Law, 156
New Right, 103, 114, 161
Newcomb, William, 132n80
Newcomb's paradox, 131–2
no-fault insurance, 157–8
noncontributors, 93–4, 96
norms, 52; and conception of justice, 86;
    family-/community-based, 63; of
    individual responsibility, 64; of
    reciprocity, 148
Novak, Michael, 101n4, 103n14,
    111n36, 126n65, 134n85, 141n96,
    161n132, 174n165

Offe, Claus, 125n64
Old Age, Survivors, and Disability
    Insurance, 160
old-age pensioners, 143–4; *see also*
    pensions/pension plans
open-field agricultural practices, 57–8
opportunism, 129
opportunities, 6, 10; versus incentives,
    177–80; job, 125, 126
options, 183; perception of, 182n189;
    viable, 181–2; *see also* choice(s)
original appropriation, 25–36, 47;
    justification of, 58
Orloff, Ann Shola, 124n61
Ostrom, Ellinor, 58n102
out-of-wedlock births/pregnancies,
    17–18, 102n7
overconsumption, 48, 76
overuse, 34, 35

Palmer, Tom G., 28n41
Parfit, Derek, 114n45, 128n73
Patashnik, Eric, 165n142
Pateman, Carole, 124n60
paternalism, 124, 181n184, 182–3
patriarchy, 124, 143n101
pensions/pension plans, 69, 72,
    160n127, 161, 166n146; private,
    193; public, 192–3
people: right to extract benefits without
    contributing, 76; unable or unwilling
    to take responsibility for self/family,
    99, 100–6
perfectly competitive market, fantasy of,
    5, 166
personal responsibility, 136, 139, 145,
    150, 161; allocation of, 158; best
    exercised through collective agency,
    167; demands in, 127; ethos of, 78;
    failure to take, 133; and family
    values, 141, 142, 143; of fathers to
    pay child support, 137–8; moralized
    definition of, 139, 140–1, 144; and

personal responsibility (*cont.*)
  politics, 191; promoting through
    deterrence, 173–4; versus public
    dependency, 100–6; *see also*
    individual responsibility
"Personal Responsibility Act," 103–4
"personal responsibility agreement,
    136–7
Personal Responsibility and Work
    Opportunity Reconciliation Act of
    1966, 102n7, 103n10, 104, 105n19
personal responsibility for welfare, 100,
    114–15, 145, 179, 195; and
    economic growth, 192–3; *see also*
    taking responsibility for own welfare
personal responsibility ideal: structural
    unemployment and, 186–9
Petchesky, Rosalind Pollack, 110n35
Peters, B. Guy, 165n143
Peterson, Paul E., 178n177
Pettit, Philip, 149n109
Philadelphia: African Americans in, 65
Philippine islands, 31–2
philosophical collectivism, 146
Pigou, A. C., 127n68
Pinochet, General, 161
Pitsch, Peter K., 61n107
Piven, Frances Fox, 124n60
planning, 127–33
Plotnick, Robert D., 14, 18n22, 193n214
Pogge, Thomas, 69n133
"policy by pun," 151
policy context, 99–115
policy reform: effects of, 109–10
political collectivism, 146, 147, 155
political disarmament, possibility of,
    73–7
political philosophers/philosophy, 81–2,
    91
politics, 190–5
pollution control, 34, 170
poor (the), 94, 95; competency of, 74;
    deserving/undeserving, 156, 175,
    176–7; effect of welfare programs on,
    73–4; estranged, 102, 105–6, 125,
    192; and health care, 75;
    imprudence of, 127–8; left behind,
    14–20; meeting needs of, 62;
    nonworking, 73, 179; regulating,
    124; unemployed, 192
Poor Law of 1834, 123n57, 137n92,
    174–5
Poor Law reform, 100, 100n4
Poor Law Report of 1834, 173
Poor Law(s), 100, 111n38, 156, 175
poor laws, 136, 172
poor relief, 127–8, 175; aim of, 172n159

population cap: Hutterites, 55
population policy, 114
Port Jervis, New York, 68
Porter, Michael E., 184n192
positional goods, 192
positive externalities, 45
positive-sum game: appropriation is, 30,
    36; society as, 25
poverty, 36–43, 76; babies born into,
    77–9; blame for, 101–2; cure for, 11;
    dynamic aspect of, 42–3; rules of
    thumb for keeping out of, 129n75;
    welfare programs and, 60–1; among
    women, 114–15
poverty rates, 40–1
"poverty traps," 177n175
pregnancy, 110, 111, 112–13, 132, 133
preventive medicine, 66
principle of lesser eligibility, 172–4, 177
private property, 22–3, 24, 25, 49, 95;
    justifying, 28; and taking
    responsibility, 46
privatization, 47–8, 50–1, 52–3, 54, 56,
    168–9
procreation: welfare mothers, 114
production: supply and demand in, 75
productive effort, 3, 4, 16, 24; income
    contingent on, 78
productivity, 4, 19; reduced by welfare
    programs, 60–1
projects, 127
property institutions, 22, 25, 27, 36, 46,
    48, 52, 94, 95; evolution of, 47–8
property law, 24
property regimes: first possession rule,
    83–4; positive-sum, 46; private,
    49–50, 52, 53; *see also* communal
    property
property rights, 22, 25; custom in, 58
prosperity, 6, 21, 22, 23, 30–1, 86;
    conduciveness to, 87; prescription
    for, 95–6
provident dispensaries, 66
prudence, 127–33, 167
"prudential lifespan" model, 128n72
public dependency: personal
    responsibility versus, 100–6
public goods, 162n135
public health, 105–6
public interest, 195
public policy: incentives and deterrence
    in, 172–3; notions of causation and,
    169–71; senses of responsibility in,
    151; shifting from welfare to
    workfare, 180–4
public property, 46, 48, 49; ownership
    of, 57

public works program(s), 186n197
punishment: through deterrence,
    173–7

racism, 43, 114
Rappaport, Michael B., 71–2, 163n138
Rawls, John, 21n33, 81, 86–7, 113n44
Reagan, Ronald, 103
Reagan administration, 192
reciprocity, norms of, 148; in welfare
    dependency debate, 113n44
redistribution, 190; government-
    administered, 60, 62; reduction of
    poverty through, 60–1; through
    social insurance, 165–6
regulating access, 35, 36; see also
    restricting access
regulatory statutes, 52
Reich, Charles A., 124n59
Reich, Robert B., 184n192
reinsurance, 164n140, 166nn145,146,
    167n148
relational contracts, 121
reliance, 127–33;
    appropriate/inappropriate, 138–9;
    defined, 116–17; on external forces,
    117–18, 122; on family, 117, 118–19,
    122, 134, 135, 136–8, 139, 141; as
    key word, 116–22; on others, 121,
    134; on state, 139, 141; see also
    self-reliance
"reluctant duelist," 183
reproductive responsibility, 111–12
resource creation, 36; by first
    appropriators, 29, 30
resource depletion, 159n125
resources: increasing, 88; key, 52;
    migrating, 52–3; rearranging, 6–7;
    right to remove from commons, 36
responsibility: allocating, 158n122;
    collectivization of, 23, 59; and com-
    munity, 44–59; individualized, 24;
    joint, 10; as key word, 116; for one
    another's well-being, 148–9; for one's
    own welfare, 4n1, 147; personal
    versus collective, 167; reproductive,
    111–12; senses of, 145, 149–54;
    transformed sense of, 18; voluntarily
    assumed, 77; and welfare, 20, 21–33;
    see also taking responsibility and
    under specific types, e.g., collective
    responsibility; externalized re-
    sponsibility; individual responsibility;
    internalized responsibility
restricting access, 32; in communes, 48
retirement benefits, 90; see also
    pensions/pension plans

right (the): and the good, 86–7
rights: differ from liberties, 25–6;
    guaranteed, 9; welfare, 123
rights-based entitlement, 124
rising tides, 190, 192–3; see also tide that
    lifts all boats
risk(s), 69; with capital, 193; collective,
    162–4, 166n145, 167;
    collectivization of, 158–67; gone
    wrong, 131n79; and responsibility,
    12, 13; spreading, 14, 78
risk pool: compulsory state-based
    collectivization of, 162–7
risk pooling, 160–1, 162, 164, 167, 168;
    structural unemployment, 187;
    voluntary/compulsory, 161–7
risk-pooling strategies, 159
risk rating, 165–7; retrospective,
    163n138
risk sharing, 95
Robinson, Kenneth J., 13n11
Roemer, John E., 187n200
Rohrschneider, Richard, 195n219
role responsibilities, 195
Roosevelt, Franklin D., 63, 72, 103
Rose, Carol, 34n52, 46, 57n99, 58
Rose, Richard, 165n143
Rothschild, Emma, 100n2
Ryan, Jennifer, 41n72

Sabel, Charles, 28
sacrifice, 92–3
Sagoff, Mark, 195n219
Sainsbury, Diane, 185n196
Salt Lake, 54
Samuelson, Paul S., 162n135
Samuelson, Robert, 38
San Diego, A., 31n49
Sanders, John T., 27, 30n47
Sapiro, Virginia, 115n46
Scanlon, T. M., Jr., 99n1
scarcity, 35, 36
Scarlett, Lynn, 6n4
Schansberg, D. Eric, 39n60, 40n63
Schelling, Thomas C., 154n116
Schmidtz, David, 4n3, 22n34, 27n39,
    35n54, 86n160, 128n72, 130n77,
    149, 160n126, 161n129
Schoeman, Ferdinand, 99n1
Schorr, Alvin, 144nn103,104
self (the): as key word, 116; in self-
    reliance, 133–9; sources of, 193–4
self-construction, 22n34
self-esteem, real, 20, 93–4
Self-Help (Smiles), 103n12, 126
self-reliance, 72, 103, 139, 161, 191;
    and family values, 141, 142, 143;

self-reliance (*cont.*)
    moralized definition of, 139, 140–1,
      144; the "self" in, 133–9; and
      spontaneous mutual support, 95
"Self-Reliance" (Emerson), 103n12
self-respect, 4n1, 19
Sen, Amartya, 114n45, 141n95,
    192n211
sense of self, 194
Shanas, E., 144n104
Shapiro, Daniel, 72n140, 90n165,
    129n75, 167n148
shared problems: collective solutions to,
    168–71
sharing, 75–6; of responsibility, 146–9
shirking, 48, 53
Short, Eugenie D., 12–13
Sidgwick, Henry, 127n68
Siegel, Fred, 19n26
Simon, Herbert A., 130n77
single mothers, 40, 41, 73, 115; *see also*
    welfare mothers
Skocpol, Theda, 75, 115n46
Slovic, Paul, 130n76
small events, 49, 50, 54, 55
Smiles, Samuel, 103n12, 126
Smith, Adam, 145, 146
social assistance, 121–2; means-tested,
    142n99
"social atoms," 76
social collectivism, 146, 147
social conditions: and taking
    responsibility, 11–12
social conventions, 118, 119, 122, 135
social entitlement, 122, 123
social evolution, 55
social institutions: justice first virtue of,
    81–2; *see also* institutions
social insurance, 160, 161, 164–7,
    185n196, 186; "pay-as-you-go"
    basis, 167n145, 185–6
Social insurance and allied services
    (Beveridge), 185n195
social life: "natural and appropriate"
    aspects of, 107
social limits to growth, 192
social organization, 5, 44–5
social policy, 106–15, 171; bad/good,
    139; *see also* public policy; social
    welfare policy
social policy debates: key words in,
    116–44
social safety net, 114, 124; *see also*
    welfare safety net
social security, 70, 160; private
    risk-pooling arrangements for,
    161

Social Security, 61, 89–90, 107,
    193n214; "bankruptcy" of, 164–5;
    spending on, 106
Social Security Act, 185n196
Social Security Amendments of 1974,
    137
Social Security Trust Fund, 89
social structure, 36, 185n194
social welfare: dependency, reliance
    and, 116–22; property ownership in,
    48; state responsibility for, 155
social welfare claimants, 152;
    attempting to drive to work, 173,
    177–84, 188–90; *see also* welfare
    dependents; welfare recipients
social welfare debates: dependency in,
    117–18; self-reliance in, 134
social welfare expenditures, 106–7
social welfare legislation, 103
social welfare policy, 100–6;
    personalized approaches to, 192–3;
    perverse incentives in, 172–3, 175–6;
    pronatalist, 113n43; sense of
    responsibility in, 150, 151
socialism, 64, 71; "café society," 169
society(ies): prosperous, 9; responsibility
    of, 11; welfare of, 145–6
society as cooperative venture for mutual
    advantage, 24–5, 30, 85, 88, 91, 92
society as snapshot metaphor, 6–7, 16
sociotropic voting, 195n219
Sosa, Ernest, 169n154
"sources of the self," 193–4
Spain, unemployment rate, 15
species, endangered, 32–3; with no
    market value, 33n51
spiritual well-being, 149
state (the): coercive collectivization by,
    164; focus of public life, 77; reliance
    on, 139, 141; responsibility for social
    welfare, 155; role of, 146; and social
    insurance, 164–6, 167; as
    underwriter of last resort, 167n148
static perspective, 6–7, 21, 24, 43
status quo, 34, 92–3; escaping, 88–91;
    injustice in, 91
steady-state system, 34, 35
Steiner, Gilbert, 143
Steiner, Hillel, 180n182
"stinting," 57–8
Streib, G. F., 144n104
structural unemployment, 46; welfare
    as compensation for, 184–9
suffering, 43; minimizing, 20–1
supply-side policies, 62, 192, 193
survivors' insurance, 185n196
Sweden, 113n43

taking responsibility, 8, 9, 10, 11, 22, 46, 52; in appropriation, 31–2; failure in, 4n1, 11, 99–100; as a group, 23; institutions role in inducing, 94–6; and minimizing suffering, 21; policies leading to, 62; for self/family/neighbors, 63, 94, 99; social conditions and, 11–12; for own welfare, 93; welfare programs and, 20; young mothers, 137
Tanner, Michael, 17n21, 20n32, 61n108
task responsibility, 7n5, 150–4
taxation, redistributive, 9
taxpayers, 135; in welfare state, 76–7
Taylor, Charles, 76n149, 99n1
Temporary Assistance for Needy Families, 110
territoriality, 83n156
Thatcher, Margaret, 102, 134n85
Thompson, E. P., 161n130
Thomson, Judith, 28
threat, 180, 181, 182
throffers, 180–4
Thurow, Lester C., 184n192
tide that lifts all boats, 3–4, 96, 190; sheltering people from, 16; those left behind by, 4, 5, 6
Tilton, Timothy A., 113n43
Time (magazine), 15n15
time-share condominiums, 53
Titmuss, Richard M., 107n26
Tocqueville, Alexis de, 100n2, 127n68
Tollison, Robert D., 106n22
Tongan islands, 31–2, 35–6
tort law, 52, 151n112, 152n113, 156–7, 159, 174n167
Townsend, Peter, 144n104
trade, 30, 94
trade unions, 64
tragedy of the commons, 22, 35, 58, 60
transaction costs, 49, 51, 192
triage logic, 154n116
"trickle-down" theory, 62, 192, 193
Tully, James, 35n53
Tversky, Amos, 130n76

unconditional basic income; *see* basic income
underclass, 102, 105
unemployable (the), 184
unemployed (the), 46
unemployment, 126–7, 163n136; insurance, 69, 70, 71–2, 160, 163nn137,138; 186n198; voluntary/ involuntary, 186n198; *see also* structural unemployment
unemployment rate, 15
Ungerson, Clare, 185n194
United Kingdom, 162n134
United Nations, 161n131, 162n134, 163n136, 166n146
U.S. Bureau of Labor Statistics, 15n17, 41, 42
U.S. Census Bureau, 37, 39, 40, 41n69, 42nn74,77, 106n24
U.S. Congress, 101n4, 102n7, 104n17
U.S. Department of Commerce, 32
U.S. Department of Labor, 39n62, 41n73, 42n75
U.S. Department of the Interior, 32
U.S. Family Support Act of 1988, 103n13
U.S. Fish and Wildlife Service, 32
U.S. House of Representatives, 103n10, 105n19
U.S. News and World Report, 38n58
U.S. Senate Finance Committee, 38
U.S. Treasury Department: Office of Tax Analysis, 40
unwed mothers, 104n15, 124; taking responsibility, 137; *see also* welfare mothers
unwed teenage mothers, 78

Váldes-Prieto, Salvador, 162n134
value(ing), 4n2
values, 7, 18; in personal responsibility, 139; Victorian, 102; *see also* family values
Van Parijs, Philippe, 85n158, 89
Victorian values, 102
Virginia Company, 53
Vobejda, Barbara, 104n16
voluntarism, 161
Voluntary action (Beveridge), 185n195
voluntary hospitals, 66
voluntary/involuntary dependencies, 119–20

wages, 37
Wagner, Richard E., 106n22
Waldron, Jeremy, 144n106, 189n206
Walker, James, 58n102
waste dumping, 49
wastes, toxic, 52
wealth: generated by original appropriation, 34; production and distribution of, 4n1, 20; redistribution of, 3; tide of, 3–23
Weaver, R. Kent, 101n4, 108n29
Weitzman, Lenore J., 157n120

welfare, 103; as compensation for structural unemployment, 184–9; of individuals, 3, 5, 6, 11, 21, 77, 86, 94, 96; private provision of, 161–2; responsibility and, 5, 8, 20, 21–3; of society, 4–5, 22, 145–6; of those left behind, 4, 5, 6, 14–20, 78, 93; *see also* social welfare

welfare benefits/payments: and child poverty rates, 40; as compensation, 187–8, 189; deliberately low to drive claimants to work, 173

welfare dependency, 107–15, 117, 118, 119, 120; objections to/opponents of, 121, 122, 127, 140–1; perspectives on, 124–5; planning and, 130–3

welfare dependents: perspective of, 123–7; *see also* welfare recipients

welfare fathers, 138

welfare mothers, 101–2, 105, 106, 114–15, 138; alternatives to welfare, 125; costs of, 159n125; deterrence and, 174; planning by, 132–3; "responsibility" of, 110–14; time on welfare rolls, 108

welfare policies, 22, 43; punitive, 142n98, 144; two-tier, 176–7

welfare programs, 17–20, 60–1, 63, 75–6; effect on poor, 73–4; lack of success of, 95

welfare recipients, 76–7; competence of, 72n141; lack of choice, 182, 184; opportunities and incentives, 177–80; time on welfare rolls, 108–9; who cannot help themselves, 175, 176; and workfare, 182–4

welfare reform, 90, 101n4, 126n67

Welfare Reform Act of 1996, 104, 110, 137

welfare rights, 123

welfare rights activists, 121–2

welfare safety net, 79; friendly societies as, 67; *see also* social safety net

welfare state, 16, 36–7, 73–4, 75, 76–7, 95, 160n128; alternatives to, 63; arguments against, 114–15; attacks on, 103–4; full employment in, 185–6; and individual responsibility, 64

welfare system, 104

welfare transfers, 14

what sort of people we are and want to be, 22, 93–4, 191, 193–5

widows and orphans, 101n4

Wikler, Daniel, 105n21, 106n22

Will, George, 174n165

Williams, Bernard, 128n72, 174n166

Williamson, Oliver E., 121n54, 192n210

Wilson, J. R. S., 119n50

Wilson, William Julius, 102n8, 125n63, 178n177

Winter, Sidney G., 121n54

Wiseman, J., 154n116

Wolf, Richard, 19n27, 90n166

women: autonomous household, 124

work, 10; welfare programs and, 19–20

workers compensation policies, 69, 156–7, 158, 160

workfare, 105, 180–4

"workforce exclusions," 107n26

Working Seminar on the Family and American Welfare Policy, 101n4

Worsham, James, 72n140

Yellen, Janet L., 112n40

Young, Iris Marion, 101n4, 124n61, 142n97

zero-sum game, 3, 25; appropriation is not, 29–31; human commerce as, 85; job market as, 85–6